Consequences of Peace

The Versailles Settlement: Aftermath and Legacy 1919–2010

Makers
of the
Modern
World

Consequences of Peace
The Versailles Settlement:
Aftermath and Legacy 1919–2010
Alan Sharp

HAUS HISTORIES

For Louise, David and Gwen

First published in Great Britain in 2010 by
Haus Publishing Ltd
70 Cadogan Place
London SW1X 9AH
www.hauspublishing.com

Copyright © Alan Sharp, 2010

The moral right of the author has been asserted

A CIP catalogue record for this book
is available from the British Library

ISBN 978-1-905791-74-3

Series design by Susan Buchanan
Typeset in Sabon by MacGuru Ltd
Printed in Dubai by Oriental Press

Contents

Acknowledgements

Once again I would like to express my appreciation to Dr Barbara Schwepcke of Haus Publishing for her inspirational championing of this series and for her support and encouragement. Jaqueline Mitchell has again proved to be a sympathetic and constructive commissioning editor whose expertise has proved invaluable. I have learned much from the other contributors to the series and thank them and everyone at Haus connected with the project for their sterling efforts. I owe an enormous debt of gratitude to good friends and colleagues who have read all or parts of the drafts of this book, corrected mistakes and made helpful suggestions. Baroness Ruth Henig, Dr Stephen Ryan and Professors Tom Fraser, Tony Lentin and Sally Marks have all been generous with their help and advice and without the enthusiasm and encouragement of Tom, Tony and Sally in particular there might not have been a concluding volume for the series at all. That would certainly have been true but for the unfailing support and love of my wife, Jen, who has patiently tolerated my relationship with my computer. I offer my sincere thanks to all concerned but any errors that remain are entirely my responsibility.

Alan Sharp
University of Ulster

Lloyd George, Wilson and Clemenceau

Introduction

'There is no single person in this room who is not disappointed with the terms we have drafted.'

Lord Robert Cecil, Paris, 30 May 1919[1]

The Peace Treaties signed in various Parisian palaces and suburbs at the end of the First World War have not enjoyed a sparkling reputation. In the words of Jan Christian Smuts, the South African delegate and close colleague of the British Premier, David Lloyd George, 'such a chance comes but once in a whole era of history – and we missed it.'[2] The prevailing perception remains that this was a huge opportunity spurned; that the Treaties at the end of the war to end war and to make the world safe for democracy delivered neither outcome, and that they had a large responsibility for the establishment of the dictatorships of the inter-war period and the outbreak of a second conflagration in 1939. In the post-Second World War and Cold War eras they continue to attract condemnation for their legacies in the Balkans, the Middle East, the Russian borderlands, the former European empires in Africa and Asia, and indeed worldwide, particularly in the wake of two seminal events, 11/9 (the fall of the Berlin Wall on 9 November 1989) and 9/11 (the attacks on the World Trade

Center in New York and the Pentagon in Washington on 11 September 2001).

Smuts' disappointment, shared by Lord Robert Cecil, who had also played a prominent role in the drafting of the League of Nations Covenant, was typical of many attending a meeting of British and American experts in May 1919. They were anxious to embody their Peace Conference cooperation and experience into an organisation with parallel branches in each country designed to deliver an essential aspect of President Woodrow Wilson's brave new world – an informed, aware and trusted public opinion which might encourage leaders to revisit and make the much needed improvements to the settlement. Their misgivings were expressed by Alfred Zimmern, who told Arnold Toynbee, a fellow member of the influential British Political Intelligence Department, that 'Paris disgusted and depressed me more than I can say. The Majestic and the Crillon [the main hotels in which the British and American delegations were based] were full of unease and heartbroken men'. The PID's effective leader, James Headlam-Morley, who had helped to find solutions to difficult questions such as the future of the Saar, Danzig and the protection of national minorities, added his testimony, writing to his brother on the eve of the signature of the Treaty of Versailles, that 'I have not found one single person here who approves of it as a whole. While in most cases particular clauses can be defended, the total effect is, I am sure, quite indefensible and in fact is, I think, quite unworkable.'[3]

> 'I have not found one single person here who approves of it as a whole. While in most cases particular clauses can be defended, the total effect is, I am sure, quite indefensible and in fact is, I think, quite unworkable.'
>
> **JAMES HEADLAM-MORLEY, JUNE 1919**

Their disquiet was emphasised and publicised by another former Conference participant, John Maynard Keynes, a Treasury official who resigned from the British delegation in June 1919 to write one of the most influential polemics of the 20th century, *The Economic Consequences of the Peace*, published in December 1919. This stinging attack on the Allied leaders and all their works, in particular reflecting Keynes' bitter disappointment with Wilson, has played a major role since in shaping the widely held perception of the settlement as a failure and a missed opportunity. Later memoirs by Conference members such as Harold Nicolson, Headlam-Morley, Stephen Bonsal and Robert Lansing did little to dispel the contemporary conclusion of a distinguished British soldier, Archibald Wavell, who served in both World Wars, that 'After "the war to end war" they seem to have been pretty successful in Paris at making a "Peace to end Peace".' The outbreak of a second major continental war in September 1939 seemed to confirm both Wavell's observation and the verdict of the French Commander of the Allied Forces on the Western Front, Marshal Ferdinand Foch, who allegedly declared of the Treaty, 'This is not Peace. It is an Armistice for twenty years.'[4]

The renewed conflict in Europe in 1939, which escalated into a new world war in 1941, incurred costs and consequences even more far-reaching than the inconceivable losses, by contemporary standards, of the First World War. Unsurprisingly, in those circumstances, later commentators continued to endorse the contemporary condemnations of the settlement and particularly the Treaty of Versailles. The American diplomat George Kennan wrote in 1985, 'I think it's increasingly recognized that the Second World War was an almost unavoidable prolongation of the first one, resulting from the very silly, humiliating and punitive peace imposed on

Germany after World War I.' Kennan's conclusion is echoed by the dust-jacket blurb of foreign correspondent David Andelman's 2008 book, *A Shattered Peace: Versailles 1919 and the Price We Pay Today*: 'For more than half a century, it has been widely recognised that the unfettered revenge against Germany and the Austro-Hungarian Empire that was the cornerstone of the Treaty of Versailles created the circumstances that led inevitably to World War II.' In 1996 the historian Jay Winter declared, 'The Peace Conference which ended the Great War was more about punishment than about peace. Perhaps inevitably, anger and retribution followed four years of bloodshed, ensuring the instability and ultimate collapse of the accords signed in the Hall of Mirrors at Versailles on 28 June 1919. The road to World War II started here.' According to *The Economist*'s summary of the Millennium in December 1999, 'The final crime was the Treaty of Versailles, whose harsh terms would ensure a second world war.' These indictments have been formidably supported by Henry Kissinger and Douglas Hurd, respectively a former American Secretary of State and a British Foreign Secretary.[5]

Whatever the responsibility of the settlement for this new war, by 1945 Europe was a ruined continent dominated by two extra-European powers, the United States and the Soviet Union. The rapid collapse of their victorious alliance into an ideological and power struggle between two superpowers that would last for over 40 years, transformed the rift already apparent in 1919 between Eastern and Western Europe into an iron curtain. The Cold War did freeze some of the persistent post-Versailles problems of the 1920s and 1930s but when first the Soviet Empire, and then the Soviet Union itself collapsed, many of these issues re-emerged.

There can be little doubt that 1989–91 made 1919 relevant

in a way that it had not been during the Cold War. That settlement is held responsible for the ethnic conflicts in Europe and Asia following the collapse of the USSR, and for the Balkan problems ensuing from the demise of Yugoslavia. In the wider world it has been blamed for its reinforcement of imperialism in Africa, Asia and Latin America and, in particular, for the nightmare of the Middle East because of the artificially constructed and sketchily defined states that it created and the hopelessly conflicting promises made to Jews and Arabs during and after the First World War. In such circumstances it is not surprising that the peace settlement made at the end of that conflict has had few friends.

This is hardly because of a lack of information about the war and the subsequent peace. The inter-war period experienced an explosion of published collections of documents – one of the unintended consequences of an attempt to solve an inter-Allied crisis during the Conference about the definition of what compensation the victors might seek from defeated Germany. The Germans initiated this to try to refute an accusation of exclusive German guilt for the outbreak of the First World War that Article 231 of the Treaty of Versailles never made. (The Article spoke of 'the responsibility of Germany and her allies'; and the parallel reparations clause in each of the other four Paris Treaties of 1919–20 substituted the relevant ex-enemy state for Germany in wording that apportioned responsibility accordingly.) Undeterred by such niceties German publicists and historians, often encouraged and subsidised by a special section of the Ministry of Foreign Affairs, attacked the settlement with great vigour. Not surprisingly, they redoubled their efforts after Lloyd George claimed, at the London Conference of March 1921 that, 'For the Allies, German responsibility for the war is fundamental. It is the basis upon which the structure of the treaty has been erected, and if that acknowledgement is repudiated or abandoned, the treaty is destroyed.'[6]

A plethora of published documents (carefully chosen, edited and – if necessary – falsified) followed, first from Germany, then from other participants. Overwhelmed by the weight of this evidence, the general consensus by the mid-1930s was that the First World War was an accident for which no one power was primarily accountable. This in turn further undermined the credibility of a settlement based on the premise of German responsibility.

Perhaps surprisingly the thesis of the accidental origins of 1914 survived the Second World War until decisively challenged by Fritz Fischer in the late 1950s and early 1960s, amidst huge controversy in his native Germany . Few would now dispute that the crucial decisions for war in 1914 were taken by Germany and its allies. In that sense Article 231 was right. Furthermore, from the 1960s onwards almost all the states involved have opened their archives on the war and the subsequent peace conferences to the inspection of scholars. Yet the historical studies published in the wake of these developments, which have tended, though not universally, to be more sympathetic to the peacemakers, have made remarkably little impression on the Keynesian-inspired popular perceptions of a deliberately cruel settlement constructed by three flawed men. Keynes dismissed the Italian premier, Vittorio Orlando, whose presence and influence were not insignificant, in a sentence and a footnote, and thus, in his version, it remains the dismal product of the Big Three as the formidable 'Tiger' (Georges Clemenceau) and the wily 'Welsh Wizard' (Lloyd George) took the ponderous Presbyterian (Wilson) to the cleaners and created a vindictive and unworkable settlement.[7]

John Maynard Keynes, 1 Jan 1940

Keynes was entitled to his opinion but there are alternative interpretations. This series of studies of the states and personalities involved has attempted to present more rounded and nuanced accounts of the Paris Peace Conferences and to offer some understanding of the conflicting aims and ambitions with which the peacemakers were faced. This concluding volume investigates some of the most significant, long-term legacies and contributions of the settlement at the end of the First World War. It considers first the impact of the decisions taken at the Conference on the states and regions concerned and assesses the prospects for stability after it. The major problem that occupied the peacemakers in the first half of 1919 was how to deal with Germany and the second chapter analyses the various attempts to solve the 'German problem' – how to accommodate the peaceful incorporation of a powerful state into a European and world structure. One of the most innovative aspects of the settlement was the creation of a new international organization to regulate world affairs.

The League of Nations proved to be a disappointment to its more enthusiastic supporters but the victorious allies wasted no time in creating a successor, the United Nations Organization, in 1945. The third chapter considers the history and contribution of these bodies to international relations since 1919.

The fourth chapter relates to national self-determination. In many instances the peace settlements were not the original source of the ideas and policies they implemented but rather they built upon and developed concepts that had already existed before 1919 or 1914. President Wilson attributed particular emphasis to the denial of national self-determination as a destabilising factor in international relations. His support for greater application of the principle made a significant contribution to raising the profile of an idea that has had a profound effect on the world since 1919, particularly in the 1960s and 1990s with first the collapse of the European empires in Africa and Asia and then the demise of the Soviet Empire in Eastern Europe and the Caucasus. One of the ways in which the peacemakers sought to overcome the impossible conundrums created by attempting to apply self-determination in hopelessly ethnically mixed regions was to create special privileges and arrangements for the minorities that would inevitably be left disappointed by the outcomes. The next chapter investigates minority protection, disarmament and changes to international law as further contributions made to later developments by the ideas of 1919.

The sixth chapter considers the role of ideology and the overwhelming cultural, political and economic influence of the United States since the experiences of the First World War that confirmed its emergence as a world power. The conclusion offers some thoughts on the settlement and its place in the history of the 20th and early 21st centuries.

1

The Peace Settlements: Versailles, an Overview

In 1914 certain key decision-makers in Europe, particularly those in Berlin and Vienna, decided that the current international order must be remade, even if that required employing the risky and unpredictable method of war. The conflict they provoked was not the short, sharp, successful war they anticipated and its consequences were much deeper and longer-lasting than they imagined or intended.

The Second World War would be an even greater conflict in terms of costs and geographical reach but there can be no doubt that the seminal event of the 20th century was the First World War. It consumed more men, munitions and material than anyone in 1914 had believed possible. Governments were forced to take responsibility for aspects of the economy, finance, production, transport and supply far beyond any previous experience. The cost of the war was astronomical and shattered previously held ideas of how much credit governments could raise. In 1917 and 1918 the United States alone spent more money than the accumulated total for all federal expenditure since independence.

On both sides of the lines women took the place of men in industry, agriculture, offices and commerce, creating increased expectations about the types and conditions of employment open to them, the facilities to which they were entitled in the workplace and their future political role. The war became a test not simply of military prowess but of the ability of governments to respond to the challenges of total war – war that required the state to commit not just its armed forces but the entirety of its resources to the task. Those that failed experienced defeat and revolution in varying degrees of intensity. Some of the victors had a greater chance to control the pace of social change but victory did not guarantee the survival of the existing political structures of the state, as Italy would soon discover. No matter how much people might wish to return to what President Warren G Harding termed 'normalcy', the world of 1914 was shattered and could not be resurrected.

The peacemakers assembled in Paris in 1919 had thus to treat not only what they perceived to be the root causes of the conflict, but also to find solutions to problems either created or exacerbated by the War itself. Germany was no longer an imperial or naval rival but beyond that little else was clear and, as politicians in a democratic age, they were deeply aware of the bitterness of electorates who had suffered the loss of family, friends and possessions. Four great empires had collapsed, leaving much of Eastern and Central Europe without government; and, as Margaret MacMillan argued, Paris became, in the first half of 1919, the world's emergency capital, with the huge project of restoring order to vast areas of the continent and the wider world, yet often lacking the means to enforce its decisions.[1] This put the peacemakers under great pressure, not least because they feared that

Bolshevism might fill the vacuum of power if they did not act swiftly.

As the American Secretary of State Robert Lansing noted on 4 April 1919, 'It is time to stop fiddling while the world is on fire, while violence and bestiality consume society. Everyone is clamouring for peace, for an immediate peace.'[2] Wilson, in particular, was acutely aware that the Russian revolutionary leader Vladimir Lenin could offer an alternative communist vision to his own ideal of a reformist capitalist and democratic world. His colleagues also knew that the problems of undoing the wartime measures to mobilise national resources for total war needed urgent attention, not least because these domestic issues were very likely to affect their political futures; and it is important to remember that none was yet ready to retire from power.

In Britain Lloyd George had just won an election but with the Liberals bitterly divided between factions supporting himself and former Prime Minister Herbert Asquith, he needed to build an alternative political platform perhaps based on a more permanent alliance with the Conservatives. Vittorio Orlando had no intention of relinquishing power in Italy at that point. The American Constitution did not then debar Wilson from seeking a third term, whilst even the 77-year-old Georges Clemenceau believed that a grateful French Parliament should choose him by acclamation to replace his bitter rival Raymond Poincaré as President of the Republic when the latter's seven year term ended in early 1920.[3]

Each needed to consider the political implications of his Paris decisions. Thus Wilson uneasily resisted Japanese demands for a racial equality clause in the League Covenant in deference to a perceived threat of increased Asian immigration and Orlando found himself trapped by the vigorous

THE PARIS PEACE TREATIES, 1919–1923
The five original Peace Treaties at the end of the First World War were all signed in Paris; the renegotiated Treaty with Turkey was signed in Switzerland.

28 June 1919	Treaty of Versailles (Germany)
10 September 1919	Treaty of Saint-Germain-en-Laye (Austria)
27 November 1919	Treaty of Neuilly (Bulgaria)
4 June 1920	Treaty of Trianon (Hungary)
10 August 1920	Treaty of Sèvres (Ottoman Empire)
24 July 1923	Treaty of Lausanne (Turkey)

domestic campaign for the port of Fiume (Rijeka). The British and French publics expected Germany to pay for the cost of the war. Yet, at the same time, in accepting Wilson's 1918 speeches as the basis for the eventual settlement in the 5 November 1918 pre-Armistice agreement with Germany, they had committed themselves to a higher moral standard of behaviour than previous peacemakers. When political reality and principles collided, as they often did in the complexity of the problems faced, the resulting compromises provided an easy target for critics seeking hypocrisy, not least because Wilson had created enormous expectations, some unintended and many undeliverable.

Politics is the art of the possible and the peacemakers in Paris were constrained by domestic expectations, the limits of their own power to implement decisions, the overwhelming nature of their task and the circumstances in which they operated. The lack of an agreed priority of issues or agenda certainly contributed to a feeling that the Conference was not well ordered. Anyone who has conducted sensitive negotiations at any level will affirm that 'open covenants of peace, openly arrived at' was an impossible aspiration and, although Wilson did not mean this to be taken literally, it represented another example of disappointed expectations, particularly for journalists. Direct negotiations with the Germans might have produced a better settlement, but fears that Allied unity would collapse in their course precluded that option. The absence of Russia left an enormous gap but in 1919 no one was sure who could truly be said to represent Russia. Reparations and national self-determination both generated huge controversy, arguments over principle and frustrated hopes.

Yet the Treaties did have their defenders. With the advantage of greater perspective, Headlam-Morley took a more positive view by 1925 than he had in June 1919. 'We are too timid and modest about our own achievements; there is too much criticism and not enough defence. Cannot we recognize that the settlement of 1919 was an immense advance on any similar settlement made in Europe in the past? In broad outline, it represents a peace of reason and justice, and the whole fabric of the continent depends on its maintenance.' The problem was that few people or states were prepared to agree and, as Harold Nicolson indicated to the Foreign Office on 20 February 1925, although the Treaties with the minor ex-enemy states were guaranteed by a superiority of force, 'The Treaty of Versailles possesses no such safeguard, since the preponderance of whatever man-power would be certainly

> 'We are too timid and modest about our own achievements; there is too much criticism and not enough defence. Cannot we recognize that the settlement of 1919 was an immense advance on any similar settlement made in Europe in the past? In broad outline, it represents a peace of reason and justice, and the whole fabric of the continent depends on its maintenance.'
> **JAMES HEADLAM-MORLEY, 1925**

and unhesitatingly available tells against, and not in favour of, the *status quo*.'[4]

Nicolson points to a useful guide to measuring how stable international relations are likely to be at any given time: does an analysis of the attitudes of the principal actors suggest whether they support or oppose the present state of affairs – are they *status quo* or revisionist in outlook and what is the overall balance between them? There can be little doubt that many states in Europe and beyond in the 1920s and 1930s were revisionist, but whilst they might oppose the existing state of affairs they did not agree on what should replace it; and very often their views on an alternative order were deeply opposed.

The next key question is whether singly or collectively they had the power to translate aspirations into actualities. Despite Nicolson's rather pessimistic appraisal the answer throughout the 1920s and early 1930s was that they did not, but that balance began to alter radically as the 1930s progressed. It is also interesting to note that it is normally taken that winners will favour the *status quo* and losers revision and, whilst this held true of the losers, this was not the case for many of the gainers from the post-war settlements.

At the eastern end of Europe the Soviet Union gradually emerged from the wreckage of Tsarist Russia as the Bolsheviks triumphed in the complicated struggles following the fall of the Romanovs. It posed a dual challenge to the settlement either in its guise as a centre of revolution or as a disgruntled state. In principle it was the ultimate revisionist, believing that the existing order of states was about to be overturned by the worldwide revolution which it was its function to promote and encourage. Normal diplomatic relations with other states were pointless since they would soon vanish. When Leon Trotsky was appointed Commissar for Foreign Affairs in November 1917 he announced that he proposed to go to the Foreign Ministry, issue a few decrees and shut up shop.

Yet despite brief communist control of Munich and a slightly longer-lived regime in Hungary, by 1920 reality suggested that the world was not about to turn red. Trotsky's successor in the Foreign Ministry, Georgy Chicherin, called the Treaty of Tartu with Estonia signed on 2 February 1920 'the first experiment in peaceful coexistence with bourgeois states' – an interesting early use of a phrase more usually associated with the 1950s and 1960s.[5] Even so, despite concluding border agreements with various neighbours, the Anglo-Russian Trade Treaty in 1921 or the more controversial Rapallo Treaty with Germany in 1922, the Soviet Union's international stance was always ambiguous, preceding Fascist Italy and Nazi Germany in confronting other states with the problem of interpreting whether their actions and ultimate aims were driven by ideology or *realpolitik*.

Although it was gradually able to reassert control over briefly independent areas like Georgia, Ukraine, Armenia and Azerbaijan, the USSR suffered major territorial losses as a result of the First World War, civil conflict and subsequent confrontations. Finland and the three Baltic states gained their independence and, after the dramatic events of the Russo-Polish War of 1920, its frontier with Poland ended much further to the east than that recommended by the Paris Peace Conference. Unsurprisingly the Soviet Union wished to reverse these losses, though its power to do so was, for the moment at least, limited.

Moving west, newly independent Latvia, Lithuania and Estonia together with Romania, Poland and Czechoslovakia

Europe 1914

Petrograd (St Petersburg)

Riga

Sea

Vilna

Königsberg

anzig

Warsaw
Brest-Litovsk

Moscow

RUSSIAN EMPIRE

Kiev

Budapest

Odessa

GARY

ROMANIA

Belgrade   Bucharest

SERBIA   BULGARIA

NEGRO   Sofia

Black Sea

ALBANIA

Constantinople

GREECE

OTTOMAN EMPIRE

Athens

Europe 1923

FINLAND

Petrograd (St Petersburg)

Tallinn
ESTONIA

m

Riga
LATVIA

Moscow

c Sea

LITHUANIA

anzig

Vilnius

Königsberg
EAST
PRUSSIA

UNION OF SOVIET
SOCIALIST REPUBLICS

Warsaw · Brest-Litovsk

POLAND

Kiev

OVAKIA

Budapest

NGARY

Odessa

ROMANIA

Belgrade · Bucharest

Black Sea

OSLAVIA

BULGARIA
Sofia

na
LBANIA

Istanbul

GREECE

TURKEY

Athens

IRAQ

SYRIA

CYPRUS

might have been expected to be *status quo* in outlook but each had unfulfilled ambitions which made relationships between them difficult. In some cases they owed their very existence to the unpredictable near simultaneous collapse of Austria-Hungary and the German and Russian Empires; and, even if Austria-Hungary had disappeared, it seemed inevitable that Russian and German power would eventually revive. In those circumstances it was essential that they cooperate to preserve their mutual independence but, failing to heed the old adage about needing to hang together to avoid hanging separately, many fell victim to the events of 1938–9. Disputes about territory and resources, like that between Czechoslovakia and Poland over Teschen, bedevilled relations between what the Germans referred to as 'season states' – states with limited life-spans. When Adolf Hitler dismembered Czechoslovakia in 1938 and 1939 the actions of neighbours who swooped to satisfy old territorial scores was symbolic of this disunity, which the French, hopeful of creating some sort of menace on Germany's eastern borders to compensate for the loss of their pre-war Russian alliance, viewed with despair, convinced as they were that Germany would attack the settlement in the east before turning west.[6]

Hungary was the really big European loser in the post-war settlement. Under the Treaty of Trianon Hungary lost two-thirds of its pre-war territory and nearly 60 per cent of its people, consigning some one-third of its Magyar population to become minorities in neighbouring states. It was a bitter revisionist throughout the inter-war period, moving closer to Hitler's Germany and eventually joining the Axis powers in the Second World War. Unlike Germany, however, Hungary did not have the power to support its demands for the revision of a settlement that emerged in June 1920 partly from decisions already taken about other states at a time when, as one Hungarian official perceptively remarked, the Allies 'were frightfully bored by the whole Paris Peace Conference.' In the words of its leading modern poet, Gyulla Illyés, writing in 1980, 'Trianon to us bears the meaning of a human slaughter-house: it is there that every third Hungarian was crushed into subsistence under foreign rule; it is there that the territories of our native language were torn to pieces.'[7]

The other remnant of Austria-Hungary, the tiny German-speaking rump state of Austria, had no wish, in 1919, to be independent, instead wanting to join Germany, something that the French, in particular, opposed. Given the difficulty the Allies had experienced in defeating Germany, and no matter what the tenets of self-determination might suggest, they were never going to allow Germany to increase its population by 8 million Austrians or 3 million Sudetenlanders from Czechoslovakia, or to gain strategic advantages ensuring domination of the Balkans. Despite this unhappy beginning, compounded by enormous financial and economic problems, the Austrian Republic came to value its national sovereignty before Hitler's forced *Anschluss* in March 1938 and re-emerged as an independent state after the Second World War. It might be classed, therefore, as one of the unexpected successes of the settlement.[8]

Germany clearly did not regard the settlement as a success; and throughout the period of the Weimar Republic the electorate made it plain they expected their leaders to seek revision of the Treaty, preferably by peaceful means. Most, including Hitler in *Mein Kampf*, accepted the loss of Alsace-Lorraine and few resented the transfer of part of Schleswig to Denmark, after a plebiscite, promised by Otto von Bismarck in 1864 but long postponed. The territory ceded to Poland was a very different matter. Germans regarded Poland as a failed state whose people had proved incapable of self-government in the 18th century and saw the transfer of Germans to Polish rule as intolerable. They resented the forced disarmament imposed by the Treaty and saw reparations as a harsh burden. Gustav Stresemann, often portrayed as the acceptable face of Germany in the inter-war period, made no secret of the initial changes he wished to implement in the wake of the Dawes Plan, which seemed to have provided an answer to the problem of reparations, and the Locarno Agreements under which he had accepted Germany's western frontiers – the return of Upper Silesia, Eupen-Malmédy and Danzig, a renegotiation of the access rights of the Polish Corridor, the reinstatement of full German sovereignty over its own territory and policies, proper protection for German minorities abroad and the recognition of Germany as a major power, to be symbolised by a permanent seat on the League of Nations Council and the right to hold colonial mandates. He hinted at further demands once Germany regained its military strength. Germany may have suffered much fewer losses proportionately than Hungary but its greater international weight meant that it was the most important revisionist state even before Hitler came to power.[9]

German National Socialism's ideology was an adaptation and development of Social Darwinism, with its gradation of races, its justification of imperial rule and its belief that life was a struggle in which races and states were either increasing their power or in decline. Since Hitler made it plain that the restoration of Germany's 1914 frontiers and possessions would not be sufficient to satisfy his vision of its world-power status, he can hardly be called a revisionist, no matter how carefully he disguised his early demands in that light. His aim was rather the reversal of the result of the First World War and then further German expansion and conquest. Historians dispute whether his ambitions were bounded by Europe and its 'near abroad' or were limitless.

Fearing for the future of France, with its smaller and ageing population, Clemenceau declared to the Senate on 11 October 1919, 'The treaty does not state that France will have many children, but it is the first thing that should have been written there. For if France does not have large families, it will be in vain that you put all the finest clauses in the treaty, that you take away all the German guns. France will be lost because there will be no more French.'[10] He was acutely aware of the disparity both in population and birth rates between Germany and France, and thought that, no matter what adjustments the settlement might make, a restored Germany would be much more powerful than a France which owed its present victory to a coalition of powers secured by a combination of skill and luck. In an ideal world France too would be a revisionist power – seeking to make the Treaty even tougher – and indeed Poincaré's occupation of the Ruhr basin in January 1923 may have had this amongst its aims.[11]

For the most part, however, French leaders accepted that Clemenceau had negotiated the best deal he could get, given that he had (apparently) secured a guarantee of French security from Britain and the United States, a long-term occupation of the Rhineland with the right to remain if Germany did not execute the Treaty, a share of reparations, various restrictions on Germany's military and economic capacity, diminutions of German resources, including the product of the Saar coalfields for France, and a reduction of Germany's population and territory. In these circumstances France was thus the major *status quo* power of the inter-war period and the main defender of the post-war settlement in Europe though not necessarily elsewhere, for example in the Near East. Its hope was that Britain would be its major partner in executing the Treaty, even if it was one neither might have created but for the critical interventions of President Wilson and his advisers, now departed. That hope would be sadly disappointed.

Even before the Treaty was signed there was a strong move in the British delegation to alter the draft terms handed to the Germans on 7 May. Joint meetings of the delegation and the Cabinet, summoned to Paris for the purpose on 1 June, empowered Lloyd George to return to his negotiating partners to seek amendments to the clauses on the fate of Upper Silesia, reparations, the length and cost of the Allied occupation and German membership of the League. On the whole he did not enjoy huge success, except in obtaining a plebiscite for Upper Silesia, some reduction in occupation costs and rather bland statements about reparations and the League. But this did not deter those who believed that revision was required and it has been argued that the inter-war British policy of appeasement – seeking to redress wrongs perceived to have been done to Germany – began in Paris.[12]

The publication of Keynes's attack on the settlement underlined and reinforced unease about its terms. Britain was thus generally open to revision, tending to believe German leaders when they asserted that certain aspects of the Treaty could not be fulfilled, but it also pined for a previous golden age in which it had, apparently, been able to divest itself of European responsibilities and concentrate on its destiny as a worldwide empire. It was difficult to convince the British that recent events had demonstrated that, without security in Europe, there could be no imperial security and that they had an active role to play in preserving European stability. They also found it hard to forget a past in which the enemy was France. There was a tendency to believe that Germany was no longer a menace but that France, in building submarines and a bomber force whilst maintaining the largest continental army, was reverting to type. As Paul Cambon, the veteran French ambassador in London remarked wanly to his successor, 'The misfortune is that the English are not yet aware that Napoleon is dead.' [13] Given that both were desperate to avoid any recurrence of the terrible costs and losses of the recent War, this failure of the two principal European powers to cooperate on a firm policy of either Treaty execution or revision was a tragedy.

Like France, Belgium sought modest territorial gains, reparations, and security guarantees. A smaller and weaker power, it was entitled to particular consideration given its wartime experiences and losses but found its main ambitions at the Peace Conference blocked by Britain and France. Territorially, it hoped to regain areas lost in 1839, notably Luxemburg and parts of Holland, with the Dutch gaining German territory in compensation. But Paris in 1919 was not Vienna in 1815. Such arrangements were now out of fashion and the peacemakers, like the Dutch, would have none of it. Thus it gained only small amounts of German territory in Europe and Africa. Though compulsory neutrality was not formally cancelled, this 1839 imposition, by tacit assumption, soon evaporated. Unlike other small states, Belgium, having gained a share of reparations with special concessions (which rapidly shrank) and a seat on the postwar Reparations Commission, participated in the occupation of western Germany and the 1923 Ruhr incursion. It thus undertook a thankless role in the post-war decade's endless Anglo-French quarrels about Germany. However, its desire to balance between

Britain and France with security guarantees from both was frustrated by France's determination to reduce it to a satellite and Britain's assumption that it already was one, producing a hostile British policy which pushed Belgium reluctantly in France's direction. An active but always realistic supporter of the League, Belgium effectively reverted to neutrality in 1936 as the international climate worsened, primarily because domestic politics prevented rearmament until its limited military arrangement with France was ended.[14]

Amongst the victors Italy was perhaps the most intense of the revisionist powers, choosing to regard a settlement in which it had made substantial strategic gains, not all of which could be justified in terms of self-determination, as the reflection of a 'mutilated victory'. The award of South Tyrol gave Italy an Alpine frontier on the Brenner Pass with the added advantage that this was no longer with the Austro-Hungarian Empire but with the tiny state of Austria, whilst its gains in Dalmatia and Istria offered opportunities for further penetration of the Danubian basin and the Balkans. Yugoslavia, even with its French patron, did not present the same challenge to Italian influence as the pre-war powers had done. Whilst Italy did not make all the imperial gains it sought, though certainly in the case of Smyrna (Izmir) this represented a stroke of luck, the issue which caused deep resentment at home and huge problems both in Paris and beyond, was Fiume. Wilson, in particular, was determined to make no concession to the Italian demand for the city, which was not part of the bargain agreed in the 1915 Treaty of London and which was deemed to be an essential outlet to the Adriatic for Yugoslavia. Orlando's failure to convince his colleagues of the Italian case led him to quit the Conference in April 1919, only to return empty-handed in early May, and was one of the reasons behind the downfall of his government on 19 June. Resentment at Italy's treatment, anger that its sacrifices were not sufficiently recognised and disappointment with the settlement, together with the deep divisions that entry into the war had already created, were major factors in the crisis of Italian liberal parliamentarianism which brought Benito Mussolini and fascism to power in October 1922. Throughout the 1920s, and with increasing boldness in the 1930s, Mussolini's Italy was, as far as it dared to be, a revisionist state, determined to show the greater efficacy of fascist government in attaining its rightful dues.[15]

In the Balkans, where the First World War was the third in a series of conflicts that reconfigured the region over a ten-year period, Bulgaria was the most dissatisfied of several unhappy states. Like the Germans, but possibly with more realistic expectations, the Bulgarians had hopes that they might benefit from the application of the principle of self-determination. They did not, losing Western Thrace to Greece, and with it access to the Aegean, and also some strategically important land to Yugoslavia. Proportionate to its size and wealth Bulgaria faced the largest reparations bill of all the Central Powers, though in the event it did not pay much; and although Bulgaria actually lost little of its pre-war territory or population, it suffered because meanwhile its neighbours Greece, Romania and Yugoslavia all expanded enormously, profiting from the collapse of Russia, Austria-Hungary and the Ottomans. Greece had 50 per cent more territory and population after the war than before, Romania doubled its size and people and Yugoslavia had three times more territory and population than pre-war Serbia.

Even so none was completely satisfied and each continued to seek readjustments to the settlement. Greek ambitions in Asia Minor suffered bloody defeat by Mustafa Kemal's (Atatürk) revived Turkey, including the massacre of the Greek population of Smyrna, leading to a painful forced exchange of populations. Only one of Yugoslavia's seven frontiers was undisputed, whilst its wider ambitions clashed with those of the Italians. Its claim to the Banat of Temesvar was fiercely challenged by Romania, creating one of the most complicated tangles for the Conference to settle, with massaged statistics, carefully distorted maps, great power rivalry and threats of the use of force all having an influence on the eventual partition of the area. This left 75,000 Romanians and 65,000 Slavs on the wrong sides of the new frontier, emphasising the impossibility of any perfect ethnographical solution to such problems in a region of intermingled populations.[16]

The defeat of the Ottoman Empire in 1918 was, apparently, complete and irreversible. Perhaps for that reason the Turks found themselves at the end of the queue of states awaiting their peace terms, the Treaty of Sèvres signed in August 1920 being the last of the original five Parisian settlements. By then, however, as Kemal's nationalist revolt in Anatolia gathered momentum, circumstances were so different it was doubtful if the Sultan's signature had any binding value. Sèvres was never ratified and by the autumn of 1922, following a near renewal of hostilities after a confrontation between British and Turkish forces at Chanak, the Allies found themselves engaged in formulating the only negotiated settlement after the First World War with the victorious Kemal's representatives. The Treaty of Lausanne, eventually signed in July 1923, recognised the new secular Turkish Republic, restored much of the territory in Europe and Asia Minor ceded under Sèvres, removed all the financial and extra-territorial privileges previously enjoyed by the great powers and, with the exception of new rules for the passage of warships through the Straits and a small demilitarised zone there, Turkey was restored to full sovereignty. Lausanne, negotiated by parties who had experienced both victory and defeat, proved to be the most successful and longest lasting of all the post-war Treaties, leaving Turkey as a largely satisfied power throughout the inter-war period.[17]

The same could not be said of the successors to the former Ottoman possessions in the Middle East. Here serious and enduring local rivalries were compounded by the ambitions of outside powers, most notably Britain and France, which had made a number of conflicting wartime promises or implied commitments to a variety of potential clients and to each other. The Hashemite clan dreamt of an independent Arabia including much of the Levant (the area of the eastern Mediterranean). Their ambitions, apparently endorsed by British undertakings in 1915 given in the hope of encouraging an Arab revolt against the Ottomans, foundered on the determination of the British and French to control the area, on family feuds and on their own inability to defeat other Arab leaders with similar aims to establish hegemony.

The British refused to recognize Hussein, the Sherif of Mecca and titular leader of the Arab revolt, as the King of the Arabs, accepting him only as the King of the Hejaz. Increasingly estranged from his sons, Feisal and Abdullah, whose success in acquiring their own thrones he resented, Hussein made a fatal blunder in 1924 by declaring himself Caliph, provoking the formidable Ibn Saud to invade and conquer the territory, thus driving him into exile. Ibn Saud eventually combined the Hejaz and Nejd into the Kingdom of Saudi Arabia in 1932, embittering still further his relations with the Hashemites. Hussein's third son, Feisal, the effective leader

Turkey and the Near East 1923

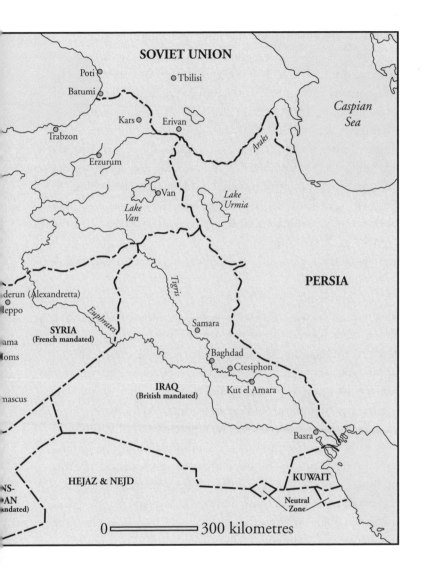

of the Arabs throughout the military campaign and peace negotiations, tried to establish a kingdom in Syria, but this collapsed under French military pressure in July 1920. His subsequent and unforeseen reappearance as the King of Mesopotamia (Iraq) in 1921 came about as part of a British attempt to retain control of the region but to limit the costs involved after a serious revolt the previous year. His brother Abdullah was recompensed for renouncing any claim on Iraq and for behaving better towards the French by becoming the Emir of Transjordan (Jordan) in 1923. Feisal and Abdullah both retained ambitions to wrest control of Syria from the French; each harboured dreams of leading a unified Arab state and neither was an especially easy client for the British to handle.[18]

The establishment of Transjordan meant that the British, by dividing historic Palestine along the line of the Jordan River, were partially reneging on the promise given to the Jews in the Balfour Declaration to make it their national home. As many had warned, the practicalities of managing Jewish immigration and land purchase without alienating the existing population or exceeding productive capacity were extremely problematic. The repercussions of events elsewhere in the Arab world further complicated matters, spilling over into Palestine. Communal disturbances leading to deaths in Jerusalem in 1920 and Jaffa in 1921 seemed to confirm the pessimistic predictions of British Ministers opposed to involvement in the area that they would be left holding the line between discontented Arabs and disappointed Jews.[19]

Nonetheless the British sought and accepted the League of Nations Mandate for Palestine on 24 July 1922 which charged them with the awesome task of placing it 'under such political, administrative and economic conditions as will secure the establishment of the Jewish National Home ... and the development of self-governing institutions, and also for safeguarding the civil and religious rights of all the inhabitants of Palestine, irrespective of race and religion'. Immigration raised the Jewish population from 83,000 in 1922 to 181,000 by 1932 but that figure more than doubled by 1936 as Jews fled Europe and particularly Hitler's Germany. This increased communal tensions in Palestine, where already violent clashes in 1929 had caused over 200 Arab and Jewish deaths, and created new political headaches for the British when a three-year Arab revolt began in 1936. These problems led to serious, but as yet inconclusive, consideration of the principle of partitioning Palestine into Jewish and Arab states with Jerusalem under British control. Before any final decision was reached the outbreak of a new major European war pushed Palestine much lower on the political agenda but it was clear, even before the appalling genocide of the Holocaust, that the *status quo* in this area was unsustainable.[20]

The First World War left the British Empire both more secure and yet more vulnerable since it was so large and difficult to police. The major conventional outside threats from Germany or Russia had dissipated and its other potential rivals were, for the moment at least, its allies. The sea routes through the Mediterranean and the Suez Canal, or round the Cape of Good Hope, were secure. South Africa now controlled South-West Africa and Australia New Guinea, and together with New Zealand, various islands south of the equator in the Pacific, removing any pre-war German menaces. Yet for each of the Dominions their wartime experiences and sacrifices had increased their sense of a separate identity and an awareness of interests which did not necessarily coincide with those of the 'mother country'. Even though it was King George V's right to ratify the Treaty of Versailles simply on the advice of his Westminster Parliament, it was judged politic to allow each of the Dominions to consider and approve the settlement before he did so. The marked lack of response from the Dominions to Britain's appeal for aid against Turkey during the 1922 Chanak crisis was a further indication that the world of 1914 had gone forever. Additionally, in India in particular, but also elsewhere in Africa and Asia, less official voices calling for self-determination were growing in strength, with the war exposing the myth of European invincibility and Wilson's apparent endorsement reinforcing existing and emerging movements. Violent unrest in Egypt and Ireland, which some attributed to the power of Bolshevik propaganda and influence, stretched British resources and emphasised that the major threats were now internal and ideological. These twin themes of increasing Dominion independence at one level and colonial discontent at another suggested interesting times ahead.[21]

In Asia the major loser, despite being an Allied power, was China whose hopes of regaining control of Shandong (Shantung), leased to the Germans under pressure in 1898 and reassigned to Japan under agreements forced upon it by the Japanese in 1915, were disappointed at the Conference. This unleashed a portentous student protest in Beijing on 4 May 1919 and left a legacy of great bitterness in a deeply divided and troubled land. The immediate effect was that China refused to sign the Treaty of Versailles; in the longer term it increased its suspicion of the West and encouraged more militant Chinese nationalism.[22]

The major winner in the Far East was Japan which emerged as an important regional power, temporarily gaining Shandong, which it returned to China after American pressure in

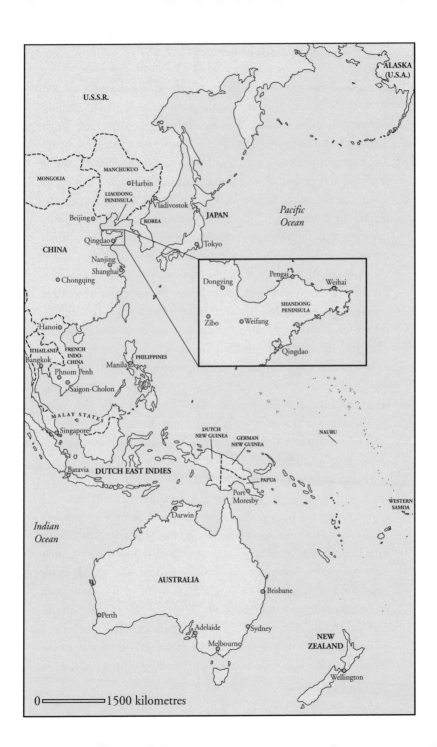

1922, and the German islands north of the equator in the Pacific. Its proposal of a racial equality clause in the League Covenant embarrassed Wilson and Cecil who were both aware of the strong opposition on the American west coast and in Australia and New Zealand to any measure that might increase the possibility of Japanese immigration. When the Japanese delegate, Baron Makino, insisted that the question be put to a vote, 11 of the 17 members of the League Commission were in favour and none against with six abstentions, allowing Wilson to claim on a dubious technicality that, since the vote on such an important issue was not unanimous, the motion fell. The payback came when Wilson, already under pressure from the Italian withdrawal from the Conference, conceded, in order to avoid the departure of a second major ally and against his principles and better judgement, that Japan rather than China should have Shandong. At the same time, Japan's demands upon and treatment of China and its expansion into the Pacific, taken together with the naval implications of its alliance with Britain, underlined growing uncertainty in the United States about the ambitions of this coming regional power.[23]

In addition to their concerns in the Far East, many Americans were deeply worried about the League of Nations and its implications for the United States; and there was, among Irish- and German-Americans in particular, anti-British and French sentiment. Wilson also had many bitter political opponents. Even so, given some judicious and properly presented concessions, he might have fulfilled his assurance to Smuts that he could pass the Treaty through the Senate. Instead on 19 November 1919 and again on 19 March 1920 a combination of a stubborn unwillingness to compromise together with sheer political ineptitude, perhaps born of a querulous invalid's growing sense of betrayal, ensured that he failed. America, whose financial, economic and, finally, military intervention in the war had been decisive, and whose contribution to peacemaking had been profound, now sought to withdraw, politically and militarily at least, into its pre-war shell.

The implications were enormous and far-reaching. America withdrew from all aspects of Treaty enforcement, whether in terms of the occupation of Germany or of the membership of various commissions. If Lloyd George's strategy really was to play for time and count upon the Americans to assist Britain to ameliorate Germany's reparations bill, it collapsed because, instead of an American chair in a commission of five powers (America, Belgium, Britain, France and Italy) there were now only four members, with the French chair having a casting vote in the unlikely event that the Italians would risk the unnecessary alienation of France by siding with Britain against the usual Franco-Belgian combination. Any hope of packaging reparations and inter-allied debts into an overall settlement was destroyed by America's determination to enforce the repayment of its wartime loans. Most important of all, Wilson's League, widely touted as the safety mechanism which would correct the inevitable mistakes made in the pressure cauldron of Paris, was orphaned, left in the reluctant care of Britain and France, which disagreed at Geneva as they did elsewhere.[24]

It is clear that in the wake of the Peace Conferences there were more powers dissatisfied with their lot than those that were satisfied. On the other hand, even with the lamentable absence of the United States from the ranks of those responsible for Treaty execution, Britain and France, whether or not supported by Italy, held the main levers of power in the post-war world and would continue to do so throughout the 1920s. It is also indisputable that, in September 1939, a second major conflict did begin and the key indictments against Versailles must centre on those terms that allegedly made such an outcome inevitable – perhaps including reparations, some of the new frontiers (particularly the Polish-German border) and the general treatment of Germany. Yet inevitability is a concept that sits very uneasily with most historians and it must be questionable whether it is reasonable to hold the peacemakers of 1919, the last of whom left office forever in October 1922, accountable for the decisions taken by their successors who might have followed many alternative turnings on the road that it is claimed led directly from 1919 to 1939. As Gerhard Schulz pointed out in 1967: 'There is a serious lack of logic in all verdicts passed on the peace treaty which ignore the fact that the pre-war policies could not prevent war, and which fail to appreciate the essential continuity of the pre-war period, the war, peace-time and the era of revision.'[25]

Three important recent studies approach the 1920s from different perspectives. Zara Steiner's magisterial volume, *The Lights That Failed*, offers a comprehensive coverage of the League, the economic recovery and European relations, including the role of some of the smaller states whose importance is often overlooked in a story dominated by Britain, France and Germany, together with Russia and the United States. Patrick Cohrs' *The Unfinished Peace after World War I* advances the thesis that, whereas the peacemakers in Paris failed, a cooperation between the financial and economic power of the United States and Britain's political leverage created the basis for a stable European peace until scuppered by the onset of the Great Depression. Robert Boyce argues challengingly in *The Great Interwar Crisis* that the combination of economic and political crises that ultimately proved fatal to European peace should be analysed as linked rather than coincidental occurrences. What all three accept is that it was what Steiner calls 'the hinge years' of 1929 to 1933 that created a decisive change to the world's future. The peace settlement at the end of the First World War was thus part of a much larger picture which must take account, above all, of the coming to power of Hitler and the Nazis in Germany.[26]

From 1933 onwards increasing numbers of Europeans feared that they were indeed living in an inter-war period. Hitler's initial moves were cautious and defensive, like the 1934 Non-Aggression Pact with Poland – an amazing policy for Germany, let alone Nazi Germany, given the rhetoric about the unacceptability of the 'bleeding frontier' with Poland, but one driven by a concern to prevent the Polish pre-emptive strike, that, in its shoes, Hitler would have launched against himself. What were left of the Versailles restrictions on Germany vanished with the reintroduction of conscription, the announcement of an air force, the Anglo-German naval deal, the remilitarisation of the Rhineland and then the annexation of Austria. War was avoided in 1938 at the expense of Czechoslovakia, dismembered by the Munich Conference whose guarantees for what remained of the state were proved hollow in March 1939 when the Germans marched into Prague. Six months later, relieved of any potential threat from Stalin by the Nazi-Soviet Pact, Hitler invaded Poland forcing Britain and France, with great reluctance, to declare war.

The Second World War confirmed that the attempt to place European international relations on a more stable and peaceful footing after the First World War had failed. A contemporary French cartoon showed German mice nibbling away at the Treaty of Versailles and this reflected much of the experience of the inter-war period. Germany's revenge for the 1918 Armistice came in the same railway carriage in the same clearing at Compiègne with the signature of the ceasefire that acknowledged French defeat in June 1940. Many of the Armistice terms were simply those of 1918 reversed and Hitler danced a jig as he left the carriage after the signature. Versailles was dead – and yet the European territorial settlement in 1945 retained a remarkable similarity to that of 1919 and the victors were swift to revive the idea of a new international organization to replace the League, despite its poor record in the 1930s. The Nuremberg and Tokyo Trials of Nazi and Japanese leaders resurrected, with greater success, the post-1919 attempt to extend the concept of war crimes beyond the operational to those responsible for political and military decisions. The legacy of 1919 would continue beyond 1945.

2

The German Problem

'We must stop the Germans clanking about the middle of Europe.'
A P Thornton[1]

In 1990, on the eve of German reunification, Hans-Dietrich Genscher, the West German Foreign Minister quoted the great novelist, Thomas Mann, stating: 'What we seek is a European Germany, not a German Europe.' He was articulating an aspirational solution to a conundrum that had dominated international relations in Europe, perhaps since 1871 and certainly since the 1890s. By then the rural agricultural German Empire created by Bismarck in the wake of Prussia's victory against France had transformed itself into a restless, urbanised, industrial giant with a rapidly growing, vigorous, educated and inventive population which threatened to disturb the European balance of power. Given also that its boundaries, particularly in the east but also in the west, were not readily definable in terms of geographical features such as mountain ranges or large rivers, its neighbours became increasingly apprehensive about their security. Yet at the same time, perhaps with less justification, given the relative strengths involved, the Germans were also concerned about threats to themselves.

The threat of German domination was a common thread in both the First and Second World Wars and, despite the contrary opinion of some later historians, it was no illusion. Theobald von Bethmann-Hollweg, the German Chancellor in 1914 made it very clear, in a private letter, that 'The aim of this war is not to restore the European balance of power, but precisely to eliminate for all time that which has been termed the European balance of power and to lay the foundations for German predominance in Europe.'[2] The 'German problem' was thus how to incorporate such a state into a European system which granted it the fair exercise of its enormous strengths and talents and the satisfaction of its legitimate claims to enjoy the status of a great power and yet not allow it to overwhelm its neighbours. If some (though certainly not all) European and world leaders were more confident at the end of the Cold War that, in the European Union, they had discovered the answer to that problem and hence could contemplate with some equanimity the rejoining of East and West Germany into a single state, this could be said to owe more to developments post-1945 than those post-1919, though it is possible to discern some early indications of changes in thinking about economic and political cooperation, particularly in the 1920s.

The peacemakers after the First World War knew that, amidst all their other concerns, the key question on which the peaceful and prosperous future of Europe depended was what to do with Germany. The first six months of negotiations in Paris were dominated by this question. All, even if with some reluctance on the part of Georges Clemenceau who might have wished it were not so, recognised that Germany would remain a major force in post-war Europe. Indeed for Woodrow Wilson and David Lloyd George Germany was not merely the problem but also had to be part of the solution. Their difficulty lay in finding a means that would allow Germany to reconfigure its industries to peacetime production and resume its position as a dynamo of European economic development and trade and yet inhibit the re-emergence of the military menace so recently unleashed on the world. The conflicting aspects of these objectives proved very hard to reconcile, as the history of the Conference reveals.[3]

Lloyd George's Fontainebleau memorandum in March 1919 summarises very well some of the dilemmas facing the peacemakers if they sought to create a European system that was not based entirely on perpetuating Germany's immediate and artificial post-war weakness. Recognising that new states like Poland had the right to exist and that the French had legitimate security concerns, he was nonetheless anxious to limit the number of Germans who would find themselves living in a different country as a result of the territorial adjustments made in Paris. He was acutely aware of the political minefields surrounding the whole question of German compensation payments to the Allies and he insisted, at least in this document, that these must be based upon a realistic assessment of Germany's changed circumstances and ability to pay. Above all he sought to avoid planting the seeds of a future European war whilst, in the shorter term, he feared that too harsh a settlement might drive the Germans to desperation and cause them to join with the Russian Bolsheviks in a revolutionary crusade against the West.

Yet at the same time Lloyd George knew that his fellow peacemakers had well-founded apprehensions as well as ambitions. They wished to curtail Germany's armed forces and envisaged that its territory would be depleted by the claims, some more legitimate than others, of its neighbours.

As democratically elected politicians they were anxious to satisfy the perceived demands of their constituents for retribution against those responsible for unleashing the death and destruction of the First World War upon mankind. Speeches advocating the trial and execution of Kaiser Wilhelm II and other prominent German leaders appeared to play well in the British General Election campaign immediately after the Armistice in late 1918, as did others seeking German contributions towards the astronomical expenditure required to win the war. The Allied leaders were aware that the war had only briefly been fought on German soil and that damage to German industry and property was miniscule compared to that in the devastated regions of France and Belgium where Germany's deliberate sabotage of mines, factories, orchards and other property in the 1918 retreat and even after the Armistice compounded the collateral destruction associated with industrialised warfare. The Germans had also systematically pillaged the industries of the areas they occupied for machinery and resources. In that sense compensation payments from Germany to the Allies might represent a mechanism for rebalancing its potential post-war advantage as France and Belgium struggled to rebuild their economies both literally and figuratively.

If Lloyd George and his fellow leaders aspired to encourage a democratic Germany to become a good European neighbour their efforts were hampered by two main obstacles – their own approaches and methods and German attitudes and perceptions – both of which need to be set firmly in the context of the events of the war and its immediate aftermath. While Lloyd George's allies might endorse his wish to avoid creating a peace which would encourage future wars there were serious disagreements amongst them as to how this might be accomplished and very different views of what might constitute acceptable terms or the priority of needs – one state's security requirements could represent an intolerable loss of territory or resources for another. For example the Polish Corridor linking the restored country's heartland to the Baltic seaport of Danzig, deemed essential to its survival, represented an unacceptable and festering legacy of the settlement for the majority of Germans, separating, as it did, East Prussia from the main body of Germany. Clemenceau was also quick to point out that Lloyd George's pleas for more generous treatment of Germany did not envisage concessions over the naval, mercantile marine or colonial questions judged to be vital to Britain's interests – someone else should pay whatever price was required.

The problems that created the First World War, or were made more numerous and complex by it, were exacerbated by confusion about how to organize the peace. Although the French always envisaged dictating peace terms to Germany this was not the initial expectation of British and American delegates who anticipated that the terms agreed by the Allies amongst themselves would form the basis for later negotiations with Germany and the other former enemy states. In the event direct negotiations with the Germans never occurred: they were handed the Allied draft terms on 7 May; permitted to make written observations which resulted in some minor amendments; and then on 22 June told, in Clemenceau's words, that they could either sign or not sign the text as it stood.

The main reason why the Allies did not negotiate with the Germans was because they knew that their agreed positions were very fragile and that their unity might be undermined by such direct contact. The model to which many referred

was the Vienna Congress in 1815 at the end of the Revolutionary and Napoleonic Wars. Then the skilful French diplomat, Talleyrand, succeeded in setting the former allies
against each other, and the fear in 1919 was that even a less
talented German could easily expose the differences in Allied
approaches. By March 1919 the assumption was that there
would be no face-to-face detailed discussions with German
delegates, but by then a number of Allied expert commissions
had established their demands on the contrary understanding that these needed to contain scope for concession and
compromise in an anticipated negotiation. Their proposals
were thus based on maximalist positions, from which they
expected some retreat in the course of later dialogue with
the Germans. Harold Nicolson, then a young British diplomat, highlighted some of the consequences of this confusion:
'We were never for one instant given to suppose that our recommendations were absolutely final. And thus we tended to
accept compromises, and even to support decisions, which we
ardently hoped would not, in the last resort, be approved.'[4]
Instead the sum of these demands, drawn up by the various
commissions, most working independently of each other and
with little or no overall coordination, became the draft Treaty.

The British in particular were aghast and Lloyd George
was authorised to try to alleviate some of what were seen
as excessive demands. His most notable success (which later
returned to embarrass him) was to change the original decision to assign all of Upper Silesia from Germany to Poland
and instead implement a plebiscite. The Germans were unimpressed and resented deeply the treatment they received both
in the formal sessions to receive and sign the Treaty and in the
arrangements for the accommodation of their delegates. One
intercepted telephone call declared, 'We are kept caged here,

like in a zoo. They look at us through the bars.' They resented even more the terms of the draft Treaty. Enforced disarmament with an army of 100,000 men, a tiny navy and no air force, the loss of Alsace-Lorraine to France and, in particular, territory ceded to Poland with the 'corridor' to Danzig separating East from West Prussia, the demands for the surrender of the Kaiser and other German leaders for trial and an unspecified bill for reparations seemed an unbearable burden. 'The Saar basin, ... Poland, Silesia, Oppeln ... 123 milliards to pay and for all that we are supposed to say "Thank you very much" ' shouted one delegation member, so loudly that the French listeners could not catch all his words. Ominously another caller suggested that any German signature would be meaningless and simply a tactic to gain time.[5]

It was a tough peace. The Treaty imposed huge cuts on Germany's armed forces: the 4 million men of 1914 were reduced to an army and navy totalling 115,000, deprived of an air force, tanks and a general staff. There was the uncertainty of a potentially massive reparations bill because the Reparations Commission was not due to deliver a figure until 1921. When it did so, in theory at least, the controversial inclusion of military pensions nearly doubled the sums asked of Germany but, equally, most of the apparent demand for £6,600 million ($32,000 million) was patently 'phoney money' – window dressing to make the bill palatable to Allied public opinion but whose payment was never seriously expected. Of the three series of bonds the Germans were to issue, over £4,000 million ($19,440 million) were C bonds which could, joked the Belgian Premier Georges Theunis, be stuck 'in a drawer without bothering to lock up, for no thief would be tempted to steal them'.[6] Germany's real debt, under the A and B bonds, was therefore about £2,500 million ($12,150 million), well within the margin of British and American estimates of its capacity to pay and less than an earlier German offer, admittedly with a number of unacceptable caveats, to pay £5,000 million ($24,300 million).

Germany did lose territory and population in 1919 – most accepted the loss of Alsace-Lorraine but the cession of land to Poland was a bitter blow. The conventional estimates are that Germany lost between 13 and 10 per cent of its territory and people respectively, but Robert Boyce has recently argued for a reassessment. He suggests that, discounting territory conquered in the last 50 years, the non-Germans in transferred lands and the movement of Germans in those areas to Germany itself, losses of 9.4 per cent of its land and 1.8 per cent of its pre-war population would be more accurate.[7] Such calculations would, of course, be irrelevant to the perceptions of Germans who wished to perceive the settlement as wicked and unfair. To take one example, what others might see as a desirable extension of the definition of war crimes to include not simply operational infringements but the responsibility of Wilhelm II and others for political and strategic decisions, Germany saw as 'shame clauses', topped by Article 231, the 'war guilt' clause.

The Allied benchmarks for measuring Weimar Germany's credentials as an honest post-war partner required it to acknowledge three things: that its pre-war behaviour was the main cause of the war; that it had fought the war using foul means; and that the military outcome was a decisive defeat. Unfortunately, Germany accepted none of these and here one comes up against one of the fundamental problems of the settlement. On 11 December 1918 the Republic's new leader, Friedrich Ebert, told returning German troops, 'No enemy has overcome you'; and this refusal to acknowledge reality helped to foster the myth that Germany had been 'stabbed in the back' by dissident elements at home which had undermined its victorious armed forces and encouraged the government to be seduced by Wilson's false promises. There may well have been aspects of the Treaty that were unreasonable or unfair to Germany but, despite the eloquent and sustained criticisms of Jan Smuts, Winston Churchill's proposal for a 'split the difference' peace, or later suggestions that the Allies should have at least attempted to negotiate with the Germans on the basis of their counterproposals, it is difficult to envisage any treaty concluded on the premise of German defeat that the Germans would have accepted as just and appropriate. In that sense Weimar's politicians were as self-deluding in expecting the Allies to treat them as entirely lacking in responsibility for the policies or the consequences of the defeat of Wilhemine Germany as were the leaders of the bomb plot against Hitler who anticipated that they would be able to retain at least some of the territories gained under the Nazis.[8]

It is also one of the paradoxes of the settlement that, although some of the participants assumed that this was a zero sum game in which Germany would be deprived of resources and its neighbours strengthened as a result, the reality was that, although its immediate circumstances were unpromising, a recovered Germany would be in a potentially stronger position than 1914. Then Germany had three great powers – Austria-Hungary, France and Russia – as neighbours and its freedom of action was thus limited if it wished to avoid confrontations with them. Now, in addition to its pre-war neighbours Denmark, Holland, Belgium, Luxemburg and Switzerland, Germany had frontiers with Poland, Czechoslovakia, Lithuania and the rump state of Austria.

With Poland separating Germany from Russia, only France remained of the great power neighbours, its credentials to that status undermined by its wartime casualties, the damage to its territory and demographic trends which indicated that its population was both ageing and nearly static.

The peacemakers were realistic enough to know that the Treaty was the beginning, not the end, of a process and some, if not all, were willing to consider adjustments to the settlement with a Germany that made a genuine attempt to execute it. But, as Gerald Feldman pithily remarked, 'No one has accused the Germans of honestly and forthrightly attempting to fulfil their obligations under the Treaty, and there is a general consensus that the policy of fulfilment had, as its purpose, the demonstration that fulfilment was not possible.'[9] With the abdication of its responsibilities by the Senate's refusal to ratify the Treaty, America left France and an increasingly reluctant Britain to implement peace conditions that neither would have negotiated in their present form had it not been for the role played by Wilson in 1918 and 1919. The early post-war years were thus marked by confrontation and frustration as Germany exploited the conflicting Anglo-French perceptions of its Treaty execution failures.

There were occasions, as at the Spa Conference in July 1920 when Anglo-French unity forced the German government to conform and perhaps offered a model that they should have followed more often; but in general the British tended to accept Germany's pleas that it could not fulfil certain conditions, whereas the French judged that it was more a matter of will than capability. In January 1923, in order to prove their point, French and Belgian troops occupied the Ruhr district, heartland of Germany's coal and metallurgical industries, in an attempt either to force Germany to pay reparations or to extract goods of comparable value. Germany's policy of passive resistance and printing money to pay workers from mines, factories and railways to withdraw their labour exacerbated massive inflation and led to the eventual collapse of the currency such that by December 1923 one US dollar was worth 4,200,000 million marks. Germany's capitulation in the late summer of 1923 was a Pyrrhic victory for France. Poincaré had missed his opportunity and found himself deserted by Belgium and Italy, coming under further pressure in early 1924 when the French currency lost 80 per cent of its 1914 value, as Britain and the United States expressed their disapproval of the occupation by refusing to support the franc.

Two initiatives emerged from this crisis which heralded a more cooperative phase in Franco-German relations. The British Foreign Secretary, Lord Curzon, seized upon American intimations of willingness to assist and brokered arrangements under which an international expert committee chaired by Charles Dawes, an American businessman, recommended a new reparations schedule backed by American financial aid. This initiated a process whereby American loans facilitated Germany's payments to France and Britain who were, in turn, able to begin to redeem their wartime borrowings from America. This more benign, though potentially precarious, cycle of debt repayment encouraged economic prosperity in Europe and helped create the conditions for the political initiatives which culminated in the Locarno Agreements of October 1925. Under the terms negotiated during that year by Aristide Briand for France, Austen Chamberlain for Britain and Gustav Stresemann for Germany, Britain and Italy undertook to guarantee Germany's frontiers with France and Belgium. France, Germany and Belgium undertook not to attack each other, thus ruling out any repeat of the Ruhr incursion, even had the French retained the will. The first of the three stages of Allied withdrawal from the Rhineland would begin on 1 December 1926 and Germany would enter the League as a permanent Council member. For his part Stresemann accepted that these frontiers and the Rhineland demilitarization were agreed rather than imposed conditions. The veteran British statesman Arthur Balfour congratulated Chamberlain, declaring, 'The Great War ended in November 1918. The Great Peace did not begin until Oct[ober] 1925.'[10]

Others were less sanguine, referring to 'Locarney-Blarney' and there were significant weaknesses in the agreements reached. The French view was that any new German aggression would be directed first to the east and hence they were apprehensive at Stresemann's refusal to extend the idea of agreed frontiers to Eastern Europe. They were also concerned at the limits which Locarno set on Britain's commitment to Europe. From being an ally and joint enforcer of the Treaty system, Britain now appeared to be reverting to its traditional policy of power balancer, with ambiguous obligations to defend the Franco-German frontier against a threat coming from either direction. The British also made it plain that whilst they reluctantly might concede that events in Western Europe had relevance for their security, they would make no commitments in Eastern Europe. Henry Kissinger's later verdict was that 'Locarno had not so much pacified Europe as defined the next battlefield'.[11]

Stresemann's immediate priorities were the removal of the Allied occupation and a renegotiation of the Polish Corridor but his longer term ambitions reflected German nationalist resentment against the terms of the Versailles Treaty. He wanted Upper Silesia, Eupen-Malmédy and Danzig returned, protection for the German minorities created by new frontiers and recognition of Germany's right to hold colonies under League mandates. Germany must regain full sovereign control over its territory and policies and be accepted as an equal partner in Europe. He did, however, recognize that an understanding with France was vital, though French insecurity and uncertain parliamentary support at home made his task difficult and, ultimately, impossible. His French counterpart, Briand, was torn between his conviction that Germany must be accommodated and a reluctance to surrender the security offered by Versailles.

For Britain, Chamberlain's main concern was to prevent a resentful Germany, restored to military strength in the 1960s or 1970s, from threatening European peace. His estimate of the timing of Germany's military revival proved wildly inaccurate and, as a convinced Francophile, he was never evenhanded; but he was anxious to cooperate with his colleagues and to create a Franco-German-British concert to regulate European affairs. He put his faith in the spirit rather than the detail of Locarno, trusting that it would create an atmosphere conducive to the peaceful resolution of disputes.[12]

The problem was that there were still so many unresolved issues emanating from the Versailles settlement. The tensions caused by Germany's attempts to remove the unwelcome restraints on its sovereignty pushed Briand increasingly on the defensive at a time when Britain's focus was on events in the Far East and elsewhere. Briand needed a new initiative. There had been a number of proposals to improve Franco-German economic cooperation since the war, some emanating from official approaches, others based on private initiative. Some had been aimed at providing a direct restoration of France and Belgium by German labour and services but these were not always welcomed by French and Belgian leaders, fearful of resentment from their own unemployed workers, nor, indeed by British leaders anxious to maintain and expand their European markets. On the political level ideas of a federal Europe began circulating in small, but influential groups like Count Coudenhove-Kalergi's Pan-European Union. In 1927 Briand became its president and at the League Assembly in September 1929 he spoke in favour of the principle of a federal Europe.

Briand understood that the restraints on German sovereignty imposed by Versailles were becoming increasingly fragile and needed to be replaced by an alternative system to guarantee French and European security. Germany had a much larger population and greater resources than France; and he feared that, left to its own devices, it would come to dominate the continent. His proposal (which was characteristically vague) envisaged an economic and political federation based on a closer Franco-German relationship aimed at creating a new European order once Stresemann's pleas for 'the liquidation of the war' had been met. The hope was that this would constrain Germany within a wider European organization, incidentally strengthening western democratic civilization against the threats posed by the Soviet Union. It might also help Europe to counter a growing fear of American economic power and penetration – Georges Duhamel's *America The Menace* and Raymond Aron and Armand Dandier's *The American Cancer* were both popular books in France in the 1930s.

In Britain, however, Briand's ideas were not welcomed. Officials denounced 'M. Briand's pan-European clap-trap' but also raised concerns about 'the Europe which France is organising' from which Britain might be excluded. If this initiative presaged the later post-Second World War developments that created the European Union, its motives and some of the reactions to it would also have been familiar to commentators after 1950.[13]

Within a month of Briand's speech, of which he had welcomed and stressed the economic rather than the political aspects, Stresemann was dead. Later that same October the American stock market collapsed and the ensuing economic, financial and political chaos ushered in what Zara Steiner has labelled 'the hinge years' of 1929–33. Briand's idea was an early casualty, but this first proposal of a voluntary European union raises the fascinating historical question of why an aspiration which had existed in various guises for centuries should reach such a prominent place in the international political agenda at a particular moment. Meanwhile soaring unemployment in Germany, among other factors, prompted disillusioned voters to seek extremist solutions, with the Communist KPD and Hitler's NSDAP the major beneficiaries, although Hitler's eventual appointment as Chancellor in January 1933 owed at least as much to intrigues and jealousy within the German ruling elite as it did to democratic support.

The next six years saw Hitler's Germany grow in strength and confidence from a position in which he concluded an unlikely Non-Aggression Pact in January 1934 with Poland in order to safeguard Germany to one in which the even more unlikely Nazi-Soviet Pact of August 1939 set the scene for a new war of aggression. Britain, and an increasingly reluctant and sceptical France, sought to tackle this new manifestation of 'the German problem' by trying to identify and rectify Hitler's real or alleged grievances with the present order. They were encouraged in this task of appeasement by frequent reminders from Hitler about the unacceptability of that order and the increasing boldness of his actions. Buoyed by the Saarland's overwhelming vote to be reintegrated into Germany in January 1935, Hitler reintroduced conscription and announced the existence of a German air force in March 1935. A year later German troops marched back into the Rhineland, which the last Allied occupying forces had left in June 1930, remilitarizing it in defiance not just of Versailles but also of Locarno.

By this time the great experiment of the League of Nations had foundered, first over Japanese actions in 1931 in Manchuria, about whose status there was some dispute, and finally over the Italian invasion of Abyssinia (Ethiopia) in October 1935, an act of aggression against a fellow League member about which, despite Abyssinia's dubious human rights record, there could be no doubt. Britain's policies of inadequate support of the League condemned it to failure, at the same time alienating Italy, a potential member of a group that might restrain Germany.[14] Instead Mussolini entered an increasingly close relationship with Hitler.

Two years later, in March 1938, Hitler reunited his homeland of Austria with Germany, exposing a new and vulnerable frontier for Czechoslovakia, whose 3 million German speakers in the Sudetenland offered him another opportunity to exploit Allied guilt over the way self-determination had been implemented in Paris. He duly annexed the Sudetenland after the Munich Conference in September 1938. In March 1939, abandoning all pretence of defending a German minority, he seized the remainder of Czechoslovakia, and on 1 September attacked Poland, causing Britain and France to declare war two days later.

The Germans were once more clanking about the middle of Europe, initially with enormous success. Rapid victory against Poland in the autumn of 1939 was followed by equally sudden and devastating defeats of Norway, Denmark, Belgium, Holland and France in the spring and early summer of 1940, leaving Britain isolated and seemingly doomed, despite the miraculous evacuation and repatriation of many of its troops but little of their equipment from Dunkirk. Even when a combination of the Royal Air Force's victory in the Battle of Britain and the Royal Navy's control of the English Channel forced Hitler to abandon his plans to invade there seemed little prospect of reversing Germany's huge continental gains. When Hitler attacked the USSR in June 1941 and reached the edge of Moscow in December things appeared even bleaker, but the Russian winter and an improving performance by the Red Army stabilized the front. On 7 December Japan attacked American naval forces in the Pacific at Pearl Harbor, Hawaii and on 11 December, for reasons that are still difficult to comprehend, Hitler declared war on the United States.[15]

Germany now faced three of the pre-war great powers, two of which were about to transform themselves into superpowers but it would take a considerable time to bring the full weight of Allied economic superiority to bear and to produce combat troops and equipment capable of undoing a German Europe. For much of 1942 the initiative remained with Germany and Japan, but then the tide of war turned and the Allies began first to stop losing and then to start winning.[16] May 1945 was *die Stunde Null* (absolute zero hour) for Germany, bombarded relentlessly from the air, invaded and occupied by Anglo-American forces from the west and, with particular brutality and rapine, by an avenging Red Army from the east. This time defeat was unambiguous and surrender unconditional.

A victorious coalition once again faced the dilemmas of what to do with Germany and of maintaining a unity of purpose now that the main enemy had been defeated. The complexities of the former problem contributed to the unsuccessful outcome of the latter as the two major Allied powers, the US and USSR, fell out. Although both American President Franklin D Roosevelt and Soviet leader Joseph Stalin envisaged that their wartime cooperation would continue, both did so on the basis of fundamental and mutual misunderstandings of the aims, strengths and weaknesses of the other. Their intention at the Yalta Conference in February 1945 was to divide Germany, once defeated, into zones of military occupation but to administer the country as a single unit under Four Power control (at British Premier Winston Churchill's insistence, France was included as one of the partners).

Despite various wartime proposals to reduce Germany to an agricultural state, depriving it of its industrial might or even to break it up into smaller units, there seems to have been no serious consideration at the end of the war of dividing Germany in two, nor any thought that the military zones of occupation would be of particular political significance. As with the arrangements for the United Nations, the proposals for the future administration of Germany, and particularly the city of Berlin, an island of Four Power control in the midst of the Soviet zone, presupposed the continuation of a working partnership between the major Allies.

With Roosevelt's death in April 1945, Harry S Truman replaced him as President, but the underlying realities remained. There was little that the allies could do to prevent the Soviet Union from redesignating Poland's frontiers, pushing the country bodily over one hundred miles further west, so that its border with the USSR was now very close to that proposed by the Paris Peace Conference in 1920, and that with Germany the line of the Oder-Neisse Rivers. Nor could they prevent the Baltic states of Latvia, Lithuania and Estonia and much of Eastern and Central Europe from falling under Soviet domination. All this and the fate of the Polish government in exile, many of whose members were arrested when they returned from London to Soviet-dominated Warsaw in 1945, raised concerns about Soviet aims and ambitions; but the period between March 1946 and March 1947 proved to be the crucial year in which relations between the US and USSR turned sour.

On 5 March 1946, Churchill, now the former British Prime Minister, spoke in Truman's home town of Fulton, Missouri, warning of an 'iron curtain' that was descending across Europe and appealing for an Anglo-American alliance to thwart Soviet ambitions. Reaction in the United States was extremely hostile and Truman was forced to deny prior knowledge of Churchill's intentions. Yet, almost exactly a year later, on 12 March 1947, Truman announced, without serious opposition, that 'it must be the policy of the United States to support free peoples who are resisting attempted subjugation by armed minorities or by outside pressures'. The 'Truman Doctrine' never named the USSR, but no one was in any doubt against whom it was directed. It, and the announcement by Secretary of State George Marshall on 5 June of the European Recovery Programme better known as the Marshall Plan, offering economic assistance to 'any government that is willing to assist in the task of recovery', were key episodes in the development of the Cold War between the US and USSR, intensifying, whether deliberately or by unintended consequence, the split between east and west in Europe.[17]

The growing difficulties of administering Germany as a single unit were important factors in this change of heart. The Anglo-Americans resented in particular the Soviet extraction of reparations from their zones (which they administered increasingly as a single unit), mainly in the form of industrial equipment, with no reciprocal food deliveries from its own zone which included much of Germany's agricultural land, and indeed the confiscation of the very rolling stock in which the equipment was delivered. The British government had to introduce rationing for bread, something which had not happened during the war itself, and then explain to its people why this was necessary to feed the Germans with whom they had recently been fighting. The Soviet devaluation of the joint occupation currency was a further concern. More generally, Americans worried about the constituency for communism that might be created by homeless and hopeless populations, evidenced by impressive communist showings in Western European elections, and the danger to their own prosperity should their European markets collapse.

In an atmosphere of increasing mutual suspicion and resentment the joint administration of Germany collapsed long before the Soviets formally withdrew from it in March 1948. On 1 January 1947 the Anglo-Americans combined their zones into Bizonia, which the French soon joined, effectively dividing Germany into western and Soviet zones. The inclusion of the western zone amongst those parts of Europe eligible for Marshall aid strengthened the growing split between east and west, whilst American resolve to remain in Europe was boosted by Stalin's blockade of road and rail access to Berlin between June 1948 and May 1949 (which was overcome by a massive Anglo-American airlift of food and supplies to the beleaguered western zone of the city). In 1949, with the creation of the Federal and the German Democratic Republics, Stalin's prediction of January 1948 came true: 'The West will make Western Germany their own and we shall turn Eastern Germany into our own state.' [18] Neither East nor West would contemplate a united Germany controlled by the other; instead it was split into two unequal parts, with West Germany (the Federal Republic of Germany) constituting roughly two-thirds of the territory.

For some this outcome was unexpected but not unwelcome. The division of Germany might, in the new language of the atomic age, deprive it of its critical mass and prevent further explosions; but now the pressures of the Cold War, both within and beyond Europe, in particular the outbreak of the Korean War in June 1950, encouraged America to require West Germany to make a greater contribution to western economic and military security. Once again the problem was how to facilitate such a West German role without it developing strengths which it might turn on its European neighbours, especially the French who were understandably nervous.

A possible answer came from a man who had been involved with two of the more hopeful aspects of the 1920s. Jean Monnet, a Frenchman of many talents, was the first Deputy Secretary General of the League of Nations and had been one of those advocating greater Franco-German economic cooperation. The crucial lessons he learned from these experiences were 'that it is impossible to solve Europe's problems among States which retain full national sovereignty' and that what was required was some new mechanism which could, in certain circumstances, compel its members to undertake actions or policies – the concept of supranationality. Yet he understood the jealousy with which national governments guarded their sovereignty so he had a very delicate path to tread.[19]

Jean Monnet – the First Citizen of Europe

JEAN MONNET (1888–1979)

Jean Monnet was a man of many parts. He was born in Cognac in France where his family were brandy merchants. Before the First World War he worked in London and travelled widely to North America, Russia, Egypt and Scandinavia for the family business. During the war he helped to coordinate Allied economic efforts, in particular in wheat production and the management of transport. From 1920 until 1923 he was the first Deputy Secretary General of the League of Nations before resigning to resume an eventful and colourful business career in banking, finance, liquor sales and railways in America, China and Europe during which he made and lost several fortunes. In the Second World War Monnet played a major role in coordinating Allied purchasing and American production, acting as a member of the British Supply Council in Washington. An early follower of General Charles de Gaulle after the defeat of France in June 1940, he suggested the idea of an Anglo-French union that Winston Churchill proposed on 16 June 1940. From 1943 Monnet served on de Gaulle's National Liberation Committee and his ideas for the economic reconstruction of France, encapsulated in his 1945 Plan, were highly influential after the war. Although his early post-war policies concentrated on the French exploitation of German resources Monnet believed that in order to enjoy a proper and equal relationship with the United States, which he much admired and whose cooperation he deemed vital, the western European states must pool their efforts. He was aware, however, of the sensitivity of states where their national sovereignty was concerned and hence adopted a gradualist approach to his eventual goal of European union. His proposal to merge Franco-German coal and steel production became the basis of the European Coal and Steel Community, established by the 1951 Treaty of Paris and which he served as the first President of its High Authority. Although his later suggestions of European Defence and Political Communities failed, he was the inspiration for the Treaty of Rome which created the European Economic Community or Common Market in 1957 and has since developed into the European Union which now comprises 27 countries. On 2 April 1976 the European Council named Monnet as the first 'Honorary Citizen of Europe'.

Monnet's suggestion to integrate the French and West German coal and steel industries, made to French Foreign Minister Robert Schuman in May 1950, reflected his belief that, 'We must not try to solve the German problem in its present context. We must change the context by transforming the basic facts'. He sought to do this by creating a pooled control of two of the main components of both weapons of war and the requirements of peacetime prosperity because he believed that the unrestricted exercise of German sovereignty had failed in the past but that it was unrealistic to seek to curtail German sovereignty unilaterally. By choosing steel and coal (industries in which Franco-German cooperation was a necessity because it was impossible to exploit the resources of the Ruhr, Alsace-Lorraine and the Saar independently of each other) and renouncing the failed idea of complete control of these assets by either France or Germany, Monnet picked an area of the economy which was highly symbolic and deeply practical and which he could use as a first step to a larger goal. As he told Schuman in a short sentence of enormous profundity, 'This proposal has an essential political objective: to make a breach in the ramparts of national sovereignty which will be narrow enough to secure consent, but deep enough to open the way towards the unity that is essential to peace.' [20]

Four other states, Italy, together with Belgium, the Netherlands and Luxemburg (collectively known as Benelux) joined France and West Germany in the European Coal and Steel

> 'This proposal has an essential political objective: to make a breach in the ramparts of national sovereignty which will be narrow enough to secure consent, but deep enough to open the way towards the unity that is essential to peace.'
> JEAN MONNET, 1950

Community (ECSC) created by the 1951 Treaty of Paris. Britain declined to become a member. The Community's High Authority introduced an element of supranationality requiring its members to act as a community rather than national decision-makers, though the almost insatiable contemporary demand for coal and steel made their task much easier. Monnet sought to build on the ECSC's success by suggesting a European Defence Community (EDC) as a way to allow West Germany to make a military contribution without creating a German army, with a European Political Community (EPC) as a necessary partner. These proved steps too far and instead, encouraged by Britain's agreement to commit to west European defence even if not to the new institutions, West Germany was permitted to re-arm in 1955 as a member of an expanded North Atlantic Treaty Organisation (NATO), originally established in the wake of the Berlin Blockade in 1949 with the purpose, according to its first Secretary-General Lord Ismay, of keeping 'the Americans in, the Germans down, and the Russians out'.[21]

Undeterred by the set-backs to EDC and EPC, Monnet regrouped and, after a conference of ECSC members at Messina in June 1955, returned with two new proposals for a European Economic Community (EEC) and a European Atomic Energy Community (Euratom), hoping to use the latter, with its potential for both massive destruction or constructive power, to parallel the ECSC's symbolic significance as a statement of peaceful intent. The Treaty of Rome was signed in March 1957 and the EEC and Euratom began on 1 January 1958, still based on the original six members of ECSC. Since then the European project has grown enormously, beginning with the accession of Britain, Ireland and Denmark in 1973, and has undergone structural changes, including direct elections to a European Parliament, its rebranding as the European Union (EU) under the Maastricht Treaty of November 1993 and the nomination in late 2009 of a European President and a Foreign Minister (High Representative) as authorized by the Lisbon Treaty signed in December 2007. The EU in 2010 comprised 27 states, 16 of which shared the euro as a common currency becoming, since the end of the Cold War, much more representative of historic Europe than the nations on the fringes of Western Europe which constituted its original membership.

Monnet's ideas encompassed more than a possible solution to the 'German problem'. Although a convinced Atlanticist, he believed that the relationship between Europe and the United States must be based on equality rather than the massive American superiority of the early post-war years. He was also mindful of the threat posed by the Soviet Union. It certainly would be simplistic to suggest that the EU and its predecessors constitute the only reason for Western Europe's years of peace since 1945 – many would cite the overarching American security presence and the unacceptable stakes of a nuclear conflict in the context of the Cold War as of great significance in that regard. Nonetheless Monnet's institutions have provided an effective framework for Franco-German cooperation and the wider development of Germany's European identity, even though there remain continuing tensions between the dual bases of authority within the Union, intergovernmentalism and supranationalism.

Were he still alive Monnet might be disappointed by the enduring strength of national sovereignty and he would certainly have been surprised by the rapid and unexpected collapse of the Soviet empire and then the Soviet Union itself. Divided Europe was, for Monnet, a given, with divided

THE BERLIN WALL
In 1945 the former German capital, which lay deep in the zone of Germany occupied by the Soviet Union, came under the four power control of Britain, France, the US and USSR. The Cold War division of Germany into East and West was paralleled in Berlin except that here travel between the two zones was relatively easy, with many East Berliners commuting to work in the west of the city. As increasing numbers began to use Berlin as an escape point from the communist world in the 1950s, political tensions about the future of the western enclave rose, leading to several crises in East-West relations. To stop the exodus, which totalled over three million people, the German Democratic Republic (East Germany) constructed a post and barbed wire fence separating the two parts of the city overnight on 12/13 August 1961. For 28 years East and West Berlin were separated by a barrier that evolved into an elaborate concrete wall and security zones with tank traps and mine fields in which intruders were shot on sight. Escapes continued, some using tunnels and one, famously, a hot-air balloon; but over 100 people lost their lives in failed attempts. The opening of the Wall on 9 November 1989 symbolized the end of the Cold War as incredulous East Berliners, watched by millions of television viewers across the world, surged unimpeded through the checkpoints.

Germany its most powerful – and potentially its most dangerous – symbol. The 1948 Blockade highlighted Berlin's central role in East-West relations and through the 1950s and early 1960s the Soviets engineered a number of crises over the future of the city, threatening to end the rights of the Western powers to access West Berlin by concluding a separate peace treaty with East Germany. The West made it clear that this was not acceptable, but the Soviets enjoyed a massive superiority in conventional weapons so there was a strong likelihood that any conflict might rapidly become nuclear. West Berlin was a particular threat to the Soviet Union in a number of ways: as a showcase for Western consumerism, culture and political philosophy, but also as an accessible escape route

Strengthening the Berlin Wall, November 1961

for increasing numbers of East Germans who wished to leave the communist system and by 1961 over three million had done so. Two key events brought this period of high stakes nuclear roulette to an end: the building of the Berlin Wall in August 1961 which sealed off East Berlin from the West, and the Cuban Missile Crisis of October 1962 (see Chapter 6).

Relations between the two German states eased in the 1970s, with each recognizing the other; and although the rhetoric of reunification on both sides of the inner German border continued, the division of Germany seemed to be permanent until the dramatic events within the Soviet Bloc in 1989. US President Ronald Reagan may have challenged the Soviet leader in a speech in June 1987, 'Mr Gorbachev, tear down this wall!', but an infectious opening of borders between East and West in the summer of 1989 took everyone by surprise and was not universally welcomed.

Britain's Premier, Margaret Thatcher, had very different advice for Gorbachev in September 1989: 'We do not want a united Germany. This would lead to a change to post-war borders, and we cannot allow that because such a development would undermine the stability of the whole international situation and could endanger our security.' Others spoke of the dangers of a 'Fourth Reich'. Even after the fall of the Wall on 9 November 1989 Thatcher remained sceptical, telling Gorbachev, 'I am convinced that reunification needs a long transition period. All Europe is watching this not without a degree of fear, remembering very well who started the two world wars.' François Mitterand, the French President, was also initially opposed but realised that the process was unstoppable. In October 1990 East Germany acceded to the Federal Republic, reunifying the post-war German territory.[22]

Germany, like West Germany before it, remains the most

> 'I am convinced that reunification needs a long transition period. All Europe is watching this not without a degree of fear, remembering very well who started the two world wars.'
> **MARGARET THATCHER, 1989**

populous member of the European Union and an economic giant within the system; but, in the second half of the 20th century and the early years of the present century, it has not tried to repeat the tragic attempts in the two World Wars to create a German Europe. The Versailles settlement did not provide an adequate response to the 'German problem', though the extent to which its failure was responsible for a second conflict is certainly debatable. With defeat in 1945, the shocking revelations of Nazi criminality and the continuing presence of the major winners of the Second World War in its territory, Germany was in no position, even had it wished to do so, to mount a new military challenge and indeed the Basic Law (constitution) of the Federal Republic committed it, as a moral imperative, to pursue peace and European unity. There can be little doubt that the more imaginative approaches of the post-1945 era, early signs of which may be detected in the 1920s, have helped to make Thomas Mann's aspiration more of a reality and to fulfil the exhortation of the distinguished historian and Second World War veteran, A P (Archie) Thornton.

3

The League of Nations and the United Nations

'What are the purposes that you hold in your heart against the fortunes of the world?'

Woodrow Wilson[1]

The 20th century witnessed two attempts to create a new order in international affairs, the League of Nations after the First World War and the United Nations Organization in the wake of the Second. Inevitably each was much influenced by the circumstances in which it originated but there was a real ambition on both occasions to produce an institution that would inhibit, if not prevent, mankind from resorting to war – a task that took on added urgency after the explosion of atomic bombs on Hiroshima and Nagasaki in August 1945 announced the arrival of weapons which really did have the capacity to destroy life and civilizations on a global scale. In many ways, however, the nuclear age was only the realization of fears which the inter-war period also entertained. The British government's grossly inflated pre-1939 estimates of the scale of civilian casualties expected from sustained German bombing, probably also using gas and chemical weapons, were already little short of cataclysmic.

There was thus a determination, after both these unprecedentedly destructive conflicts, to establish structures and codes of conduct that would encourage alternative modes of dispute resolution. The League did not fulfil the expectations of its advocates, which were overambitious and unrealistic, yet the great powers still established a replacement after the Second World War. In its turn, the United Nations has also suffered disappointments and experienced frustrations when rendered powerless by the determination of the major powers either to block the initiatives of rivals or to act independently. Nonetheless, despite their inability to deliver the world peace their most hopeful supporters envisaged, both the League and UN have helped to transform the norms and conduct of international relations and represent a remarkable evolution from pre-1914 diplomacy.

The League of Nations was the most ambitious of the attempts by the peacemakers in 1919 to ensure that the dreadful experiences of the First World War would not be repeated. Taken at its face value the League Covenant represented a revolution in international relations, the abandonment of concepts like the balance of power or exclusive alliances in favour of a system of collective security under which its members promised, in Article 10, 'to respect and preserve as against external aggression the territorial integrity and existing independence of all members of the League'. It was a startling commitment, based on the idea that peace was indivisible and that it was the responsibility of all to safeguard the security of each of the members. However, Robert Cecil's pertinent question – 'Yes, but do any of us mean it?' – expressed the doubts of many inter-war decision makers who were reluctant to discard the methods with which they were familiar for an unknown and untested ideal and who were wary of the implications of such an undertaking.[2]

Woodrow Wilson believed, however, that his rapturous receptions in Paris, London and Rome in December 1918 and January 1919 signified support for his proposal. 'I find in my welcome the thought that they [the Allied nations] have fought to do away with the old order and establish a new one.' The proposed basis of this new order was the last of his Fourteen Points of 8 January 1918: 'A general association of governments must be formed under specific covenants for the purpose of affording mutual guarantees of political independence and territorial integrity to great and small States alike.' He was convinced that 'the great game, now for ever discredited, of the Balance of Power' was no more.

His European colleagues were less sure. While there was clearly a body of intellectual and popular support for a new system of international relations to replace the mechanisms that had failed in 1914, that enthusiasm was not necessarily shared by the political elites. The public, desperate for any organization that could prevent a repetition of the First World War, expected its leaders to support the League. Those leaders were, for a variety of reasons, not entirely willing to do so but equally would not dissociate themselves from the League through a strong sense of electoral self-preservation. One of the fault lines running through the whole system in the 1920s and into the 1930s was this dichotomy between what political leaders told their electorates and what they really believed. In 1935 the Abyssinian crisis would bring the British government, in particular, face-to-face with the consequences of this problem.[3]

The outbreak of war in 1914, reinforced by its seemingly interminable duration and dreadful toll, had encouraged calls for a radical revision of the existing structures of international relations. Sir Edward Grey, then the British Foreign Secretary, was convinced that had he been able to force colleagues in Berlin and Vienna to attend and abide by the decisions of a European conference of great powers the war could have been avoided. As recently as 1913 the London Conference on the Balkans had suggested that the 19th century Concert of Europe was still capable of preventing general war, as its admirers claimed it had done since 1815. But the Concert was a voluntary system, depending upon the willingness of the powers to participate without any mechanism to force them to consult. Grey thus favoured a new international security architecture with powers to demand consultation and delay before war could be declared, but it was Wilson who became the most effective advocate of a new system even if not its most influential designer.

Underlying every aspect of Wilson's policies was his fundamental belief in the basic goodness of mankind. Empowering the people would produce a prosperous and peaceful future. They should choose the state in which they lived and then control its government. Being good and also rational they would choose wise governments, facilitating domestic harmony and economic progress. The League of Nations, an organization designed not to outlaw war but to prevent the sort of rapid slide into conflict that had happened in the summer of 1914, would create a space for calmer reflection, enabling the people to extend their wise counsel to the field of international relations. Making the world safe for democracy would also make the world a safer place, because democratic governments would heed the warning voices of their informed public opinions and not allow disputes to deteriorate into war.

Wilson placed great faith in the persuasive strength of his democratic, self-determining world. 'My conception of the League of Nations is just this, that it shall operate as the organized moral force of men throughout the world and that whenever or wherever wrong and aggression are planned or contemplated, this searching light of conscience will be turned upon them and men everywhere will ask, "What are the purposes that you hold in your heart against the fortunes of the world?"' Cecil echoed this belief 'What we rely upon is public opinion ... and if we are wrong about that, then the whole thing is wrong.' The French, who sought more tangible military safeguards, were unconvinced. Their delegate to the League Commission Ferdinand Larnaude was heard to mutter, 'Am I at a Peace Conference or in a madhouse?'; while Georges Clemenceau growled '*vox populi, vox diaboli*' (the voice of the people is the voice of the devil) and paid Wilson the dubious compliment of referring to 'la noble candeur de son esprit' (the high-minded naivety of his thought).[4]

> 'My conception of the League of Nations is just this, that it shall operate as the organized moral force of men throughout the world and that whenever or wherever wrong and aggression are planned or contemplated, this searching light of conscience will be turned upon them and men everywhere will ask, "What are the purposes that you hold in your heart against the fortunes of the world?"'
>
> **WOODROW WILSON, 1918**

The key to collective security was that aggression would be met by automatic and unequivocal sanctions. One of the earliest study groups investigating the subject proposed that any member going to war without exhausting the League's procedures 'will become *ipso facto* [automatically] at war with all the other Allied states ...', and Wilson's own first draft stated 'Should any Contracting Power break or disregard its covenant ... it shall thereby *ipso facto* ... become at war with all the members of the League.' This encapsulated the central idea of his alternative international organization – the automatic guarantee by all the members of a universal alliance to defend the political independence and territorial integrity of other member states in the face of unprovoked aggression. Wilson's wording, however, exposed the central problem of the system – the clash between the sovereignty of the member states and the requirement that any guarantee be absolute, unconditional and automatic. His proposal meant that the most fundamental decision for any sovereign government – that of going to war – would not only be made for it by another government but by one which had broken its international pledges.

Wilson's advisers reminded him that this was incompatible with the constitutional right of the United States Congress to determine any American declaration of war and his European allies found it equally unacceptable. He thus changed Article 16 of the Covenant to read: 'Should any Contracting Power break or disregard its covenant ... it shall thereby *ipso facto* be deemed to have committed an act of war against all the members of the League.' By restoring the discretion to individual member governments to determine their response to any such situation he was bowing to the inevitable victory of national sovereignty over the idea of any supranational authority, but this did rob collective security of the immediacy upon which any credible guarantee depended.[5]

In reality the main members of the League were not prepared to forsake the existing system of international relations and did not see it as a replacement but more as a development and improvement of current practice; but this was complicated by ambiguities already apparent in 1919. The League was supposed to offer its members an absolute guarantee of their territorial integrity and yet, at the same time, be the vehicle for peaceful change because, for the British in particular, a system that did not allow for flexibility and change over time would simply be destroyed by its own rigidity and indeed could constitute a threat to the world peace it was designed to deliver. Wilson and Lloyd George both hoped the League would correct the mistakes that the Peace Conference was bound to make and Article 19 allowed for the reconsideration of 'international conditions whose continuance might endanger the peace of the world'. Clearly some of the many disputed new frontiers of Europe might fall under that definition; and presumably the remedy would be to alter them, thus infringing the territorial integrity of one or more states.

Yet, if the League insurance policy did not protect all states, what value could be placed on Article 10? Or did it only apply to some states under certain conditions not very clearly spelt out in the small print? It said little for France's belief in collective security that it required a separate Anglo-American guarantee against any renewed German aggression presumably already covered by the Covenant. If great powers required reassurance why should smaller powers trust the system to protect them? There were also the potentially sticky questions of what constituted 'unprovoked aggression' (it would later take the United Nations until 1974 to produce even a vague definition of aggression) and whether a potential case would always be absolutely clear and unambiguous.

The League was indeed 'the world's first truly international organization', but it never became the universal body that its mission demanded. Its 42 founder members in 1920 consisted of 29 of the victorious powers and some ex-neutrals. The major enemy states were initially excluded. Russia remained unrepresented until 1934. Its early membership, and Wilson's insistence that the Covenant become the first part of all the Paris Treaties, did give some credence to the damaging idea that it was a 'League of Victors'. In all, 63 states joined the League in the course of its existence with membership at its peak of 58 in 1934–5; but 16 states, including Japan, Germany and Italy withdrew and the USSR was expelled. The great powers were never all simultaneously in membership and America's absence – the Senate's rejection of the Treaty meant it did not join – dealt the organization a crippling blow from the outset.

The League lost American power and counsel leaving the other great powers with a much greater burden. America would thus avoid the costs of maintaining and enforcing the new system, thereby potentially gaining a commercial advantage if the League powers found that dealing with a dispute diverted their energy from normal industry and trade. It might also constitute a potential threat if, for example, the League called for a naval blockade against an aggressive state with which the Americans still wished to trade. Anglo-American relations had always been sensitive about the freedom of the seas, as the American assertion of their absolute right as neutrals to continue trading with either or both parties to a war clashed with the British naval policy of blockade to deprive its enemies of goods essential to their war effort. The 1812–14 War had been fought on this issue which threatened further conflict during the American Civil War and the First World War. Stanley Baldwin, the Conservative British Prime Minister, said he would always discuss any such blockade with Washington before allowing the Royal Navy to become the

League's enforcer. As with so many other post-war matters, America's withdrawal from the implementation of policies in whose creation it had played a vital role left Britain and France as the main players; and Geneva, where the League established its headquarters, became yet another arena in which their contested visions clashed.[6]

If Britain was concerned about the possibility of League action leading to a naval confrontation with the United States, Canada with its 3,000-mile land frontier with America was equally anxious. It made four attempts in early League Assemblies to delete or dilute Article 10, one delegate declaring, rather tactlessly, that Canada lived 'in a fire-proof house far from inflammable materials' and saw no reason to be part of an international fire brigade – so much for the indivisibility of peace! Technically these motions failed, but in 1925 the Locarno signatories recognized the reality that members' obligations under the Covenant would be limited by their 'geographical situations and special conditions'. Each state must decide what, if any, contribution to make to any collective security operation and sanctions under Article 16 were not mandatory.[7] As Gilbert Murray, the chairman of the League of Nations Union in Britain pointed out, collective security was not very secure: 'The obligation in article 10 is at once too widespread for any prudent nation to accept, and

'The obligation in article 10 is at once too widespread for any prudent nation to accept, and too vague for any prudent nation to bank upon. As the Covenant now stands, no nation would be really safe in acting on the supposition that, if it were attacked, the rest of the League would send armies to defend it.'

GILBERT MURRAY, CHAIRMAN OF THE LEAGUE OF NATIONS UNION IN BRITAIN, 1923

too vague for any prudent nation to bank upon. As the Covenant now stands, no nation would be really safe in acting on the supposition that, if it were attacked, the rest of the League would send armies to defend it.'[8]

Not surprisingly this situation was unacceptable to the French but there was little enthusiasm in Britain for attempts to strengthen collective security, first by the Treaty of Mutual Assistance and then the Geneva Protocol. The Foreign Office and the service departments, fearing undefined and unacceptable military commitments, resisted, unconvinced by optimistic advocates of these proposals who argued that they would enable and encourage mutual and continuing disarmament. The pessimistic and paradoxical doubts of opponents were later neatly summarized by the British Committee of Imperial Defence in November 1935: 'It is almost impossible to forecast the nations with which we might be brought into conflict owing to a breach of the Covenant ... It is also difficult to calculate what the composition of our ... [armed] forces should be, as no reasonable warning of the conditions under which we might have to operate can be given. Consequently ... [a]s the result of the principle of collective security we must be more instantly ready for war than before.'[9]

It became clear very quickly that the League would be an adjunct to existing international relations mechanisms and often one to be kept at arm's length; Britain and France had no intention of allowing Treaty enforcement to become a League responsibility. The Foreign Office resisted, for example, any attempt to pass to the League the resolution of problems arising from unauthorized German troop numbers in the Ruhr district in the wake of the Kapp *putsch* in Germany in March 1920. Nor, in 1921, despite the provisions of Article 213 of the Treaty, were Britain and France prepared to see the

League as a credible replacement for the Inter-Allied Military Mission Control Commission as the major enforcer of German disarmament. These matters were for the Allied governments to settle.[10]

The League did have its uses. Handing over the government of Danzig and the Saar to the League solved tricky problems of reconciling the national self-determination of the inhabitants with the need to provide Poland with a port and France with coal. The awkward and demanding parcel of minority protection could conveniently be passed to Geneva; and Britain and France were driven to seek League intervention after they could not agree on how the 1921 plebiscite results in Upper Silesia should be interpreted. Britain was unhappy with the outcome recommended by a League committee, disparagingly dismissed by Sir Maurice Hankey, the Cabinet Secretary, as consisting of 'A pro-French Belgian, two Dagos, and a Chink' – hardly an indication of great respect.[11] The League was responsible for supervising the mandates under which the former German and Ottoman colonies had been allocated to the victorious powers – in one sense a fig leaf to cover imperialism but in another an important recognition of the principle of trusteeship backed by some accountability.

The League's beneficial role in inhibiting slavery, international prostitution and the trading of drugs, in promoting the protection of refugees and minorities or preventing and controlling disease was acknowledged at the time and by later historians. What is not entirely clear is whether the 'new diplomacy' achieved substantially different results than the 'old' might have done in similar circumstances. It did enjoy some successes, most notably in the Swedish-Finnish quarrel over the Åland Islands in 1920 and in the Greco-Bulgarian dispute of 1925 but, significantly, both were in accessible parts of Europe, were between minor states, and did not involve the direct interests of a great power.

The League was much less effective where any of these criteria did not apply, for example incidents such as the Polish seizure of Vilna in 1920s or in the Bolivia-Paraguay confrontation of the early 1930s. It had no role following the Franco-Belgian occupation of the Ruhr in 1923. In the same year the Corfu incident involving Greece and Italy indicated that the exigencies of the international system, great power politics and prestige could all play their role in undermining League involvement. Instead, Italian susceptibilities were spared by the inter-Allied Conference of Ambassadors tackling the problem, despite Lord Curzon's opinion that 'if we do not back up the [Greek] appeal to the League, that institution may as well shut its doors'.[12] When the incident was remote and involved a major power, such as in Manchuria in 1931, the League struggled to make any impact and its problems were not eased by the difficulty of clearly identifying Japan as an aggressor or indeed whether Manchuria was effectively part of China.[13] It was, however, in Abyssinia in 1935 that the demands of the old and new diplomacies came into the sharpest confrontation.

On 3 January 1935 Abyssinia appealed inconclusively to the League under the auspices of Article 11 after Italian and Abyssinian forces clashed at Wal-Wal in Abyssinia in December 1934. Nine months later Mussolini, Italy's fascist leader, used this incident as an excuse to invade Abyssinia on 3 October 1935 with the intention of consolidating Italy's north-east African empire and redeeming the humiliating Adowa defeat of 1896. Such behaviour might have been acceptable to the other great powers (though not to the invaded peoples) in the 19th century, but it was not so in 1935. Italy had clearly committed an act of aggression against a fellow member of the League – ironically one whose application for membership it had strongly supported in 1923. Abyssinia, already well known in Geneva for its dubious dealings in slavery, was not the ideal test case as a deserving cause for international solidarity but the circumstances meant that the credibility of the League and the 'new diplomacy' became inextricably linked with the response to this problem.

That response would be determined by Britain and France but their positions were complicated by the demands of the 'old diplomacy'. Faced with Hitler's repudiation of key elements of Versailles, Britain and France were anxious to retain Italian support in Europe. Italy had an impressive modern fleet and Mussolini boasted of the power and size of his air force. His action in deterring Hitler from further intervention in Austria after the murder of Chancellor Engelbert Dollfuss in July 1934 by despatching troops to the Brenner frontier bolstered Italy's credentials as an important component in any European balance of power. An Anglo-French-Italian meeting at Stresa in April 1935 seemed to Britain and France to have consolidated an anti-German bloc, while Mussolini's perception was that they would turn a blind eye to the fate of Abyssinia in return for Italian support.[14]

Britain, perhaps to a greater extent than France, was caught between these two conflicting visions – collective security, the League and international morality on one hand; and on the other considerations of balance of power and an amoral approach to international diplomacy that measured ends, not means. As the crisis in Abyssinia developed so did the pressures on the British decision-making elite, torn between the public's continuing support for the League and their own scepticism and preference for the unpalatable alternative. The

British government faced an election that autumn aware that
11 million people, or over half the number that would vote,
had overwhelmingly indicated their support for the League
in a poll organized by the League of Nations Union. Perhaps
unsurprisingly 97 per cent believed Britain must remain in
the League; but, although support diminished as the questions asked implied greater sacrifices, still over 6.5 million
people said they would endorse the League using the ultimate
sanction of war. No British political party seeking election
could ignore this, no matter how sceptical its leaders might
be about collective security.

Britain did press for sanctions, but backed away from the
two that would be most likely to deter Italy (or, more alarm-
ingly, provoke Mussolini into what British leaders called 'a
mad dog act', for example a surprise attack on British naval
forces in the Mediterranean) – an embargo on supplying
oil to Italy and denying it the use of the Suez Canal. The
coalition National Government was comfortably re-elected,
but the international results were less happy. Hitler took the
opportunity to remilitarize the Rhineland and the sanctions
against Italy could not prevent its conquest of Abyssinia. The
lessons were painful.[15]

On 30 June 1936 the Abyssinian Emperor Haile Selassie
addressed the League's Assembly: 'I ask the Great powers,
who have promised the guarantee of collective security to
small states – those small states over whom hangs the threat
that they may one day suffer the fate of Ethiopa: What measures do they intend to take? Representatives of the world,
I have come to Geneva to discharge in your midst the most
painful duties of the head of a state. What answer am I to take
back to my people?'[16] For followers of *realpolitik* the answer
was obvious, as Henry Pownall, then serving in the secretariat

of the British Committee of Imperial Defence declared: 'So much for Collective Security and "moral forces" and all the rest of that stuff ... It's no good thinking that Articles 10 and 16 of the Covenant can remain. People who rely on them for safety will be let down as Abyssinia was let down. This the smaller nations are particularly alive to and are saying so vociferously in their press ... So ... we now know where we stand, the Experiment has been made and failed. How lucky that it *has* been tried out in this minor test case, lucky for all except Abyssinia.' [17]

Robert Cecil's 'Great Experiment' had ended in failure. It had been based on too many paradoxes: the attempt to create collective security in a world of sovereign national states, the hope of international democracy in a world dominated by great powers, the aim of deterring a potential aggressor and maintaining the peace with the ultimate threat of war, a guarantee of territorial integrity combined with an agency for territorial readjustment; in short a revolutionary basis for future international stability. After Abyssinia the League became an increasing irrelevance in international diplomacy. Small states looked to their own security or like Ireland and Belgium became neutral, and the larger states reverted to their more familiar policies of alliances and rearmament. When the Austrian *Anschluss* destroyed the independence of a member in 1938 the League was not even informed. Italy became the ally of Nazi Germany, driven away from the Stresa camp by a policy that had produced the exact opposite of its intentions. Anglo-French differences ensured that they neither achieved collective security nor re-established the balance of power. The ghost of the League continued to inhabit the splendid headquarters in Geneva, opened just as its authority collapsed. In 1938 and 1939 the members effectively passed all responsibility to the Secretary-General, Joseph Avenol, replaced by Sean Lester in 1940, so that the organization continued to exist, technically at least, until its dissolution on 18 April 1946.

The first charge on the League was to inhibit the use of war as an instrument of international relations. In this it patently failed, yet the United States, USSR and Britain began planning for its successor in the midst of the Second World War. Once again this owed much to the sponsorship of an American President. Franklin D Roosevelt, who had stood unsuccessfully as Vice-President in the 1920 elections on a Wilsonian ticket, persuaded Stalin, ever suspicious of capitalist entrapment, and Churchill, who preferred the idea of regional pacts, to support a new universal body. This time, however, through Roosevelt's greater political skill and a changed atmosphere in the United States, there was bipartisan support for American membership. Indeed it was the first of the 51 founder states to ratify the UN Charter on 4 July 1945, only eight days after its signature – a crucial difference, even though, as one British diplomat admitted, the new organization bore 'an almost embarrassing resemblance to its predecessor'.[18]

The League Assembly became the United Nations General Assembly and the Council became the Security Council, though with a firm nod to the realities of power, the five permanent members – China, France, UK, US and USSR – now each had a veto to prevent the UN from acting on substantive matters with which they disagreed. Originally with 11 members, the Security Council expanded to 15 in 1965 in response to changing and enlarged UN membership. The Permanent Court of International Justice became the International Court of Justice, the International Labour Organization continued, the UN Trusteeship Council assumed the mandate responsibilities of the League and the idea of an independent secretariat was retained and enhanced. A new Economic, Social and Cultural Organisation (ECOSOC) was added. The Charter entered into force on 24 October 1945 and the first meetings of the Security Council and the General Assembly took place in London in January 1946. Once again, as Wilson had originally declared in 1919, a living thing was born.[19]

If the League was designed to prevent the rush to conflict that preceded the First World War, the UN sought to discourage the territorial aggrandizement that triggered the Second and to provide an effective response 'against renewal of aggressive policy' by unnamed 'enemy states'. It banned the use of force in international relations except for self-defence or in pursuit of UN-sanctioned operations to avert a threat to peace; but its founders were determined that this body would have the teeth that the League had patently lacked. Membership entailed a responsibility to supply appropriate military forces, bases and rights of passage when the Security Council determined this was necessary. The Charter established a Military Staff Committee to assist the Security Council and to plan and coordinate a UN military force and the establishment of bases; but this ambitious and potentially revolutionary project became an early victim of Cold War disagreements between the US and USSR. Lacking its own forces the Security Council could now only request that members take military action.[20]

This clash between the two dominant partners in the victorious wartime alliance was clearly not anticipated by either, otherwise the occupation arrangements for dealing with former enemy states would have been much more carefully negotiated and the whole UN project would have had a very different shape. It did mean, however, that rather as after 1919, the new international organization risked becoming sidelined while the major powers conducted elsewhere the business that they deemed important, even though this had not been their intention. To some extent this did happen: the Soviet Union used its veto on many occasions to frustrate Security Council action – 75 times between 1945 and 1966 – and most diplomacy about the major Cold War incidents took place in other places. The UN was a marginal player at best during the Berlin Blockade, the Hungarian uprising, various confrontations over Berlin, the Cuban Missile Crisis and the Soviet invasion of Czechoslovakia, though it could be useful in allowing discreet informal contacts to be pursued and was sometimes a stage for posturing and playacting. The dream of collective security largely evaporated in this atmosphere of mutual and self-reinforcing suspicion between two superpowers who instead created massive and exclusive military alliances: the American-led NATO and the Soviet Warsaw Pact. From 1949 onwards when the Soviets also acquired atomic weapons, both had the capacity, quite literally, to destroy the world.

Their confrontation also affected attitudes to new applications for membership over which they, as permanent members, held a veto. Each looked suspiciously at any state sponsored by the other, or which was thought to be too sympathetic to the opposing camp, and 51 of the first 100 vetoes related to the rejection of a membership application. A trickle of states slipped through, three in 1946, a further six by 1953; but it was not until December 1955, when 16 new members joined, that the log-jam was broken. Thereafter, swelled by the mounting numbers of newly independent former colonies, the nature of the UN's membership changed, and the original numerical

Stuck between a rock and a hard place: Henry Cabot Lodge Jr, Gladwyn Jebb, Andrey Vishinsky

predominance of Europe and North and Latin America was overtaken by Africa and Asia as membership nearly tripled in the next 20 years. The arrival of this 'Third World' into an international arena previously dominated by the Western and communist camps undermined the hold which the United States originally held in the UN, though without this necessarily meaning that the Soviet Union now held all the cards. Nonetheless between 1966 and 1993 the Russians used the veto 14 times compared to the Americans' 69 (of which their first ever veto came only in 1970). A flurry of new members at the end of the Cold War meant that by 2010 the UN had 192 members – over 100 delegations more than envisaged by the architects of its headquarters, opened in New York in 1952.[21]

The Cold War did not entirely cripple the UN, even if it

NATO

The North Atlantic Treaty Organization was established on 4 April 1949 between the United States, Canada, the United Kingdom, France, Belgium, the Netherlands, Luxembourg, Portugal, Italy, Norway, Denmark and Iceland to provide for their mutual defence against the USSR. In the event of an armed attack on any of the members in Europe or North America the other members undertook to take such action as they deemed necessary to defend the security of the North Atlantic area, which could involve the use of military force. Its purposes were succinctly defined by Lord Ismay, its first Secretary-General, as 'to keep the Russians out, the Americans in and the Germans down' but NATO in fact became the vehicle that facilitated West German rearmament when the Federal Republic joined on 9 May 1955. Originally set very much in a Cold War context where it came to be countered by the Warsaw Pact of the USSR and its East European allies established on 14 May 1955, NATO survived the end of the Cold War. It enlarged its membership to 28 states, including some former Warsaw Pact countries and it better defined its relationship with the European Union, particularly in terms of the EU's right to use NATO assets in peacekeeping and other operations. In the 1990s NATO undertook peacekeeping and peace-enforcement roles during the various conflicts that erupted in the former Yugoslavia including military interventions and bombing missions during the Bosnian and Kosovo wars. Although the anticipated threats to the alliance were originally expected in Europe, the first invocation of NATO's collective security provisions came in the wake of the attacks on America on 11 September 2001 and included assistance with advanced warning aircraft surveillance and naval operations in the Mediterranean to inhibit the movement of terrorists or their supplies. In 2003 NATO took command of the International Security Assistance Force in Afghanistan, its first such role outside Europe and North America, and in 2006 NATO assumed responsibility for military operations in the south of Afghanistan.

often drove its supporters to despair. Chance could still play a role. Korea had been partitioned in 1945 with the Soviets controlling the North and the Americans occupying the South. When the Communist government of the North launched an invasion of the South in June 1950, the Soviet delegation was boycotting the UN because the Americans refused to transfer the Chinese seat on the Security Council from the defeated Nationalists now based in Taiwan (Formosa) to Mao Zedong's victorious revolutionary regime. This enabled the United States to gain Security Council legitimization for what was essentially an American military intervention. Even though 45 states responded to the UN call for assistance (of which 16 contributed fighting forces), the bulk of the troops were South Korean and American and all were under American command. When the Soviets returned to the UN the Americans were able to maintain its support, despite the veto, by bolstering the role of the General Assembly through the 'Uniting for Peace' resolution in November 1950 which allowed the Assembly to make recommendations for collective action in certain circumstances. Despite the unsurprisingly differing interpretations of the validity of this device, the UN continued to back the intervention in Korea, where the fighting ended with an armistice in July 1953, though the USSR took revenge by refusing to accept the renomination of the first Secretary-General, Trygve Lie, when his term expired in 1951. Lie set the pattern for an enhanced role for the Secretary-General, but became the first of several holders of that office to learn that upsetting a permanent member had a price. He was replaced by another Scandinavian, Dag Hammarskjöld.[22]

It would be over 40 years before the UN took a similar action, after the Iraqi invasion of Kuwait in August 1990, at a time when the end of the Cold War and a more cooperative atmosphere between the major powers gave rise to hopes that it could now fulfil the security role envisaged in 1945. In the meantime, however, the UN had adjusted to the changing international environment in which, although the threat of inter-state war had not disappeared, the major problems more regularly arose either from internal conflicts, the collapse of states or a combination of both. It did so by evolving a set of responses suitable both to the tasks and to its capabilities. The Charter did not mention the concept of peacekeeping, yet the blue helmets of UN forces engaged in policing boundaries between neighbours in conflict have become a powerful symbol of its role and importance. From its early days the UN was involved in observer missions in Indonesia, the Middle East and Kashmir – and there were earlier precedents under the League – but the first real peacekeeping force (and the first to wear the blue helmets) was the UN Emergency Force (UNEF) established during the 1956 Suez Crisis to create a barrier along the Egyptian-Israeli border and round the Gaza Strip.[23]

UNEF shared much in common with most later peacekeeping missions, though the UN did learn lessons and make suitable adjustments over time. The troops were lightly armed, permitted to use force only in self-defence and required only to separate the conflicting parties and not to intervene in any other way, no matter how difficult or distressing that prohibition might be in certain circumstances. The contingent came not from the permanent Security Council members, but from other powers who were more likely to be perceived as neutral by the antagonists and this was the norm, though not exclusively so, in future missions. A number of principles emerged: peacekeeping was only appropriate where the parties to the dispute accepted the UN role; it was crucial that the major powers should at least acquiesce; and the mandate had to be realistic in the light of the resources available, preferably with an exit strategy. It proved a particularly useful device in tackling disputes in newly independent former colonies, though during the mission to the Congo (1960–4) its mandate finally had to be strengthened to deal with an impossibly confused and threatening situation, thus creating one of the rare examples of UN peace enforcement.

Hammarskjöld died in a plane crash in Northern Rhodesia in September 1961 while attempting to negotiate a settlement in the Congo and was succeeded by the Burmese U Thant, during whose term of office (1961–71) the UN despatched a number of peacekeeping missions including one to Cyprus in 1964, which was the first to use civilian police in a significant role. Against this, however, U Thant also witnessed the essential powerlessness of the UN where the interests of the permanent members were engaged and where they were not willing to allow the UN to intervene. France permitted no interference in Algeria; the Soviets vetoed calls for the Warsaw Pact to leave Czechoslovakia; the United States waged war in Vietnam. U Thant also felt obliged to comply with the demand of Egypt's President Nasser that UNEF be withdrawn, setting in train events leading to the outbreak of the Arab-Israeli Six Day War in June 1967. Like the League before it the UN could only do what its members were willing to permit.

When it was successful the UN gained great credit for its peacekeeping operations but it was nearly undone by the huge increase in demand for its services as the Cold War ended, unthawing struggles that had been subsumed and frozen during this global confrontation. By June 1994 the UN had 17 peacekeeping operations in progress, stretching its capacity beyond breaking-point in some cases. Many of the locations for these problems – Iraq, Yugoslavia, Georgia for example – would have been familiar to the peacemakers in Paris in 1919, though in some cases their origins, like the deep-rooted antagonisms in the Balkans, stretched much further back in time. Most of these were internal conflicts – the Yale-Ford Foundation report in 1995 identified nearly 100 wars fought after 1989 of which only five were inter-state.[24] There were some early encouraging signs as the United States and the Soviet Union cooperated in the UN to broker an end to the long-running Iraq-Iran War in 1988. In the same year the UN played a major role in ending the war between the Soviet Union and Afghanistan, though the Soviet withdrawal did not bring much peace to Afghanistan itself where internal factions continued to fight. It also had a striking success in ending the conflict in Namibia, involving local forces as well as those from South Africa and Cuba, though it was less successful in Angola. In 1992 the UN helped to create a more stable situation in much-troubled Cambodia; and between 1989 and 1991 it monitored elections, human rights and peace agreements in several states in Central America.[25]

As UN sanctioned multi-national forces under American command moved to expel Iraq from Kuwait in January 1991, President George H Bush announced his hope for a 'new world order'; and the success of that operation, coupled with the fruits of greater American-Russian cooperation did give real hope that the UN would now enjoy a much more central role in world politics. These hopes were dashed by the messy failure in Somalia (1992–5), where American casualties and humiliation threatened the relationship between the UN and its major financial supporter, and by the UN's inability to prevent genocide in Rwanda in 1994.[26]

Meanwhile the former Yugoslavia was falling apart and the ethnic and religious tensions that had simmered for centuries in a region riven by fault-lines erupted into conflict and genocide. From its initial involvement in peacekeeping in Croatia and Bosnia in 1992 the UN was drawn deeper and deeper into a situation where its resources and political will were utterly inadequate for its often redefined mission. The crisis was also desperately embarrassing for the European Union because it proved unable to deal with a problem in Europe without assistance from the United States. The situation was not helped by ambiguities of role and purpose between the UN, the EU and NATO. The UN did make an important humanitarian contribution, helping to provide food and medical aid to stricken areas, but the capture of UN personnel and their utilization as human shields against NATO airstrikes on Bosnian Serb positions and, above all, its failure to prevent the seizure of the 'safe area' of Srebrenica and the subsequent massacre of thousands of Bosnian Muslim men by the Bosnian Serbs, left the UN's reputation severely mauled.[27]

President George W Bush (the son of President George H Bush) took office in 2001, leading a Republican Party whose relationship with the UN has frequently been fraught. Subsequent events intensified the debate in the United States and elsewhere about the role and relevance of the UN and the status of international law. On 11 September 2001 Al-Qaeda, an Islamist fundamentalist group that had declared *jihad* (holy war) against the United States, launched a series of suicide attacks on the Pentagon in Washington and the World Trade Center in New York using hijacked airliners. This precipitated an invasion of Afghanistan by the United States, supported by the United Kingdom and their allies in October to remove the Taliban government, in an attempt to eradicate Al-Qaeda bases. The UN subsequently authorized the deployment of an International Security Assistance Force (ISAF) to Kabul in December 2001 to enable an Afghani government to establish a stable state from a secure base, extending its mission to cover the whole country in October

2003. Although the Taliban were forced to flee Kabul and lost control of the state in 2001, the NATO-led ISAF continued to meet armed resistance, especially in the south of Afghanistan and Al-Qaeda retained a strong influence there and in neighbouring Pakistan.

The other main military operation launched as part of Bush's 'War on Terror' was against President Saddam Hussein of Iraq, though there was little substantive evidence to link Iraq with Al-Qaeda. Operation Iraqi Freedom which began in March 2003 had the declared intention of depriving Iraq of its alleged weapons of mass destruction and chemical arsenal, though none were subsequently discovered. The invasion by an American-led coalition with the United Kingdom as the US's main supporter had no specific UN mandate but both Bush and British Prime Minister Tony Blair argued that no new UN resolution was necessary. While few disputed the appalling nature of Saddam Hussein's tyranny or that regime change was desirable, the question of the legality of the invasion created intense debate both at the time and subsequently. Kofi Annan, then UN Secretary-General, was quite clear on 16 September 2004 when he stated 'From our point of view, from the Charter point of view, it was illegal.' Yet Bush was equally clear throughout that he intended to act in any case in a pre-emptive strike against a potential threat. Once again the UN found itself an onlooker as the world's remaining superpower made the crucial decisions – and then, again not untypically, returned to at least partial favour when the initial military success of the invasion was not matched by political, institutional and economic stabilization and the unilateralists were not averse to seeking multilateral participation in a process that remains ongoing.

Like the League, the UN continues to disappoint its most

ambitious supporters and arouses scepticism among those who condemn it as an idealistic talking-shop. Advocates and critics alike are aware that some of its ageing mechanisms need to change to reflect the realities of power and that some of the original five permanent Security Council members should perhaps vacate their chairs. While the ideal of 'one state one vote' continues to have merit, there must be some recognition that the UN's burdens are not borne equally in a situation in which ten states pay 76 per cent of the UN budget and the other 182 pay the remainder but theoretically have the democratic power to commit the paymasters. Collective security remains an aspirational concept and the history of both organizations indicates that, when it suits them, 'powers will be powers'. At the same time the League and the UN have done much to advance the cause of human rights and to promote the concept of international law. Both have helped to encourage such agreement on disarmament as has, to date, been possible. As international meeting points they have served a very useful purpose for states that could not possibly afford to maintain separate missions in every world capital and they have afforded the opportunity for informal and deniable conversations that have helped to prevent the escalation of disputes.

> 'Each man begins the world afresh. Only institutions grow wiser: they store up the collective wisdom, men subject to the same laws will gradually find, not that their natures change but that their behaviour does.'
>
> HENRI FRÉDÉRIC AMIEL, 1873, OFT QUOTED BY MONNET

Two quotations may serve as a conclusion to this chapter: President Dwight D Eisenhower's verdict that, 'With all the defects, with all the failures we can check up against it, the U.N. still represents man's best-organized hope to substitute the conference table for the battlefield'; and the point well made by the 19th century Genevan diarist, Henri Frédéric Amiel, which was often quoted by Jean Monnet that, 'Each man begins the world afresh. Only institutions grow wiser: they store up the collective wisdom, men subject to the same laws will gradually find, not that their natures change but that their behaviour does.'[28] The drafters of the Covenant in 1919 would have agreed with both sentiments.

4

National Self-Determination: Wilson's Troublesome Principle

'The phrase ["national self-determination"] is simply loaded with dynamite. It will raise hopes which can never be realised. It will, I fear, cost thousands of lives ... What a calamity the phrase was ever uttered! What misery it will cause!'

Robert Lansing

The idea of national self-determination was not conjured into being by the First World War or the Paris Peace Conference and Woodrow Wilson's speeches did not create nationalist movements out of thin air. He himself identified the main cause of war in 1914 as precisely the lack of the opportunity for a number of European nationalisms to fulfil that principle. 'This war,' he said, 'had its roots in the disregard of the rights of small nations and of nationalities which lacked the union or force to make good their claim to determine their own allegiances and their own forms of political life.' There were already, before 1914, discontented nationalist groups in many empires in Europe and further afield who wished to secede and create their own states.[1]

Nonetheless, despite earlier examples, the First World War

did provide an enormous boost to the concept, partly because both sides were driven to risk playing the potentially suicidal card of encouraging nationalist discontent in their enemies' ranks, and partly because the near simultaneous defeat and collapse of four multi-national empires created opportunities for national groups to realise their dreams leaving self-determination as the only principled alternative to *force majeure* for the Peace Conference as it sought to restructure Europe. And Wilson was a key figure: 'Absent him,' wrote Daniel Patrick Moynihan, the distinguished American politician and diplomat, 'the "principle" of self-determination would not be ratified by the United Nations Charter: it was he who put it on the agenda of international order.'[2] The war also radicalised nationalist sentiment in a number of states such that, whereas before 1914 the goals of Eduard Beneš, Tomáš Masaryk or John Redmond, were home rule for the Czechoslovaks or the Irish within their respective empires, now nothing less than complete independence would do.

Although David Lloyd George used the phrase 'national self-determination' before him, it was Wilson who as the leader of the world's most powerful state declared it to be 'an imperative principle of action',[3] becoming in 1918 and 1919 the focus of the hopes of millions of people across the globe. Hundreds of petitions from Europe, Africa and Asia seeking his support arrived at the Hotel Crillon, the American headquarters in Paris, while some delegations appeared in person, hoping for an audience. In numbers he had never imagined, they expected the President to deliver their aspirations to statehood. As an aghast Wilson admitted to the United States Senate in August 1919, 'When I gave utterance to those words [that all nations had a right to self-determination] I said them without the knowledge that nationalities existed, which are coming to us day after day … You do not know and cannot appreciate the anxieties that I have experienced as a result of many millions of people having their hopes raised by what I have said.'[4] He had tried to put some limits on the application of the principle when he suggested that 'all well-defined national aspirations shall be accorded the utmost satisfaction that can be accorded them without introducing new or perpetrating old elements of discord and antagonism that would be likely in time to break the peace of Europe, and consequently of the world';[5] but hopeful nationalists heeded neither the philosophical nor the geographical caveats that Wilson introduced or implied.

Wilson was thinking almost exclusively of European affairs when he spoke; and indeed he amended an early draft of the League Covenant to remove a commitment promising the application of the principle to future territorial settlements when advisers warned him of the possibility that this might bring colonial matters before the League and make imperial dissatisfaction a permanent feature. Yet, as his Secretary of State Robert Lansing had foreseen on the eve of the Conference, his words echoed across the colonial world with disruptive effects. National self-determination, he wrote 'is bound to be the basis of impossible demands on the Peace Congress and create trouble in many lands. What effect will it have

> 'When I gave utterance to those words [that all nations had a right to self-determination] I said them without the knowledge that nationalities existed, which are coming to us day after day … You do not know and cannot appreciate the anxieties that I have experienced as a result of many millions of people having their hopes raised by what I have said.'
> **WOODROW WILSON, AUGUST 1919**

on the Irish, the Indians, the Egyptians, and the nationalists among the Boers? Will it not breed discontent, disorder and rebellion?' He continued with a chilling (but underestimated) prediction: 'The phrase is simply loaded with dynamite. It will raise hopes which can never be realised. It will, I fear, cost thousands of lives ... What a calamity the phrase was ever uttered! What misery it will cause!'[6]

It was precisely the unpredictability of national self-determination as a weapon that deterred the belligerents, at least in the early years of the First World War, from employing it in Europe. The obvious attraction of undermining one's enemy by encouraging internal dissension in its ranks was offset by the equally obvious danger that, like poison gas, the wind might blow the idea back into the faces of multinational empires, each with its own discontented national groups. Both sides were prepared, however, to encourage disgruntled colonial subjects to rebel against their imperial masters. As early as 4 September 1914 German Chancellor Bethmann-Hollweg authorized a campaign to spread unrest in India and Egypt, though the subsequent record of ineptitude belied the stereotype of German efficiency.[7] In Britain Lord Cromer suggested in October 1914, as war with the Ottomans loomed, that 'a few officers who could speak Arabic, if sent into Arabia, could raise the whole country against the Turks'. While this was not immediately implemented, defeats

> '[National self-determination] is bound to be the basis of impossible demands on the Peace Congress and create trouble in many lands. What effect will it have on the Irish, the Indians, the Egyptians, and the nationalists among the Boers? Will it not breed discontent, disorder and rebellion?'
>
> **ROBERT LANSING, 1918**

at Gallipoli and Kut encouraged Britain to negotiate with the Hashemites, leading to the Arab revolt in the desert, romantically linked with T E Lawrence (Lawrence of Arabia), which contributed to the eventual overwhelming British victory in the Middle East.[8] To further complicate matters Arthur Balfour, the British Foreign Secretary, pledged support for a Jewish National Home in Palestine in November 1917, raising all sorts of issues about territorial definitions, the rights of the local population and those of Jewish immigrants seeking to rebuild Zion.[9]

These are apt reminders of the dangers of offering insincere long-term promises for immediate gains because it is clear that, whatever commitments the British and the French might have made to Arabs or Jews, they had no intention of abandoning their post-war control of a region rich in the new strategic resource of oil, important in terms of imperial communications and steeped in history and religious significance. Although their joint declaration of 7 November 1918 alleged that they were fighting for 'the complete and definite emancipation of the peoples so long oppressed by the Turks and the establishment of national governments and administrations deriving their authority from the initiative and free choice of the indigenous populations', the reality was very different. The British Colonial Secretary, Lord Milner, made this clear in his definition of Arab independence: 'what we mean by it is that Arabia, while being independent herself should be kept out of the sphere of European political intrigue and within the British sphere of influence: in other words that her independent native rulers should have no foreign treaties except with us.' Equally, the French were determined to maintain control over their allocated parts of the region whatever the wishes of the population. Balfour pulled no punches: 'Neither of us wants much less than supreme economic and political control, to be exercised no doubt (at least in our case) with friendly and unostentatious cooperation with the Arabs – but nevertheless, in the last resort, to be exercised.' As he later pointed out, since the French were the only possible candidates to hold the League Mandate for Syria, the inhabitants 'could freely choose, but it is Hobson's choice after all'.[10]

> 'Neither of us wants much less than supreme economic and political control, to be exercised no doubt (at least in our case) with friendly and unostentatious cooperation with the Arabs – but nevertheless, in the last resort, to be exercised.'
>
> ARTHUR BALFOUR

Having unleashed forces they later struggled to control, Britain and France found themselves enmeshed in the Middle East for decades to come.

Self-interest also came first in Europe, where the Entente powers generously apportioned as yet uncaptured enemy territories between themselves or offered them as inducements to potential allies like Italy or Romania with no thought to the wishes of the local populations. National self-determination had little attraction for the rulers of Austria-Hungary bedevilled by minority problems, Britain where the Irish question had dominated politics for half a century and who faced growing discontent in India and Egypt, or for the multinational empires of Russia, Germany and France; but it is a measure of the desperate straits to which all were driven in their efforts to prevail in the area that, eventually, both the Entente and the Central Powers succumbed to temptation.

Poland, destroyed as an independent state in the second half of the 18th century, its territory annexed by Austria, Russia and Prussia, was an obvious target for both sides.

Germany and Russia indicated support for its restoration although they tended to envisage establishing a new Poland in those Polish lands that they would, in victory, seize from their opponents – a resurrection of Napoleon's Grand Duchy of Warsaw rather than a fully independent Poland. As Georges Clemenceau admitted, 'We ... started as allies of the Russian oppressors of Poland, with the Polish soldiers of Silesia and Galicia fighting against us',[11] and it required first Russian defeat but then the eventual triumph of the Entente to create the vacuum which the new, truly independent Poland could fill. Wilson's 13th point promised just such a free state but also highlighted some of the many problems associated with self-determination. It spoke of 'an independent Poland ... [which would] include the territories inhabited by indisputably Polish populations, which should be assured free and secure access to the sea ...'. It was a very broad-brush statement, short on definitions and long on potential contradictions – what constituted 'indisputably Polish' and could the state be given access to the sea without infringing other self-determinations?

There was also growing support in the Allied capitals for the idea of other new states: Czechoslovakia, although this raised another problem – had anyone asked the Slovaks if they wanted to be part of this new polity?; and Yugoslavia, which raised similar questions about the relative roles to be played by Serbs, Croats and Slovenes. And what did all this imply for Austria-Hungary, whose continued existence seemed to be incompatible with the concept of Polish, Yugoslav and Czech secession, despite assurances from both Lloyd George and Wilson in their January 1918 speeches that its destruction was no part of their programmes? Two contradictory policies co-existed throughout much of the war:

maintain Austria-Hungary as a state and encourage it to quit the Central Powers and conclude a separate peace; and try to destroy the Empire by supporting nationalist dissidents within. Wilson's semi-official think-tank, the Inquiry, neatly summed up the paradoxical implications: 'Our policy must therefore consist first in a stirring up of nationalist discontent, and then in refusing to accept the extreme logic of this discontent which would be the dismemberment of Austria-Hungary.' [12] Confusion continued in London, Paris, Rome and Washington until the dilemma was resolved by Austria-Hungary imploding at the end of the war.

National self-determination still posed huge problems for the peacemakers, some of which were self-imposed – the contradictory promises offered to different parties and their obvious, if unstated, belief that the principle was not to be applied to their own possessions – and others which were inherent, most notably the hopeless intermingling of ethnic groups in Eastern and Central Europe – the legacy of countless migrations, invasions, wars and dynastic deals. There was an added complication in that the peacemakers, and in particular Wilson – inevitably for the President of a nation of immigrants – emphasized choice in terms of nationality which Western liberals tended to confuse with citizenship while in the Eastern European tradition nationality was determined by race, language and religion. Whereas for Wilson someone born in Ireland or Italy could become an American – i.e., the concept of civic nationalism; for Poles ethnic nationalism ruled: you either were or were not Polish, and this had nothing to do with choice.

The Banat of Temesvar offers an interesting example of the difficulties of applying the principle. In 1914 it was Hungarian, now it was claimed by two Allied powers – the fledgling state of Yugoslavia and Romania to whom it had been promised by the 1916 Treaty of Bucharest, which the Romanians claimed remained valid despite their conclusion of a separate peace with the Central Powers in 1917. It was impossible to draw any frontier that did not leave substantial minorities on either side, while great power rivalries further complicated matters. The Italians, always hostile to any Yugoslav ambition, backed Romania and this helped to strengthen French support for the Yugoslavs. The interested parties produced carefully designed maps to highlight their claims. Each was prepared to accept a plebiscite – but only if its voting conditions meant the outcome was bound to support their cause, and each contemplated using force. Eventually the Conference allowed Hungary to retain the area around Szeged; Romania got most of the rest but Yugoslavia gained some land in the west. This left 75,000 Romanians in Yugoslavia and 65,000 Slavs in Romania. Both countries resented the arrangements made by the League to protect these minorities. No one was satisfied – it was an apt microcosm of the frustrations and resentments generated by the 1919 negotiations.

The Allies claimed that 'Every territorial settlement of the Treaty of Peace has been determined after the most careful and laboured consideration of all the religious, racial and linguistic factors in each particular country', and it is certainly true that much study and research was devoted to some of the new frontiers with, for example, James Headlam-Morley and Charles Haskins physically inspecting the border they proposed between the Saarland and Germany.[13] The peacemakers were agonisingly aware that some of their decisions contradicted the principle and were often frustrated that the only constant factor when considering whether a new frontier should reflect linguistic, administrative, economic, military or communications priorities was that none of these coincided.

Yet to the Germans the Allied claim sounded hollow. Even if they accepted defeat in the west (and, with the growing strength of the 'stab in the back' myth, this was certainly not a given), Germans considered they had clearly won the war in the east. How, therefore, was it fair to assign Germans to the rule of Poles who had signally failed to govern themselves? Did self-determination apply only in favour of the victors? Why were the territories of the German-speakers of the Sudetenland or Austria denied the right to merge with Germany? Why were strategic considerations invoked to justify the transfer of Austrians to Italian rule in the South Tyrol? Why was territory they asserted was German given to Poland to create a corridor to the sea? These were not unreasonable questions but it was clear that self-determination was not the only consideration and that the Allies were never going to allow its application to increase the strength of a Germany they had already struggled to defeat. The German perceptions of the denial of Wilson's 'imperative principle of action' offered them further justification for revision and bolstered nationalist resentment.

The Parisian settlements reduced the number of people living in a European state in which they were not the majority ethnic group from around 60 million in 1914 to about 30 million or from about 50 per cent of the total population to 25 per cent. Since each one of those remaining 30 million, of whom some 13 million were German, constituted proof that the principle had not been or could not be fully applied, it is unlikely that the problem was really halved. In certain cases it might even have increased. An admittedly biased source, Kurt Schuschnigg, the last Chancellor of independent inter-war Austria, claimed that, whereas in 1914 minorities in the

Austro-Hungarian Empire totalled 27,419,000, after 1919 in the same area the figure was 27,600,000. Given that many previous masters now found themselves the minority and that the new dominant groups often lacked magnanimity, the potential for disruption was obvious. The peacemakers sought to mitigate against this in two ways: first by conducting plebiscites in some regions to discover the wishes of the local populations; secondly, where minorities were created, to provide protection through the auspices of the League.

At first sight it seems the obvious solution that the local population should be asked to decide in situations where the line of a new boundary is uncertain. There were, and are, complicating factors. Inhabitants may be wary of expressing their true wishes for fear of reprisals. The manner in which the question is posed, who is asking it or the way in which the votes are tallied (for example by town, region, province or overall) may well affect the outcome. There were five decisive plebiscites in the immediate aftermath of the Peace Conference – in Schleswig, Klagenfurt, Allenstein, Marienwerder and Oedenburg. The later 1921 plebiscite in Upper Silesia resulted in an overall majority for remaining German but engendered a bitter Anglo-French dispute about how to interpret the result and draw the new frontier. There was provision for future plebiscites to be held in the Saarland, Smyrna (Izmir) and East Galicia but events overtook the last two and only that in the Saar was held, giving Adolf Hitler his first major foreign policy triumph in 1935.

Some of the results made an interesting commentary on the assumption that nationality was determined by language. In Allenstein 46 per cent of the population spoke Polish, yet only 2 per cent voted to join Poland. In Upper Silesia 65 per cent spoke Polish but Germany gained an overall majority and

PRESIDENT WILSON'S FOURTEEN POINTS, 8 JANUARY 1918

The program of the world's peace, therefore, is our program; and that program, the only possible program, as we see it, is this:

I. Open covenants of peace, openly arrived at, after which there shall be no private international understandings of any kind but diplomacy shall proceed always frankly and in the public view.

II. Absolute freedom of navigation upon the seas, outside territorial waters, alike in peace and in war, except as the seas may be closed in whole or in part by international action for the enforcement of international covenants.

III. The removal, so far as possible, of all economic barriers and the establishment of an equality of trade conditions among all the nations consenting to the peace and associating themselves for its maintenance.

IV. Adequate guarantees given and taken that national armaments will be reduced to the lowest point consistent with domestic safety.

V. A free, open-minded, and absolutely impartial adjustment of all colonial claims, based upon a strict observance of the principle that in determining all such questions of sovereignty the interests of the populations concerned must have equal weight with the equitable claims of the government whose title is to be determined.

VI. The evacuation of all Russian territory and such a settlement of all questions affecting Russia as will secure the best and freest cooperation of the other nations of the world in obtaining for her an unhampered and unembarrassed opportunity for the independent determination of her own political development and national policy and assure her of a sincere welcome into the society of free nations under institutions of her own choosing; and, more than a welcome, assistance also of every kind that she may need and may herself desire. The treatment accorded Russia by her sister nations in the months to come will be the acid test of their good will, of their comprehension of her needs as distinguished from their own interests, and of their intelligent and unselfish sympathy.

VII. Belgium, the whole world will agree, must be evacuated and restored, without any attempt to limit the sovereignty which she enjoys in common with all other free nations. No other single act will serve as this will serve to restore confidence among the nations in the laws which they have themselves set and determined for the government of their relations with one another. Without this healing act the whole structure and validity of international law is forever impaired.

VIII. All French territory should be freed and the invaded portions restored, and the wrong done to France by Prussia in 1871 in the matter of Alsace-Lorraine, which has unsettled the peace of the world for nearly fifty years, should be righted, in order that peace may once more be made secure in the interest of all.

IX. A readjustment of the frontiers of Italy should be effected along clearly recognizable lines of nationality.

X. The peoples of Austria-Hungary, whose place among the nations we wish to see safeguarded and assured, should be accorded the freest opportunity to autonomous development.

XI. Rumania, Serbia, and Montenegro should be evacuated; occupied territories restored; Serbia accorded free and secure access to the sea; and the relations of the several Balkan states to one another determined by friendly counsel along historically established lines of allegiance and nationality; and international guarantees of the political and economic independence and territorial integrity of the several Balkan states should be entered into.

XII. The Turkish portion of the present Ottoman Empire should be assured a secure sovereignty, but the other nationalities which are now under Turkish rule should be assured an undoubted security of life and an absolutely unmolested opportunity of autonomous development, and the Dardanelles should be permanently opened as a free passage to the ships and commerce of all nations under international guarantees.

XIII. An independent Polish state should be erected which should include the territories inhabited by indisputably Polish populations, which should be assured a free and secure access to the sea, and whose political and economic independence and territorial integrity should be guaranteed by international covenant.

XIV. A general association of nations must be formed under specific covenants for the purpose of affording mutual guarantees of political independence and territorial integrity to great and small states alike.

in Klagenfurt 68 per cent of the population were Slovenes, yet only 40 per cent voted to secede from Austria. Like national self-determination, the principle of the plebiscite was double-edged. A senior British official minuted in some alarm, 'Obviously the conference has nothing to do with territories owned by the allies before the war ... plebiscites taken in countries in our possession ... might be very inconvenient and certainly should not be encouraged.' In such circumstances it is unsurprising that, as H W V Temperley, the first major historian of the Conference, noted, 'On the whole, plebiscites were more talked about than conceded'. Instead, as Headlam-Morley observed, the Conference simply decided: 'I sometimes ask whether the people on the spot are ever to be consulted, but I am always told that this is out of the question. Self-determination is quite *démodé*. Leeper and Nicolson [two British officials] determine for them what they ought to wish, but they do it very well.'[14]

The peacemakers shunned most attempts at forcible transfers of populations, except in one major instance in the later Treaty of Lausanne involving the Greeks and Turks in Asia Minor. It may be that a more brutal policy in the short term might have saved longer-term difficulties but their liberal philosophy predisposed them to seek to make their maps fit the people rather than the reverse and it is hard to fault them for that. They were aware, however, that discontented minorities could offer neighbouring kin states excellent moral excuses to disrupt the international order should they wish to do so. Hence they instituted a system of minority protection to encourage the new states to treat all these potentially reluctant citizens fairly and, in turn, to foster loyalty to those states on the part of the transferred populations. (See Chapter 5 for a fuller discussion of this development.)

In the short term it was the French and British who experienced the bulk of the problems from discontented groups unconvinced of the advantages of being parts of larger empires at the very moment when those empires reached their widest extent following the redistribution of German and Ottoman possessions. France rapidly discovered that Curzon was right to predict 'they do not know what they are in for' as revolts in Syria and elsewhere tested its imperial resolve, and Britain found itself facing so many problems worldwide that it, rather fancifully, suspected Moscow of orchestrating them.

Eschewing the seats they had won to the Westminster Parliament in the 1918 British general election, Irish Republicans established their own assembly, *Dáil Éireann,* in January 1919 and sent an unsuccessful delegation to Paris to seek recognition for the aspiring state and to claim membership of the League of Nations. Neither Wilson nor Clemenceau would receive the delegates, but Lloyd George still faced the major crisis postponed in 1914 by suspending the Irish Home Rule Act for the duration of the war. Since then the situation had been made more complicated by the consequences of the Easter Rising in Dublin in 1916 and the unsuccessful attempt to apply conscription to Ireland, which enhanced the position of *Sinn Fein,* the revolutionary Irish independence movement. Meanwhile, loyal nationalists and Unionists believed that the sacrifices they had made for Britain during the war entitled their contradictory aspirations for autonomy or continued links to Britain to be satisfied. In 1920 the Irish Republican Army mounted a sustained insurgency campaign against British Crown forces in Ireland, creating an increasing cycle of violence and counter-violence, terror and counter-terror, which eventually concluded with the partition of Ireland into a Free State in the south, while in the north six of the nine counties of historic Ulster remained part of the United Kingdom.

Commenting on the Anglo-Irish negotiations the British Colonial Secretary Winston Churchill alleged they 'had played a considerable part in loosening for the first time the traditional policy of the British Empire in refusing to bow to outrage and rebellion'.[15] This was a rather distorted historical judgement, but if Ireland was not the first case, it was certainly not the last. In Egypt, where nationalists were similarly frustrated in their hopes to advance their case at the Conference, widespread anti-British disturbances in March 1919 were the prelude to three years of violence, which the British sought to suppress before imposing a form of partial independence in 1922 in which they retained control of defence and the Suez Canal. There were also problems as Britain battled to realise its ambition to control new areas of the Middle East without incurring crippling costs. In March 1921 Churchill's solution to dealing with Britain's mandates in the area was to make the most prominent of the Hashemite Arab wartime leaders, Feisal, King of Iraq (then Mesopotamia) while his brother, Abdullah, later became Emir of Transjordan (the future Kingdom of Jordan). In 1932 Britain relinquished its mandate (though not certain military facilities) and independent Iraq became a member of the League. Meanwhile in Palestine, the twice or thrice 'promised land', Britain found itself fulfilling Robert Cecil's gloomy prediction that, 'We shall simply keep the peace between the Arabs and the Jews. We are not going to get anything out of it. Whoever goes there will have a poor time.'[16]

In Palestine self-determination was complicated by the competing claims of the indigenous inhabitants and immigrant Jews seeking refuge in their promised National Home.

At the Conference Chaim Weizmann, the spokesman for the Zionists, had neatly sidestepped the question of whether they were seeking to build a state. He denied this, but added, 'Later on, when the Jews formed the large majority, they would be ripe to establish such a government as would answer to the state of the development of the country and to their ideals'.[17] Inter-communal violence in the 1920s became worse in the 1930s when Jewish immigration rocketed in response to Hitler's systematic persecution, which began almost as soon as he became Chancellor of Germany in January 1933. The British contemplated and then rejected a policy of partition and the establishment of separate Jewish and Arab states, an idea which found some favour with the Jews but none with the Arabs. The war postponed further consideration of the idea.

There was always a danger that events in the Middle East might excite Muslim sympathy in India, the real heart of the British Empire, and threaten Britain's ability to recruit Punjabi Muslims into the Indian army, a pillar of British power. India was vital to Britain as a base, as a market and as a resource for manpower. Politicians and officials in London and India had struggled before, during and after the First World War to balance Britain's need for control with the responsibility to prepare India for greater self-government, even if this was not envisaged as an early possibility. One step towards this had been the establishment of the Indian National Congress in 1885 as a forum in which an elite of educated Indians could conduct a dialogue with the British government. Although the Congress was initially entirely loyal to the Crown, Curzon's ill-fated attempt to partition Bengal before the war, together with growing frustration about progress towards self-government and the war itself, all helped to radicalize elements of the Congress where Bal Gangadhar Tilak became the leading advocate of *swaraj* (home-rule).

The Indian National Congress had no formal power and its attempt to nominate Tilak as its representative in Paris in 1919 was simply brushed aside. Instead India was represented at the Peace Conference by Edwin Montagu, then Secretary of State for India, and Lord Sinha of Raipur, with the Maharajah of Bikaner as an alternate member of what was officially a delegation of two. Both Indians had served on the Imperial War Cabinet and both believed in greater autonomy for India within the Empire but on a gradual basis. Bikaner represented the 600 Indian princes who had sworn allegiance to the British Crown and whose lands comprised about a third of India. Sinha, the first Indian to become a British peer, was a Bengali lawyer who had become President of the Indian National Congress in 1915. He represented British India, the remaining two-thirds of the subcontinent then governed by an uneasy partnership of Montagu in London and the Viceroy in Delhi, Lord Chelmsford.

Bikaner and Sinha could congratulate themselves that India was separately represented in Paris and that it became a founder member of the League, though they shared Japanese disappointment at the rejection of a racial equality clause in the Covenant. Sinha also spent much time in London, playing an important role in assisting Montagu to pilot the Montagu-Chelmsford Reforms through Parliament as the British conceded further degrees of Indian control in the provincial governments to those already established by the earlier Morley-Minto Reforms of 1909. There was, however, a growing body of opinion in India that was not satisfied with such a gradualist approach; and the British, increasingly nervous of this and possible Muslim resentment of the treatment of parts of the former Ottoman Empire, imposed the Rowlatt Acts in March 1919 which enabled them to imprison without jury trial persons suspected of terrorist activity. Congress, now led by a British-trained lawyer, Mohandas Gandhi, reacted by staging the first of a series of non-cooperation campaigns designed to encourage Britain to leave India. The ill-judged actions of General Dyer in April 1919 in firing without warning on a crowd in Amritsar, left at least 379 Indians dead and over 1,500 wounded, provoking political outrage in India and controversy in London. The pattern of concession mixed with coercion together with an element of religious divide-and-rule was typical of the policies of various British governments in the inter-war period as they sought to retain control. On the whole they were successful, though the overall trend was of a weakening connection between India and Britain, not only politically but also economically.[18]

Like Britain, the other European imperial powers found themselves torn between various policies to maintain control of their colonies. They were prepared to use force, ruthlessly on occasion, but they also experienced an increased sense of the need to promote economic, political and social development of their possessions, encouraged, if not decisively shaped, by the responsibilities imposed by the League mandate system. In France, whose empire was second in size only to that of Britain, the politician and former Governor-General of French Indochina Albert Sarraut wrote in 1922 that his country's colonial policy 'fundamentally beg[an] with the great idea of human solidarity' and that 'its efforts must be as beneficial to the colonies as to itself'. He shared some of the ideas expressed in Britain by Lord Frederick Lugard in his influential study, also published in 1922, *The Dual Mandate in Tropical Africa*, which helped to make imperialism more respectable while simultaneously opening new opportunities for left-wing European parties, now becoming more involved in colonial affairs, to hold governments to account for alleged abuses and for failures to translate their ideals into practical policies.[19]

There was growing unrest in the 1930s in Indo-China itself, which the French sought to control by a combination of direct rule and client states. This was provoked by a combination of resentments against taxation, exploitation and economic conditions that Ho Chi Minh, a Marxist and Vietnamese nationalist, sought to channel into the nascent nationalist cause whose case he had unsuccessfully tried to submit to the Peace Conference in 1919. The French vigorously repressed the disturbances, which included a military mutiny, and suppressed much political activity but, with their attention turning to the growing threat from Japan, they did not pursue alternative policies to conciliate the local population. Their problems were even more marked in Syria where they struggled between 1925 and 1927 to suppress the revolt led by Sultan Pasha al-Atrash. In their North African possessions (Algeria, Tunisia and Morocco) the influential settler populations were a powerful barrier to reforms that were increasingly necessary but that inter-war French governments were too weak to impose. As in Indo-China, nationalism was not yet the force it would become and faced the added complication of establishing what role, if any, Islam should play in its identity. Even so one quarter of the inter-war French army was based in North Africa and it saw action on a number of occasions, notably in suppressing the Rif revolt led by Abd-el-Krim in Morocco after his early successes against Spanish forces in the area. He was defeated in 1926 and sent into exile but his guerrilla tactics influenced other revolutionaries and nationalists like Ho Chi Minh, Mao Zedong in China and Che Guevara in Latin America.[20]

The decisive changes to empire and European imperialism came after 1945, but the events of the First World War, the experiences of those who served in the armed forces and the expectations raised by Wilson promoted increasing demands for self-government, albeit mainly among the ranks of the urban, educated elite. Many of the future leaders of Vietnam, Algeria, Tunisia, Indonesia, Burma, Sri Lanka, India, Pakistan and African states such as Kenya and Senegal first made their mark in the inter-war years; some, like Ho Chi Minh or Gandhi establishing their status by falling foul of laws imposed by the colonial governments. Imperialism was under further self-imposed pressure as Sarraut pointed out in 1931: 'In the mind of other races the war has dealt a terrible blow to the moral standing of a civilization which Europeans claimed with pride to be superior, yet in whose name Europeans spent more than four years savagely killing each other.' Nonetheless, despite its problems, European colonial rule was not yet doomed. Indeed by the 1930s governments perceived the major threats to their continuing control coming not from internal opposition but from other aggressive states seeking to dispossess them. It would take another major war, coupled with new domestic priorities, to see self-determination applied to most of these possessions in the quarter-century after the end of the Second World War.[21]

Meanwhile in Europe the 1930s in particular saw the exploitation of discontented minorities by revisionist neighbouring kin states in the manner that the peacemakers had hoped could be avoided by a mixture of special privileges for the minorities and good governance by their host states. The Nazis enjoyed an overwhelming success in the January

1935 plebiscite in the Saar district which voted decisively to be reincorporated into the *Reich* despite the obvious political and racial discrimination already being practised there. The March 1938 *Anschluss* with Austria could be portrayed as the belated granting of a self-determination denied by the peace-makers, even though the outcome of Schuschnigg's threat-ened plebiscite might well have endorsed continuing Austrian independence.

This opened the door for Hitler to increase the pressure on Czechoslovakia over the future of the Sudetenland. On 28 March he told Konrad Henlein, the leader of the Sudeten German Party, that 'He could no longer tolerate Germans being oppressed or fired upon.' Henlein understood this to mean that in negotiations with the Czech government, 'We must always demand so much that we can never be satisfied. The Führer approved this view.' [22] Despite the subsequent attempts of the Czech President Eduard Beneš to reach an accommodation, Henlein stuck to his instructions and helped Hitler create the crisis resolved by the dramatic interventions of the British Premier Neville Chamberlain in September 1938, culminating in the Munich Conference, the secession of the Sudetenland and the effective dismantling of the Czech state, though its rump would linger for another six months.

It is interesting to speculate what might have happened had Hitler next turned his attention to the Polish Corridor, where another German minority offered some cloak for Nazi aggres-sion. Instead he launched the blatantly imperialistic occupa-tion of Prague in March 1939 while disgruntled neighbours also demanded their shares of the Czech carcase. After Prague there was no room for further doubt and Chamberlain now tried to deter Germany by offering carefully worded guaran-tees of political independence, though not always territorial integrity, to Poland, Greece and Romania. The failure of this policy, which needed the cooperation of the Soviet Union to give it any possible military credibility, coupled with the shameless Nazi-Soviet Pact in August 1939, signalled the end of national self-determination for most of Europe for a considerable period – certainly until the defeat of the Axis Powers in 1945, and for many people, for much longer than that.

Leaving aside the question of how far the states within the Soviet bloc after the Second World War were truly independent, the irony of that new settlement was that, although clearly not based on the principle of national self-determination, it actually delivered a much more ethnically homogeneous East European state structure than the peacemakers in Paris were able to achieve. They would have condemned the brutal means by which this was accomplished – extermination, the redrawing of boundaries for political purposes and the forcible transfer of populations. The Holocaust reduced the Jewish population of most East European states to a tiny proportion, for example only 0.003 per cent in both Poland and Czechoslovakia. Only 2 per cent of the Polish population were Germans; and, following the expulsion of 3 million Sudetenlanders, only 50,000 Germans remained in Czechoslovakia – 0.5 per cent of the total population. The Hungarians in Slovakia were the only sizeable minority left. Meanwhile Poland was shunted over 100 miles west, losing a fifth of its pre-war territory and a third of its population, with only a few hundred thousand Ukranians and Belorussians left in the state. Post-1945 Hungary was now 92.1 per cent Magyar and Austria even more clearly German. By 1970, in seven East European states where the national minority populations constituted 25 per cent of the total in the 1930s, the figure was now 7 per cent.[23]

If the First World War had both increased the imperial territories yet weakened the power of the European victors, the Second World War, as many had feared and predicted, marked the beginning of the end for overseas empires. Japan was hardly a shining beacon for national self-determination as it extended its empire across Asia and the Pacific but its initial defeats of the colonial powers undermined their self-confidence and shattered any remaining sense of awe on the part of the colonial peoples. After the war a growing demand for self-government in the colonies was matched by a decreasing will within the metropolitan states to maintain their control, faced as they were by the need to reconstruct devastated cities and industries and to match the rising social expectations of their electorates from the diminished resources of their wrecked economies.

The revulsion against Nazism and fascism meant imperialism was out of fashion and could only be tolerated on a temporary basis. Although decolonization was not stated as a specific goal of the United Nations (UN), Article 73 of its Charter reminded the imperial powers of 'their sacred trust... to promote the well being of the inhabitants of these territories' and their responsibility 'to develop self-government ... and to assist them in the progressive development of their free political institutions ...' The Soviet Union, despite itself establishing a new East European empire, used these obligations as a convenient stick to beat its Western opponents, while the other principal victor, the United States, found itself uneasily poised between its own anti-imperial rhetoric and its fear that the collapse of the European empires in Asia and Africa would result in Communist expansion.

In the immediate aftermath of 1945 the British found the burdens of their Palestinian Mandate and their Indian empire too great to sustain, but the end of British control in both areas highlighted the problems and ambiguities of national self-determination in a particularly stark and tragic manner. Faced with mounting Jewish militancy and fierce Arab resistance to increased immigration by survivors of the Holocaust, Britain sought – without great expectations – the assistance of the UN. The resulting report from its Special Commission on Palestine (UNSCOP) proposed to partition the territory into two states, one Arab the other Jewish, leaving Jerusalem an international city under UN control. Despite enormous American pressure and the support of the USSR the proposal only just achieved the necessary two-thirds majority in the General Assembly on 29 November 1947, presaging further unrest in Palestine and increased preparations for war.

On 14 May 1948 the British relinquished their mandate, the new state of Israel was proclaimed in Tel Aviv and President Truman announced American recognition. The next day war broke out between Israel and six Arab states, united in their wish to destroy the Jewish state but otherwise hopelessly divided. The resulting Israeli victory secured the new state, enlarged its territory and created the Palestinian refugee problem. Some 200,000 Palestinians fled to the Gaza Strip, then in Egyptian hands, others to the West Bank, which, in 1950, became part of the new Kingdom of Jordan. 150,000 more remained, with great reluctance, in Israel itself. Many found themselves living in conditions of great deprivation in camps or grossly overcrowded shanty towns. Their continuing demands for self-determination coupled, in their most extreme form, with a refusal to recognize the state of Israel constituted an ongoing legacy which has contributed to deep unrest, several wars in the region, acted as a justification for terrorism and remains a potential threat to world peace.[24]

At midnight on 14 August 1947 India achieved its independence from Britain but the subcontinent was not ceded as a single state, instead being divided into India and Pakistan, itself split into two separate enclaves, East and West Pakistan. In 1971 East Pakistan became independent as Bangladesh. Clement Attlee's Labour Government reluctantly accepted the policy of partition proposed by the new Viceroy Lord Mountbatten, because it proved impossible to resolve the religious and political difficulties that divided Mohammad Ali Jinnah the leader of the Muslim League from Mohandas Gandhi, Jawaharlal Nehru and the other leaders of the mainly Hindu Congress Party. Whereas the Congress sought to maintain Indian unity, Jinnah became an increasingly adamant advocate of a separate, Muslim Pakistan. Growing inter-communal violence preceded the handover of power but in the months that followed it has been estimated that some 14.5 million people moved from one to the other jurisdiction, hoping to find safety with their co-religionists. Up to a million people died from violence, exhaustion, hunger or disease and countless more became homeless refugees as they tried to accommodate themselves to new frontiers drawn by politicians on a map.[25]

The following year Britain left Ceylon (Sri Lanka) and Burma (Myanmar), thus completing the first stage of its disengagement from its Asian empire. Malaya, the next major territory in the region to achieve independence, illustrated how decolonization created its own complications for the principle of national self-determination. In Paris Harold Nicolson had complained, 'it is appalling, those three ignorant and irresponsible men cutting [territories] to bits as if they were dividing a cake'. Many of the European empires comprised territories that had been created by drawing relatively arbitrary lines on maps, taking little account of tribal loyalties or local history. The general assumption of British governments, as they prepared their colonies for independence, was that these new states would be able to accommodate differing ethnic, religious or racial groups and create acceptable political and economic structures to ensure harmony and development.

British Malaya was an artificial construct consisting of various groups of jurisdictions; while the development of its rubber and tin mining industries had encouraged immigrants from China and India, creating an ethnic mixture in which by 1941 the Chinese with 43 per cent of the population outnumbered native Malays with 41 per cent. Indians, at 14 per cent, made up the majority of the rest. The failure of Britain's attempt to reconstitute the area into a more coordinated colony after 1945 was further complicated by an insurgency campaign conducted mainly by Chinese guerrillas which was eventually defeated by a combination of military strategy, political and economic measures and effective propaganda. Malaya became independent in 1957 but by then Britain had essentially abandoned its attempt to create a multiracial political entity.[26]

Meanwhile the French were drawn into a long struggle to retain control of French Indo-China where revolt broke out in December 1946. Unusually among the campaigns conducted by colonial nationalists, this developed from a guerrilla insurgency into a full-scale conventional military confrontation between March and May 1954 at the battle of Dien Bien Phu which the French lost. They had already granted independence to Laos in 1947 and Cambodia in 1953; now Indo-China was divided into two states, North and South Vietnam, after the 1954 Geneva Peace Talks.

The French trauma continued in North Africa where, despite relatively peaceful transitions to independence for Morocco in 1956 and Tunisia in 1958, another bitter struggle occurred in Algeria from 1954, complicated by the large (12.5 per cent) settler population which had dispossessed the local peasantry. The brutality of this colonial war, which eventually engaged half a million French troops, provoked deep division in France itself and in June 1958 contributed to the return as Prime Minister of General Charles de Gaulle to the political stage he had quit in disgust in 1946. In October he became President of the new Fifth Republic. His policy of phased withdrawal from Algeria disappointed and surprised those who believed de Gaulle supported continued French rule and led to military revolt, assassination attempts and the execution by firing squad of Colonel Jean Bastien-Thiry. Algeria became independent in July 1962.[27]

It was, in part, their belief that Colonel Gamal Abdul Nasser, the Egyptian leader, was providing support to the Algerian rebels that encouraged the French to participate in the disastrous Anglo-French Suez expedition in 1956. In 1954 Britain agreed to end its 'temporary' occupation of Egypt that had begun in 1882, negotiating a deal which it believed safeguarded its interests with the new nationalist Egyptian leadership that had seized power in 1952. When Nasser nationalized the Suez Canal in 1956, however, the enraged British Premier Anthony Eden planned, with his French counterpart Guy Mollet and in collusion with the Israelis, to use the pretext of separating Egyptian and Israeli forces following an Israeli attack to justify an Anglo-French intervention which would also overturn Nasser. When the Americans refused to support them the initial military success of the operation in November 1956 became a humiliating political failure which perhaps scarred Britain more deeply than France. Two years later, a bloody coup destroyed the Hashemite monarchy in Iraq (though the British were able to assist King Hussein to survive in Jordan). Britain's post-1918 dreams of a new Middle Eastern empire had finally collapsed.[28]

The fall-out from Suez contributed to the accelerating process of British decolonization in Africa which began with the independence of Ghana (the Gold Coast) in 1957. In 1960 14 French, three British, two Belgian and one Italian colonies (including Cameroon, Mali, Senegal, the Congo, Somalia and Nigeria) became independent to be followed by 15 more states in the later 1960s. Between 1956 and 1968 51 new members joined the UN, mostly from Asia, Africa and the Caribbean and they swelled the ranks of those who, in 1960, had supported Resolution 1514, which condemned continuing colonialism and advocated self-determination.[29] It is one of the ironies of history that the poorest and one of the least powerful of the European imperial powers, Portugal, would be the last to face the inevitability of decolonization. The British Empire, which after the First World War, comprised a quarter of the world's population and its surface, was reduced by 2010 to 14 overseas territories, mostly small islands scattered about the world's oceans.

Even more than Asia, Africa had been divided between the European powers on the basis of arbitrary lines on a map, and several newly independent states faced crippling ethnic and tribal divisions, leading, particularly in the Congo, Nigeria and the Horn of Africa, to attempted secessions and civil wars. In July 1960, shortly after Belgium hastily granted independence to the Congo, two crises rocked the new state – an army mutiny, which Belgian troops re-emerged, uninvited, to suppress; and the attempted secession of the copper-rich province of Katanga. The UN intervened and persuaded the Belgians to withdraw but was reluctant to move decisively against Katanga and civil war erupted, lasting another two years before the defeat of Katanga's ambitions.

In Nigeria, to which the British bequeathed a federal structure based on three provinces (north, south-west and east, each more or less corresponding to ethnic and religious divisions), the Eastern Province attempted to secede in May 1967 naming itself Biafra. Over the next three years the Ibo in Biafra were defeated, at the cost of over half a million lives on both sides, by the Hausa from the north and the Yoruba from the south-west. The war ended in January 1970. In contrast Eritrea did succeed, after a long struggle lasting from 1963 until 1991, in seceding from Ethiopia and was admitted to the UN in 1993. It was able to do so partly because of another long war in the Horn of Africa between Ethiopia and Somalia about disputed boundaries which weakened Ethiopia and virtually destroyed Somalia as a state.[30]

The most horrific instances of attempts to rid states of unwanted inhabitants in Africa occurred in Rwanda and neighbouring Burundi in a series of conflicts between the Hutus and Tutsis, peoples whose separation seems to be based more on a combination of social class and colonial policy than ethnic difference, though there are several disputed explanations for the division. In both states before independence from Belgium the Hutu constituted the majority population but the minority Tutsi were the dominant political force. After independence the Tutsi retained control in Burundi but were ousted by the Hutu in Rwanda. Both states have witnessed a number of attempted genocides in the past 50 years. In Burundi in 1972 the Tutsi army killed some 100,000 Hutus, and in a further outbreak of violence after 1993 an estimated

500,000 Burundians from both groups perished. In Rwanda an earlier Hutu attack on the Tutsi in 1959 was eclipsed by the terrible violence of 1994 when, in a three-month period, some 800,000 people, mainly Tutsi, were murdered despite the presence of a UN peacekeeping force in the country, dealing a fatal blow to any hopes of a 'New World Order' after the end of the Cold War.[31]

During the Nigerian conflict Secretary-General U Thant took a firm stance, stating that the UN 'has never accepted and does not accept and I do not believe it will ever accept the principle of secession of a part of its member state'[32] and to date Eritrea remains the only example of a successful secession in Africa, despite a series of civil wars sometimes encouraged by neighbouring states seeking to gain resources or territory. Yet despite U Thant's clarity the underlying question remains. The settlement in 1919, as indeed that after 1945, was based on the principle of the sovereign state as the foundation of the international system. Both the League and the UN were deliberately not designed as superstates but as international organizations required to request rather than demand their members to act. Given the prominence given by Wilson and by later peacemakers to the principles of democracy and self-determination, their role in the legitimacy of states has become increasingly important. The key question here is whether, in any state but especially in a democracy, discontented groups have the right to secede.

The 1975 Helsinki Final Act declared that 'all peoples always have the right ... when and as they wish' to exercise self-determination and in 1990 the distinguished British international lawyer Professor Sir Ian Brownlie stated, 'The present position is that self-determination is a legal principle' and possibly has the special status as a law of overriding force.[33] This places a very real uncertainty at the heart of the international system. If the sovereignty and territorial integrity of states is not secure, how can the international system, itself built upon and from those states, enjoy a firm foundation? Yet if a state is perceived by its inhabitants to be treating them unjustly, wherein lies its moral legitimacy?

These are questions lacking easy and simple answers. One of U Thant's successors, Boutros Boutros-Ghali, struggled to come to terms with the issues in his 1992 *Agenda for Peace*. He wrote: 'The United Nations has not closed its door. Yet if every ethnic, religious or linguistic group claimed statehood, there would be no limit to fragmentation, and peace, security and economic well-being for all would become ever-more difficult to achieve.' Tellingly, however, he offered no concrete agenda to achieve his aspiration that, 'The sovereignty, territorial integrity and independence of States within the established international system and the principle of the self-determination of peoples, both of great value and importance, must not be permitted to work against each other in the period ahead.'[34]

> 'The sovereignty, territorial integrity and independence of States within the established international system and the principle of the self-determination of peoples, both of great value and importance, must not be permitted to work against each other in the period ahead.'
> BOUTROS BOUTROS-GHALI, 1992

The clash of these principles continues to exercise us today. Although it was still possible in 1989 for the historian Michael Howard to write of Versailles that 'the states established by the settlement have remained viable ever since',[35] the subsequent collapse of the USSR undermined that claim. Eighteen new or revived states, in addition to Russia (which took over the USSR's Security Council chair), Belorus and Ukraine (which were as Soviet puppets founder members of the UN), have since emerged. Quarrels and disputes frozen by the Cold War thawed often to disastrous effect; and the historian Eric Hobsbawm blamed the peacemakers of 1919, claiming that 'The national conflicts tearing the continent apart in the 1990s were the old chickens of Versailles coming home to roost.'[36] Some, like the ethnic and religious divisions of the Balkans, were even older than that and this was reflected in the bitterness and brutality that ensued from the disintegration of Yugoslavia, resulting in hundreds of thousands of deaths in battles or through the hideous euphemism of ethnic cleansing – murder by a fancy name. Czechoslovakia was more fortunate. Its division by velvet divorce on 31 December 1992 created without bloodshed two new states, the Czech and Slovak Republics; but this still left 300,000 Slovaks and 60,000 Czechs on the wrong side of the new borders, thousands of German speakers in the Sudeten area of the Czech Republic, and half a million Hungarians in Slovakia. Nationalist groups in Hungary continue to assert their interest in the fate of these exiles, and of a further 2.5 million Hungarians living in six other bordering states.[37] There are 26 million Russians scattered about the wreckage of the old Soviet empire. A latter-day Hitler would not find it difficult to find a plausible cause to cloak his ambition to disrupt the current order.

> 'From the Baltics to the Adriatic, from the Ukraine to the Balkans, oppressed millions have given new life to his imperative – and often troublesome principle. Indeed if results are the measure, Wilson has proved a more successful revolutionary than Lenin.'
>
> **KARL MEYER, 1991**

Before the worst of the Balkan atrocities the *New York Times* columnist Karl Meyer wrote, on 14 August 1991, that Wilson's dream of national self-determination once more held the floor, a lifetime after the Paris Conference. 'From the Baltics to the Adriatic, from the Ukraine to the Balkans, oppressed millions have given new life to his imperative – and often troublesome principle. Indeed if results are the measure, Wilson has proved a more successful revolutionary than Lenin.' In some cases, however, the costs have been or would be very high, a striking reminder of Lansing's 1918 warning that, 'The gift of clever phrasing may be a curse unless the phrases are put to the test of sound, practical application before being uttered ... Think of the feelings of the author when he counts the dead because he coined a phrase!' If Wilson encouraged the genie of self-determination to emerge further from its bottle it has proved impossible since to get it to return inside.[38]

5

Minority Protection, Disarmament and International Law

The creation of the League of Nations was the most obvious and innovative attempt by the peacemakers in Paris to ensure that 1914–18 became indeed 'the war to end all wars', but they also took other steps to avoid conflict and to discourage potential disturbers of the peace. The League was, and its successor the United Nations remains, closely associated with three of these initiatives: minority protection, disarmament and international law. Each, whilst built upon existing experience and practice, was given new prominence and significance by the First World War settlements.

Minority protection was intended to deny would-be revisionists a plausible excuse for actions taken with ulterior motives. The peacemakers were painfully aware that they were bound to disappoint the hopes for self-determination of many, particularly in Eastern and Central Europe with its kaleidoscopic array of ethnicities, languages and religions. To diminish the possibility of aggressive neighbouring states using the alleged mistreatment of their kinsmen as an excuse for territorial revision and aggrandisement, they proposed special collective privileges and protection for the disappointed and reluctant citizens of states to which they had been unwillingly consigned by the new boundaries approved by the Conference. Disarmament would serve a double purpose – removing both a possible reason for conflict and the means to wage it. Sir Edward Grey, the British Foreign Secretary in 1914, believed that 'great armaments lead inevitably to war … The enormous growth of armaments in Europe, the sense of insecurity and fear caused by them – it was these that made war inevitable.'[1] At least some of the peacemakers shared this conviction and the Treaties, whilst initially imposing unilateral disarmament on the defeated powers, contained the promise of future multilateral reductions of military forces and expenditure. Finally, by asserting the criminal responsibility of enemy military and political leaders for starting the war and the manner in which it was waged, the peacemakers extended the scope of illegality in warfare from purely operational misconduct and introduced the concept of crimes against humanity. The hope here was that fear of future retribution might inhibit leaders from embarking on military adventures.

Minority protection

'[I]t is essential, if man is not to be compelled to have recourse, as a last resort, to rebellion against tyranny and oppression, that human rights should be protected by the rule of law.'

Universal Declaration of Human Rights, 10 December 1948

The concept of minority protection existed long before the Paris Conferences. There are examples of provision for safeguarding religious groups at least as far back as the 16th century, usually involving a neighbouring state sharing the religion of the minority which was prepared to act on its behalf, and the Treaty of Westphalia in 1648 included international religious guarantees. The three major 19th century settlements – Vienna in 1815, Paris in 1856 and Berlin in 1878 – all included rights for people transferred to a different state. Religion rather than nationality remained the main object of protection but a very significant 19th century development meant that, in theory at least, protection became a joint responsibility of the great powers. The main driving force for this was the gradual dissolution of the Ottoman Empire and the emergence of new independent states in the Balkans. At the Congress of Berlin in 1878, the great powers – Austria-Hungary, Britain, France, Germany, Italy and Russia, together with the Ottoman Empire – recognised the sovereignty and independence of Serbia, Montenegro and Romania. With the earlier independence of Greece in 1830 and Bulgaria making significant progress towards full sovereignty, the 19th century saw five new states in the area and it was acknowledged that such developments were of general European interest. Before they would recognize such a new state the great powers demanded that it give a formal undertaking to comply with certain principles of governance (a 'standard of civilization' in the contemporary phrase), in particular that it would guarantee religious toleration and undertake not to exclude individuals from public office or civic rights on religious grounds.

The precedents set in the 19th century thus suggested that the protection of the civic rights of minority religious groups was something imposed on the small states of Eastern Europe when the great powers recognised their independence or agreed to major changes in their territorial boundaries. The great powers did not apply the same principles to themselves – no such demands were made of the newly unified states of

Italy or Germany – the assumption, not always true, being that such states needed no external monitoring to behave in a proper manner towards all their citizens. Nor were they eager to act against states which did not comply with their undertakings. Given that the Jews constituted the major religious minority group scattered about Eastern and Central Europe it was upon them that the main focus of protection fell and, in the case of Romania in particular, the great powers saw their authority flouted. Article 44 of the 1878 Treaty of Berlin forbade discrimination against Jewish citizens of Romania but the powers did nothing when Romania thwarted this by what was, essentially, a simple declaration that no Jew could be a Romanian citizen. Good intentions were undone by a combination of great power rivalry, competition for client states in the Balkans and indifference to issues not of direct concern to themselves. There was also the consideration that, whilst the powers understood that these conditions for recognition implied their right to intervene in the internal affairs of the new states, such action might constitute a very unwelcome precedent weakening the long-standing principle of non-interference in the domestic affairs of other sovereign states established by the 1648 Treaty of Westphalia. The peacemakers in Paris were informed by these developments and followed many of the same principles and precedents and it is indeed probable that, but for the diligence of the League of Nation's Minorities Questions Section, there might have been equal inattention to the enforcement of their decisions after 1919 as there had been before the First World War.[2]

Although there were other vocal minority groups in the various Allied states which pressed their leaders to incorporate guarantees of their rights into the settlement, the most powerful lobbies, especially in the United States, France and Britain, were Jewish organisations anxious, in particular, about the fate of Jews in Eastern and Central Europe. Their campaigns were of great importance in reminding the peacemakers of a challenging and complex duty. The Jewish voice was, however, split between Zionists seeking a separate homeland and those more concerned with protecting Jews who wished to remain in their present locations. This blurring of the margins between religion and nationality is indicative of a widening focus for protection, emphasised by Wilson when he spoke of 'national minorities', the creation of which would be the inevitable result of the application of national self-determination in ethnically mixed regions. Yet the prominence of the Jewish issue is evidenced by the final wording of the Treaties which referred not to national minorities but to minorities of 'language, race and religion'. As a later commentator remarked, this Jewish suggestion was based on the argument 'that if you can prevent a Jew from being persecuted on the score of his race, his language, or his religion, you will have made it impossible to get at him at all'.[3]

The original plan of Wilson and his British colleague on the League Commission Lord Robert Cecil was to include in the League Covenant general guarantees of equality of treatment for 'all racial or national minorities' and of freedom of religious expression for all beliefs 'whose practices are not inconsistent with public order or public morals'. This attempt to create a universal system alarmed those in the American and British delegations concerned that imprecise and wide-ranging definitions might encourage discontented subjects within their own and other jurisdictions to seek to appeal to the League over the authority of the state – the examples often cited of potential appellants were African-Americans and the Irish. Racial equality, of which the Japanese became particular sponsors, raised difficult political issues about immigration for Australia and New Zealand, and for Wilson on the Pacific seaboard, compounded in his case by the smouldering issue of colour in the southern states. To his deep embarrassment he had first to abandon his racial and religious drafts and then to resort to dubious technicalities of procedure to block a Japanese proposal to reinstate a racial equality clause in the Covenant. The attempt to create a global system of minority rights had failed and the problem would have to be resolved on a country-by-country basis.[4]

This left the peacemakers, already faced with a major crisis as various interlinked and apparently insoluble problems threatened to scupper the entire Conference, with little time or energy to rethink their approach. They found themselves under renewed pressure from Jewish groups, particularly after a massacre of 35 Jews in Pinsk by Polish soldiers in early April, and they were reminded that if they wished to require new or enlarged states to conform to international economic, postal and transportation agreements as well as to expected standards of behaviour, they must reach such arrangements with the states concerned before they were granted international recognition in the Peace Treaties. The German delegation was already at Versailles when belatedly on 1 May 1919 the Allies established the New States Committee with the remit of tackling these various issues.

The initial hope was that the Committee could still draw up detailed provisions based upon American suggestions for the protection of minorities in Poland in time for them to be included in the draft German Treaty but this proved impossible. Instead a clause was inserted binding Poland to accept whatever terms the Allies deemed necessary to safeguard minority rights there, leaving the Committee with more time to consider what these requirements might be. By 14 May it had assembled a draft Treaty with Poland that became the model for all the other minority Treaties. Under it Poland was obliged to enact fundamental laws which could not be abrogated establishing provisions for the protection of the life and liberty of 'all inhabitants of Poland without distinction of birth, nationality, language, race or religion'. To avoid any repetition of the Romanian example the articles defining citizenship were carefully designed to ensure that all inhabitants of the new state automatically became full and complete Polish citizens. All citizens should be equal before the law and non-Polish speakers were guaranteed free private use of their own language and the right to use that language before the courts. All Polish citizens should enjoy equal rights to establish religious, charitable and social institutions and schools where their own language and religion could be practised.

In addition to these provisions, which applied all over Poland, there were others that applied only to specific areas and which were not fundamental. Where a considerable proportion of the population spoke a language other than Polish the state would fund primary education in that language. The state would also ensure that minorities received an equitable share of any public funds distributed for educational, religious or charitable purposes. Where the minority language was German these provisions applied only to areas that had been part of Germany on 1 August 1914. Finally there were a number of Jewish clauses which were specific to the Polish Treaty. Jewish educational committees would administer their proportionate share of state funds for education and organize and manage their schools. The Sabbath was protected excepting only the needs of military service, national defence or the preservation of public order. No elections or electoral registration could take place on a Saturday.

Poland recognized that these arrangements for the protection of people belonging to 'racial, religious or linguistic minorities' were matters of international concern to be placed under the guarantee of the League of Nations and that they could not be altered except by a majority vote in the League Council. Council members had the right to draw attention to infractions or the danger of infractions of these provisions and the Council could then take what steps it deemed necessary to correct the problem.

The Council of Four accepted these recommendations on 17 May as the basis for the Polish Treaty and for other subsequent Treaties with Romania, Greece, Yugoslavia, Czechoslovakia, Austria, Hungary, Bulgaria, Turkey, Albania, Lithuania, Latvia and Estonia as well as Iraq. The defeated states had the Treaties imposed upon them as part of the settlement; the others accepted them in return for the formal recognition of their gains by the powers or as part of the terms of their admission to the League. At the 31 May plenary session Romania, Czechoslovakia and Yugoslavia objected strongly, arguing that these provisions abrogated state sovereignty and implied the inferiority of the East European states. Given that Britain, Italy, France, Denmark, Belgium or even Germany were not required to give similar undertakings they had a point, but Wilson was adamant: 'Nothing, I venture to say, is more likely to disturb the peace of the world than the treatment which might in certain circumstances be meted out to minorities. And therefore, if the great powers are to guarantee the peace of the world in any sense, is it unjust that they should be satisfied that the proper and necessary guarantees have been given?' On 28 June Poland signed first the Treaty of Versailles and then the Polish Minority Treaty and subsequently the other East European states bowed to the inevitable when it came to their turn to formalise the peace.[5]

The peacemakers had widened the definition of minority protection to include some provision for linguistic and cultural rights, offering recognition of their importance as symbols of national identity. This was, of course, a double-edged sword because the Treaties did not specify whether the underlying objective was the preservation of minorities or the encouragement of assimilation. We may infer that the peacemakers' intention was to introduce limited, preferably temporary, arrangements enabling national minorities to become reconciled to their new states whilst, at the same time protecting, as far as possible in the interests of national and international harmony, the sovereignty of those host states. The British Foreign Secretary Austen Chamberlain told the League Council in 1926 that 'the object of the minority treaties ... was ... to secure for the minorities that measure of protection and justice which would gradually prepare them to be merged in the national community to which they belonged.'[6]

> 'The object of the minority treaties ... was ... to secure for the minorities that measure of protection and justice which would gradually prepare them to be merged in the national community to which they belonged.'
> **AUSTEN CHAMBERLAIN, 1926**

Chamberlain's language betrays the ambiguities inherent in the western liberal tradition's confusion of nationality and citizenship – the minorities might be citizens of their new states but neither they, nor their hosts, necessarily perceived them to be members of the 'national community', and the measures that the peacemakers hoped would encourage assimilation seemed to the host states simply to encourage and perpetuate the separateness of the minorities. The wider ambiguity about the Treaties' objectives was highlighted in a bitter 1925 debate in the League Council over whether minorities owed any duties towards their host states. Mello Franco, the Brazilian representative, reflecting the assimilationist philosophy of his country, argued that the peacemakers could not have intended to create a system in which groups in certain states regarded themselves as permanent strangers. These were clearly measures 'which might gradually prepare the way for the conditions necessary for the establishment of a complete national unit'. Gustav Stresemann, the German leader, took a very different view – minority protection must be permanent, not simply 'a transition period instituted to overcome temporary difficulties'. He had no desire to see Germans in Poland or elsewhere assimilated into alien states.[7]

The British placed great faith in the force of circumstances. James Headlam-Morley hoped that 'if the passionate nationalism diminishes, as it probably will, all the states will get to see that if the frontiers are all permanently settled and if it is definitely agreed that no change of frontier can be made by methods of war and revolution, without the consent of the League of Nations, it will generally be recognised that it is for the advantage of the state itself to treat these national minorities with the greatest consideration'. His colleague Lord Hardinge expressed the reciprocal point: 'All these difficulties are likely to disappear as soon as the frontiers have been definitely decided by the peace conference and the Germans of Bohemia realize that they will have to live in amity with their Czech neighbours or go elsewhere.' Majorities and minorities would have to live together in the new and permanent frontiers of Eastern Europe. Unfortunately the optimistic assumptions upon which these conclusions rested were unfounded. Majorities, often seeking retribution for their earlier ill-treatment at the hands of their former rulers, regarded minorities with suspicion; the minorities, sometimes looking to neighbouring kin states for support, did not become reconciled to their lot; and many frontiers were very definitely not accepted as final.[8]

The peacemakers had carefully restricted the right to raise concerns about minority treatment to League Council members but, in practice, there was no great enthusiasm amongst the victors to take up these matters. When Headlam-Morley suggested to the Foreign Office that Britain had an obligation to pursue flagrant violations of the Treaties one of his colleagues responded that whilst Britain had the right to inform the League, 'I do not agree with Mr Headlam-Morley that [it has] the *obligation* to do so ... I do not see why H[is M[ajesty's]G[overnment] should be called upon to champion the cause of minorities as a matter of course, and to incur the odium of lecturing the various offending governments.' The French took a similar attitude and so, to breathe some life into it, the system was amended in 1920 to allow minority groups themselves to petition the League, though the treaty-bound states took a very dim view of this, in some cases threatening complainants with accusations of treason.[9]

Given that the original intention of the peacemakers was to reduce potential sources of international friction the outcome was not a success. The inter-war period witnessed confrontations between minorities and their host states and interventions by revisionist kin states. Germany and Hungary in particular were assiduous exploiters of the real or imagined grievances of their exiles. The treaty-bound states retained a deep resentment of the special provisions imposed upon them. In 1934 Poland denounced the Minorities Treaty, effectively destroying the League system, though the ultimate cynical use of a minority to engineer revision of the settlements came with Hitler's demand in April 1938 that Henlein and the Sudeten Germans must never be satisfied, no matter what concessions were made to them by the Czech state, thus justifying his intervention on their behalf and the destruction of Czechoslovakia at Munich.[10]

The belief, as one observer put it, that 'every protected minority will ultimately find its Henlein' helped to discredit the idea of group rights and to shift the focus after the Second World War towards the protection of individual human rights and the unity of states. The UN's 1970 Declaration of Principles on Friendly Relations Between States emphasized that 'nothing ... shall be construed as authorising or encouraging any action which would dismember or impair, totally or in part, the territorial integrity or political unity of sovereign and independent States conducting themselves in compliance with the principle of equal rights and self-determination of peoples ... and thus possessed of a government representing the whole people belonging to the territory, without distinction as to race, creed or colour'. Whilst there was still plenty of scope for argument about what constituted proper conduct by a government, the message was plain – it was preferable to preserve the integrity of states. Indeed between 1945 and 1989 the only mention of

> 'Nothing ... shall be construed as authorising or encouraging any action which would dismember or impair, totally or in part, the territorial integrity or political unity of sovereign and independent States conducting themselves in compliance with the principle of equal rights and self-determination of peoples ...'
>
> UN'S DECLARATION OF PRINCIPLES ON FRIENDLY RELATIONS BETWEEN STATES, 1970

minority rights in a UN document was a clause in the 1966 Covenant on Civil and Political Rights which allowed states to define what constituted a minority. Many took advantage of this loophole to redefine groups as aboriginals or immigrants rather than as minorities.

Individual human rights rather than special provision for groups were also preferred because they were deemed to be compatible with population transfer or the assimilation of minorities – again measures that were not uncommon in the wake of the Second World War and which, it was hoped, would strengthen the stability of states whilst (in a manner that the Paris peacemakers almost entirely eschewed) 'fulfilling' the self-determination of those forcibly transferred to their kin states. The new peace treaties signed by several of the former Axis powers in 1947 required each to 'take all necessary measures to ensure that everyone within its jurisdiction, without distinction as to race, sex, language or religion, enjoyed fundamental human rights and liberties, including freedom of thought, press, publication, culture, opinion and meeting'. The European Convention on Human Rights signed on 4 November 1950 and which entered into force in September 1953 specified a wide range of political and civil rights relating to the individual. There was no mention of group minority rights and, despite some discussion of the need to consider the issue in the Council of Europe, this remained the norm for the period of the Cold War, although the 1975 Helsinki Final Act did, in a very limited way, acknowledge that minorities might be entitled to special consideration.[11]

This European experience was paralleled by the American Convention on Human Rights which was agreed by the Organization of American States (OAS) at San José, Costa Rica, in 1969 and came into force on 18 July 1978. It stressed individual rather than group rights, though some of its provisions were more far-reaching than its European counterparts. The equivalent African document, the Banjul Charter on Human and Peoples' Rights that was adopted in 1981 and came into force in 1986, did make some provision for peoples' rights in addition to the usual political and civil rights. These peoples' rights included the right to self-determination though, given the sensitivity of many of the African frontiers that were created by the colonial powers, this has been usually interpreted to mean a right that should be exercised without infringing the current territorial integrity of states.[12]

After 1989 the freeing of frontiers in Europe created an opportunity for people to join their kin and the early 1990s witnessed massive population movements whilst the unfreezing of antagonisms suppressed during the Cold War reopened the question of secession of reluctant subjects of Czechoslovakia, the USSR and Yugoslavia. Fearing the potential security risks involved, the Council for Security and Cooperation in Europe (CSCE – after 1995 the Organization for Security and Cooperation in Europe, OSCE) took up a number of issues in Eastern and Central Europe. It faced exactly the same questions of principle and practicality with which the peacemakers in Paris had struggled – how to create measures strong enough to satisfy and guarantee minorities without eroding the essential sovereignty and territorial integrity of states; and it came to recognize that individual rights were not always sufficient because certain rights, the use of a language for example, depended on group use.

CSCE's 1990 Copenhagen Document marked a massive shift from the post-1945 approach, recognizing, as it did, the rights of minorities to form associations within and across international frontiers; to receive official information in their own language; and to enjoy its free use in private, public, religious and educational contexts. The Document, to which 30 European states subscribed, guaranteed freedom from assimilation and prohibited forcible transfers of population. Many of its provisions have been repeated and embellished in various other conventions and proposals but its suggestion of appropriate local or autonomous administrations for minorities was, predictably, highly contentious and has not attracted much support.

Further instruments include the 1990 Charter of Paris for a New Europe, the 1991 Geneva Report on National Minorities, the 1992 Moscow and Helsinki Documents, the Council of Europe's 1992 Charter for Regional or Minority Languages and its 1994 Framework Convention for the Protection of National Minorities (FCNM) which came into force in 1998 after ratification by 12 states. By 2009 a further 27 had done so, with the notable exception of France which considers its republic one and indivisible and remains an advocate of individual rather than group rights. The FCNM, the first multi-lateral legally binding provision for the protection of European minorities, sought to help minorities retain their identities and cultures, basing its provisions very much on the Copenhagen Document's approaches. In December 1992 CSCE created a High Commissioner for National Minorities to assist member states to implement minority standards and to help resolve problems.[13]

In Europe alone it has been calculated that there are 87 peoples, 90 languages (of which 53 are not the official tongue of any state) and 329 national or ethnic groups. Every European state with a population of over a million has at least one minority: Russia with 45 has the most, followed by the Ukraine with 23 and Romania with 19 groups. The perennial problem remains how to provide fair and reasonable protection for the languages and cultures of these minorities and yet not destroy the stability of the states in which they reside or, consequentially, that of the whole international system. The European Union has struggled to reconcile the approaches and philosophies of its member states and to implement a perceived need to bolster individual human rights with an element of collective privileges. Perhaps unsurprisingly its approach has been cautious but its interest in the issue is a further indication of how its role has expanded from providing a framework to prevent international conflict to providing assistance to members in resolving internal unrest.[14]

The creation of minorities is an inevitable consequence of the application of national self-determination or simply the emergence of any new state. The protection of minorities and their rights is a further issue to which the peacemakers in Paris have made an important contribution. The problems that they either stated or implied remain part of today's agenda though it is much harder for current politicians to plead ignorance about persecuted and mistreated minorities whose plight is highlighted by media reports. Public pressure for 'something to be done' has raised the stakes and helped to blur still further the Westphalian principle that domestic matters are purely for internal resolution by the state involved. The 1999 NATO intervention against Serbia on behalf of Albanians in Kosovo marked an important breach of a principle whose definition has become increasingly uncertain. Decision-makers remain torn between the rights of states and the rights of their inhabitants in a complex series of considerations in which it is much easier to formulate the problem than it is to develop a solution. The brave words of the preamble to the Universal Declaration of Human Rights adopted in December 1948 in the wake of a second global conflict even more terrible than the first, asserted that the 'recognition of the inherent dignity and of the equal and inalienable rights of all members of the human family is the foundation of freedom, justice and peace in the world' but defining and delivering those rights remains as much of a problem today as it was for the peacemakers in 1919.

Disarmament

'It is useless for the sheep to pass resolutions in favour of vegetarianism while the wolf remains of a different opinion.'

William Inge, 1919.[15]

The disarmament provisions in the settlements at the end of the First World War were unusual in two respects. It was not uncommon for major defeated powers to have some limits set on their armed forces or their military strengths as the historian Philip Towle has argued: 'This was part of every major peace settlement from the Treaty of Utrecht in 1713, through the Paris negotiations in 1815 and 1919, to the post-war agreements in 1945.' More recently the UN undertook to disarm Iraq after the first Gulf War in 1991. It was not normal, however, to extend such requirements to the lesser members of the losing side. Yet the five original Paris Treaties all imposed stringent limitations on the size, composition and equipment of the armed forces of all the beaten Central Powers. Even more striking was the commitment made by the victors to seek to achieve the aspiration expressed in the fourth of Wilson's Fourteen Points: 'Adequate guarantees given and taken that national armaments will be reduced to the lowest point consistent with domestic safety.' The extension of the forced disarmament of the losers into a universal voluntary enterprise represented a remarkable attempt to transform international politics reflecting the beliefs of at least some of the peacemakers that if arms races were a cause of war, arms reduction could help to create a peaceful world.[16]

In 1914, on the outbreak of war, Germany had some four million men under arms and a powerful navy with 15 dreadnought battleships and over 150 other ships. The Treaty of Versailles sought to disarm Germany comprehensively. It reduced its army to 100,000 men, of whom only 4,000 could be officers. All must be volunteers with other ranks engaging for a minimum of 12 years and officers for 25. To avoid a repetition of the ploys used by Prussia to circumvent Napoleon's attempt to disarm it after Jena in 1806 the Treaty placed strict limits on the manpower and training of other state organizations like the police, customs or coastguards and restricted the numbers of servicemen who could be discharged for medical or other reasons to avoid a churn of trained personnel. It banned Germany from possessing tanks, heavy guns and poison gas or other chemical weapons and limited the amounts of other forms of armaments. Only designated plants could produce arms and munitions, and none of this material could be imported or exported. Germany was allowed no military presence of any kind in the demilitarized zone covering all German territory on the west bank of the Rhine and the strip of land 50 kilometres to the east of the river. It was forbidden to improve any of its other frontier or coastal fortifications. The Treaty demanded that Germany disband its general staff (the central planning body for the army) and forbade its reconstitution. The navy was similarly depleted, reduced to little more than a coastal defence force, deprived of its dreadnoughts and submarines and with only 36 ships and a maximum strength of 15,000 men. Germany was not allowed any military or naval aircraft. The reduction of Germany's armed forces and the destruction of weapons or military capacity in excess of the Treaty provisions would be monitored by three Inter-Allied Commissions of Control, one for each service.

For the British and Americans the removal of the German naval threat was a given requirement but, perhaps surprisingly, the Allies had not devoted much thought to the post-war military disarmament of Germany. A recent study concludes that, 'The victors' adoption of the Versailles disarmament programme was … late and sudden' and largely a consequence of the opportunity created by the crippling Armistice terms demanded by Marshal Foch.[17] Most of the questions surrounding the military and naval disarmament of Germany were rapidly resolved by the Big Four, but this disguised some very deep divisions between them. In common with many British leaders Lloyd George was concerned about the post-war balance of power if Germany was left too weak to counter whatever threat might emerge from the chaos in Russia and (though this could not be so openly professed) to inhibit an over-mighty France.

The French, not unnaturally, had a different perspective, based on their potential vulnerability to a much larger and younger German population. Wilson and Lloyd George were opposed to conscription, the latter asserting with some vigour that it encouraged militarism. Clemenceau and Orlando were offended and unimpressed but the eventual compromise that established the voluntary principle for German recruitment also entailed a much smaller German army, at best half the size that either the American or British experts considered adequate for internal and external security.

These disagreements influenced later attitudes to

enforcement, leaving the British generally more sympathetic to German pleas for a relaxation of the terms. They also had consequences for the other Treaties since it was deemed politic to reduce Austrian, Hungarian, Bulgarian and Turkish troop numbers in proportion to the 100,000 men allowed to Germany. Austria was permitted 30,000, Hungary 35,000, Bulgaria 20,000 and Turkey, under the abortive Treaty of Sèvres, 50,000. There were no such restrictions on Turkey in the renegotiated Treaty of Lausanne. Denied conscription, Austria, Bulgaria and Hungary struggled to reach even these figures and found themselves surrounded by neighbours with much more powerful armies.

The British leadership tended to view disarmament in terms of the destruction of war-making material and capacity and, to a lesser extent, the control of the numbers of German service personnel. The French definition of disarmament penetrated much more deeply, seeking additionally the more elusive goals of breaking Germany's 'military spirit' and thus achieving 'moral disarmament'. It was simpler to benchmark the British approach. It was relatively easy to count the numbers of weapons destroyed. By the end of 1920 the Allied Control Commission calculated that it had reached over 90 per cent of its target figures for the destruction of aircraft and equipment. In January 1921 the British Air Ministry declared, 'The aerial disarmament of Germany may be regarded as virtually accomplished.' By the middle of 1921 Germany had complied with all the important naval terms and, although military disarmament was more complex and fraught, Britain was reasonably sure that the key points had been achieved by late 1922.[18]

The French concept of disarmament was much more intangible. The Allies were aware that the German government, military, industrialists and individuals acting either in an official or personal capacity were seeking to evade as many of the restrictions as they could. Lloyd George had not heeded the warnings offered by Foch and others that the small professional German army he sought would provide an ideal platform for rapid expansion in the future.

This was indeed how Germany planned its new forces, training all personnel to hold ranks several higher than their present posts. After signing the Treaty of Rapallo with the Soviet Union in April 1922 Germany made secret arrangements to build and test forbidden weapons and equipment in the USSR. Krupp and other major German arms manufacturers set up clandestine plants in other countries and the German military used various pretexts to maintain the bureaucracy and information necessary to enable the rapid expansion of the armed forces. In that sense the German military spirit had clearly not been broken and the French hope of moral disarmament was not achieved though British leaders disagreed. They distinguished between two Germanys: the old, militaristic and aggressive Prussian-dominated Germany, which they believed had been discredited by the war and had disappeared along with the Kaiser; and the new, republican Germany in whose good intentions they placed much faith. The French, unconvinced of this fundamental change of heart, did not make such a distinction.[19]

Any decision about whether or not Germany had complied with the military terms of the Treaty would be based on a combination of these psychological and quantifiable grounds but was, ultimately, political. In the wake of the Locarno negotiations, under which Germany had voluntarily recognized its post-war frontiers with France and Belgium and the demilitarization of the Rhineland, the Allies decided that Germany had disarmed. There were, however, dissenting voices who feared the depth of the military tradition in Germany and who suggested 'that, from the moment control is withdrawn it would take the German authorities only one year to attain their maximum war production of 1918 in guns and munitions'. Others, however, pointed out that, even accepting this gloomy assessment, such an expansion of Germany's military capabilities could not take place in secret. Hence, should Germany attempt to do so, the Allies would have plenty of time to take counteraction – provided they had the will so to do.[20] Unfortunately, as Hitler correctly calculated, they did not.

The settlement, however, went beyond the disarmament of the former enemy states. In his Fontainebleau memorandum in March 1919 Lloyd George endorsed Wilson's wider commitment to disarmament. He accepted that, initially, the disarmament of the Central Powers would be unilateral but added, 'it is idle to endeavour to impose a permanent limitation of armaments on Germany unless we are prepared similarly to impose a limitation upon ourselves'. In their reply to Germany's observations on the draft Treaty the Allies developed this theme stating, 'their requirements in regard to German armaments were not made solely with the objective of rendering it impossible for Germany to resume her policy of military aggression. They are also the first step towards that general reduction and limitation of armaments which they seek to bring about as one of the most fruitful preventives of war, and which it will be one of the first duties of the League of Nations to promote.' This undertaking was incorporated in the preamble to the disarmament section of the Treaty which declared, 'In order to render possible the initiation of a general limitation of the armaments of all nations,

Germany undertakes strictly to observe the military, naval and air clauses which follow.' There was thus a predisposition to arms limitation and a moral obligation under the Treaty to drive this forward under the auspices of the League, which in Article 8 of its Covenant looked forward to 'the reduction of national armaments to the lowest point consistent with national safety'.[21]

This formula raised a number of key problems: who would determine that lowest point or define what constituted national safety; and, as with the undertaking in Article 10 'to respect and preserve ... the territorial and existing political independence of all Members', was there a danger of simply trying to preserve the present international *status quo*, making no allowance for redistributions of power or changing circumstances? The proposal to review matters every ten years only partially answered the latter question and, as Sir Eyre Crowe had argued in a forceful wartime memorandum indicating the pitfalls of disarmament, no matter how attractive the idea was in theory, 'To perpetuate indefinitely the conditions prevailing at a given time would

> 'It is idle to endeavour to impose a permanent limitation of armaments on Germany unless we are prepared similarly to impose a limitation upon ourselves.'
> **DAVID LLOYD GEORGE, 1919**

mean not only that no State whose power has hitherto been weak relatively to others may hope to get stronger, but that a definite order or hierarchy must be recognised, in which each State is fated to occupy a fixed place.' Among his other objections, many of which would be vindicated by events, Crowe had warned that unless states honoured their obligations to disarm, those who did so could be placed in danger if others did not. Furthermore 'unless all the world's leading military and naval powers were involved in schemes of armament limitation, disarmament could prove very dangerous to those who undertook it'.[22]

Such a universal undertaking was impossible in a difficult post-war situation in which the United States refused to join the League and no one knew what the outcome of the strife in Russia would be. Already the newest – and potentially the most powerful – of the world's military powers and a pre-war great power stood outside the system, leaving states in Eastern Europe in particular unwilling to deprive themselves of defensive capacity. As always, however, there lurked the tricky problem of perception: one state's assessment of its minimal defensive requirements might seem suspiciously like the means of aggression to a nervous neighbour. Equally, weapons that were deemed defensive by one power were perceived as offensive by others and the whole business of definitions bogged the arguments down in interminable wrangles. An exasperated Aristide Briand, taxed by an American correspondent in 1922 about France's obsession with the Rhineland, pointed out that the United States was building new battleships. When told that these were for purely peaceful purposes he wryly commented, 'Very well, but so far as I know battleships were not invented for fishing sardines'.[23]

Unsurprisingly the League struggled to make progress either in its attempts to find a scheme to facilitate land disarmament or to limit the arms trade. The first fell afoul of the insecurity of states which would not surrender their weapons until they believed themselves invulnerable and the second proved too big a hurdle for contrasting reasons. Some major arms producers like the United States feared a loss of business while smaller states which did not produce their own weapons feared they might not be able to obtain them. It also failed to persuade members to adopt a 'full and frank' exchange of information about their armed forces – another step too far for sovereign states to risk, though the League did publish, until 1938, an annual *Armaments Year Book* based on information made public by members.

On the broader front, however, first the Temporary Mixed Commission, then the Coordination Commission and finally the Preparatory Commission strove to create a convention for a general disarmament conference in the face of the widely differing views of Britain and France. Eventually, in a very unpromising international climate, the Disarmament Conference opened in Geneva in February 1932 but the delegates could reach no satisfactory conclusions on the definitions of offensive and defensive weapons and France and Germany were deeply divided. In February 1933 the Japanese representatives walked out of the League Assembly during the debate on events in Manchuria, formally withdrawing from the League a month later; while in October Hitler's Germany quit the Disarmament Conference and then the League itself. The Conference formally continued to meet sporadically until 1937, but it was effectively dead.[24]

The Washington Naval Conference of 1921–2 proved to be a more reliable signpost to future attempts at disarmament than the League's more ambitious vision. Here the major maritime powers (France, Great Britain, Italy, Japan and the United States) agreed to fix the ratios of capital ships between them, a decision which was helped in an age of submarines and aircraft by some doubts over the continuing value of battleships. In contrast it took much longer to negotiate a limitation of cruisers and destroyers, partly because of the technical difficulties that arose over tonnage and gun barrel size and partly because of the perennial problem about defining their roles and purpose. Only after the failure of the Coolidge Naval Conference in 1927 was agreement finally concluded in London in 1930. Despite all the efforts of the League, these naval limitations came about as the result of the original and independent initiative of the American President Warren G Harding in 1921 and involved only the five principal naval powers. Ominously the Japanese reaction to these agreements was extremely hostile, worsening still further the difficult political situation there as rival factions struggled for the upper hand and the assassination of military and political leaders became a regular occurrence.

The post-Second World War experience has echoed the fate of multilateral general schemes of disarmament in the 1920s and 1930s. Where there have been successes these have usually been in specific areas, relating to classes of weaponry that have some reasonable chance of an agreed definition among all the parties involved. They have often been initiated by the major powers before, in some cases, being extended more widely. The two main areas in which there has been a measure of international agreement relate to chemical and nuclear weapons.

The United Nations has built upon the progress made by the League in brokering international agreements against the use of chemical and biological weapons. The Washington Naval Conference participants also agreed that poison gas, which was extensively used in the First World War despite earlier bans, was illegal and that they would not use it against each other. The League expanded that original undertaking between five states into an absolute ban on the use of gas, chemical or bacteriological weapons agreed by 30 countries attending a conference in Geneva in May and June 1925 and the Geneva Protocol came into force in September 1929. The great powers honoured their commitment to abstain from using poison gas against each other, most notably during the Second World War, though all sides kept supplies to use in retaliation should the agreement be breached. Italy and Japan did employ gas in their respective wars in Abyssinia and China before 1939.

Since the Second World War it was used in a civil war in Yemen and by Saddam Hussein during the Iran-Iraq war and against Kurds in Iraq itself. In Vietnam the United States deployed chemicals to destroy food crops and vegetation used for cover by the Viet Cong but there have also been more hopeful indications. The original Geneva Protocol was supplemented by the 1972 Biological and Toxin Weapons Convention (BTWC) which banned the development, production or stockpiling of biological or toxin weapons and the 1992 Chemical Weapons Convention (CWC) which extends these prohibitions to chemical weapons. Both these instruments have attracted widespread support with 162 states party to the BTWC and almost every country in the world (188 in total) has signed up to the CWC.[25]

The United States conducted a successful nuclear explosion on 16 July 1945 and subsequently dropped two atomic bombs on Hiroshima and Nagasaki in Japan on 6 and 9 August, the only use to date of nuclear weapons in war. In 1949 the Soviet Union exploded 'Joe One' and joined the hitherto exclusively American nuclear club, to be followed by Britain, France, China, India, Pakistan, North Korea and, almost certainly, Israel. Early attempts in the 1950s by the US and USSR working through the UN to limit nuclear weapons were overambitious, tending also to fall foul of another perennial issue relating to disarmament – verification. Meanwhile atmospheric nuclear testing gave rise to growing concerns about the environmental impact. In the wake of the 1962 Cuban Missile Crisis the two superpowers and Britain signed the 1963 Partial Test Ban Treaty, prohibiting all but underground nuclear testing. They subsequently opened this agreement to other states who wished to accede to it. To date over 120 states have done so, with the notable exception of France.[26]

Subsequent developments in this area have been a mixture of deals between the US and USSR/Russia and multilateral agreements. Amongst the latter the 1968 Nuclear Non-Proliferation Treaty, designed to stop the spread of states with nuclear weapons, currently has 189 subscribing states. The 1996 Comprehensive Test Ban Treaty, which bans all nuclear test explosions, has attracted 181 states to sign and 148 to ratify it.

Meanwhile in 1972 in the first Strategic Arms Limitation Treaty (SALT I) the US and USSR agreed not to increase their current deployment of intercontinental missiles (ICBMs) or their submarine-launched ballistic missiles (SLBMs) and in the Anti-Ballistic Missile Treaty they limited their numbers of missile interceptors. In 1979 SALT II capped the US and USSR at equal numbers of heavy bombers, ICBM and SLBM launchers and also limited their quotas of Multiple Independent Re-entry Vehicles (MIRVs). In the 1991 Strategic Arms Reduction Treaty (START I) the two superpowers agreed to halve their missiles to some 6,000 by 1998 and in the abortive 1993 START II they planned further reductions to roughly 3,000 – 3,500 missiles each. The Strategic Offensive Reductions Treaty (SORT) of 2002 promised cuts in undefined 'strategic nuclear warheads' to around 2,000 each by 2012. In April 2010 Presidents Barack Obama and Dmitry Medvedev signed the New START in Prague, promising to further reduce their missiles within seven years to just over 1,500 and to limit the numbers of other nuclear weapons and delivery systems. Even if they do so we shall still live in an age of that most appropriate of acronyms, MAD (mutually assured destruction).[27]

Eyre Crowe, the supreme realist who had such a massive influence on the British Foreign Office in the first quarter of the 20th century, put his finger on many of the problems relating to the desirable concept of disarmament: how would one stop states from cheating; who would verify their claims; who would define offensive and defensive weapons; how could a system be evolved that would provide security, stability and yet be adaptable to change? Many of the arms limitation agreements between the USSR (or now Russia) and the US are reminiscent of the British approach at the end of the First World War – that the quantity of destroyed weapons and the limited numbers remaining would increase a sense of security. But we are still faced with the objection that the French made then that disarmament has to reach further, or as the preamble to the UNESCO Constitution asserts: 'Since wars begin in the minds of men it is in the minds of men that the defences of peace must be constructed.'[28]

International Law

'I do not want when the war is over to pursue any policy of vengeance, but we have got so to act that men in future who feel tempted to follow the example of the rulers who plunged the world into this war will know what is waiting for them at the end of it.'

David Lloyd George, Newcastle, 29 November 1918.[29]

Article 227 of the Treaty of Versailles arraigned the former Kaiser Wilhelm II 'for a supreme offence against international morality and the sanctity of treaties' and provided for the establishment of a special international tribunal to try him. The Allies undertook to pursue Wilhelm's extradition from the Netherlands where he had sought sanctuary in November 1918. Article 228 required Germany to surrender 'all persons accused of having committed an act in violation of the laws and customs of war' for trial by Allied military courts. The prosecution of operational crimes in warfare was not a new concept but when the Allies later began to assemble their lists of those they wished to try for violations of the laws and customs of war it became clear that by including the former Chancellor Bethmann-Hollweg, Admiral Alfred von Tirpitz, Field Marshal Paul von Hindenburg or General Erich Ludendorff among over 80 prominent German leaders, they were extending the scope of the idea to include those responsible for the creation and implementation of policy as well as servicemen who breached the established codes for the conduct of military operations. In the latter instance it was, in any case, the more usual practice in peace settlements to extend a mutual amnesty for acts committed under the strain of war. Article 239 stated that the Allies also had the right to try persons who had committed crimes against their nationals, thinking here particularly of actions undertaken during the extensive German occupation of Allied territory during the war. Earlier, in 1915, the Allies had accused the Turks of 'crimes ... against humanity and civilization' in their protest against allegations that the Ottomans were exterminating their Armenian subjects. Although this Allied letter lacked the authority of a formal treaty, it did form part of some extremely important new developments in thinking about international law during and after the First World War.[30]

The previous 50 years had witnessed significant progress in attempts to codify and regulate warfare. These ranged from the care of the wounded and arrangements to protect medical personnel and facilities under the 1864 Geneva Convention to the prohibition of various actions such as the bombardment of undefended towns, bombing from balloons, the use of poison gas, dum-dum bullets or the abuse of authority over the civilian population of occupied territory under the two Hague Conventions on the Laws and Customs of War in 1899 and 1907. The idea of an international criminal court embodied in Article 228 was, however, new and controversial.

There had been widespread anger in the Allied states about Germany's brutal occupation of Belgium and its use of submarines and bombing aircraft as well as the strongly expressed sentiment that someone should be accountable for the unleashing of such death and destruction upon the world. This idea played well in the British general election in late 1918 and although it was one of his colleagues who declared that he was for hanging the Kaiser, Lloyd George had privately suggested that he should be shot and publicly endorsed demands for him to be tried, not least as a deterrent to future leaders. The British Cabinet was deeply divided, despite Lloyd George's resolute support for a trial, but eventually accepted Attorney-General F E Smith's argument that, unless the Kaiser was indicted, it would be impossible to arraign other, lesser, figures.[31]

Persuading his fellow peacemakers proved almost as difficult for Lloyd George. They had no problems with holding Germany and its allies chiefly responsible for the outbreak of war or for fighting that war by 'barbarous or illegitimate means', but Robert Lansing, the American Secretary of State, was absolutely determined that the Allies had no right to establish an international court to try a head of state for a crime that he did not believe existed. To do so, said

Lansing, would be the equivalent of international lynch law. For differing reasons the Japanese and Italians agreed but Lloyd George stuck to his guns: 'I would like to see the man responsible for the greatest crime in history punished for it.' Eventually Wilson compromised and agreed to seek the Kaiser's extradition from the Netherlands for trial before an international tribunal of five judges, one from each of the five principal Allies. Had that trial taken place it would have created an interesting precedent but, perhaps fortunately for all and especially the Kaiser, the Dutch refused to relinquish their unwanted guest who remained in exile in the Netherlands until his death in 1941.[32]

The question of trying other German leaders remained highly emotive on both sides, particularly when the initial Allied lists named over 3,000 potential defendants. Even the reduced demand for 853 men and one woman shocked Lloyd George, despite his earlier enthusiasm. He remarked that the British and French, placed in a similar position (as they might well have been had Germany won) would not have complied and advised seeking the 'surrender of the most important and notorious offenders and let the rest go'. The Allies compromised. Germany itself should try those named and the final list indicted only 45 people, all for alleged operational crimes or for cruelty to prisoners or people in the occupied territories. None was a prominent military or civilian leader. The German Supreme Court at Leipzig produced a series of farcical acquittals or lenient sentences and in 1922 the Allies repudiated the court, leaving the French to convict over a thousand Germans, in their absence, by December 1924. The British, originally the main instigators of the trials, quietly walked away.[33]

Meanwhile, in dealing with the Turks, the Allies were

confronted with a similar legal problem to that identified by Lansing, one which would also face Allied leaders at the end of the Second World War. In December 1918 Arthur Balfour told an Allied conference that, since the Armenian massacres occurred under Ottoman sovereignty, the perpetrators 'strictly speaking had committed no definite legal offences … It was necessary to consider how they could be got at.' He believed that this was a new category of crime requiring a new legal statute making such atrocities a crime against humanity but the Turks had already themselves, in February and March 1919, arrested over 50 prominent members of the previous government, including some held responsible for the Armenian massacres. Two officials from the Yozgat district were tried by court-martial and found guilty of illegally ordering the deportation and murder of Armenians 'against humanity and civilization'. One, Major Tewfik Bey, the police commander, was sentenced to 15 years hard labour; the other, Kemal Bey, the lieutenant governor, was sentenced to death. Following his execution, Kemal's funeral attracted over 1,000 indignant nationalist mourners, an indication of the growing problems facing the Sultan's government; but it still persisted, on 27 April 1919, in opening the trial of the Turkish wartime leaders, some *in absentia*.[34]

When, in May, the British heard that charges against many of the men were about to be dropped, they seized 68 of them and moved them to Mudros and Malta. The Ottoman court-martial was left with hardly any actual defendants but it did convict a number of prominent Young Turk leaders, including Talaat and Enver Pasha, sentencing them to death in their absence. 'This trial has long been a farce,' wrote one diplomat, a view shared by most British officials in Constantinople; but now they found themselves faced with the difficult question of what to do with the men in their custody. It was a slow process as they struggled throughout 1919 and into 1920 to establish a legal mechanism to express their revulsion against the atrocities in Armenia. Article 230 of the Treaty of Sèvres of 10 August 1920 required the Ottomans to surrender the persons 'responsible for the massacres committed during the continuance of the state of war on territory which formed part of the Turkish Empire on August 1, 1914'. They would be tried by a court of the Allies' choosing, possibly a League of Nations tribunal if it could be created in time. The reality, however, was that the Sultan's signature on the Treaty was worthless, Mustafa Kemal's nationalist revolt was gathering momentum and the British were releasing prisoners for lack of evidence though some officials still hoped to mount prosecutions over Armenia. These hopes were ended when, faced with a choice between leaving British prisoners in Kemal's hands or releasing the remaining alleged war criminals, the British government, acknowledging that it was yielding to blackmail, swapped its prisoners for Kemal's.[35]

Neither the German nor the Turkish example seemed to set an auspicious precedent for the effectiveness of war crimes trials and indeed during the Second World War Churchill advocated the summary execution of the main Nazi leadership, though he blanched at Stalin's figures of 50,000 or 100,000 shootings. But despite the collapse of the post-First World War experiments legalism was firmly embedded in the thinking of the democratic states. Roosevelt, after a brief flirtation with summary justice, insisted that there must be trials even though the inter-war attempts to establish an international court by the League or by private pressure groups had made only limited progress. The Nuremberg and Tokyo trials of the German and Japanese leadership built upon these earlier experiences but were much more effective, not least because following total victory and the occupation of the defeated powers the Allies were able to arrest and then themselves try those accused of war crimes.

Nuremberg established what Leipzig and Constantinople had failed to do: that aggression was a 'crime against peace' and violators bore legal responsibility for their actions; that the perpetrators of genocide had committed crimes against humanity; that obedience to superior orders did not constitute a defence; and that the main political and military leaders were liable to prosecution under international law. Some were disappointed that the main American objective was to try the Nazi leadership for waging war rather than for their crimes against humanity. There were also very marked differences in the approaches of the Soviet and the Anglo-American representatives. At an American dinner party A J Vishinsky, the Soviet prosecutor who had conducted the Moscow show trials in the late 1930s, proposed a toast to the defendants, 'May their paths lead straight from the courthouse to the grave!', shocking those who had drunk the toast before it was translated. Nonetheless, concludes one authority, despite accusations that this was victors' justice, 'Legalists are justified in seeing Nuremberg as a famous victory, even if they forget that the margin was razor-thin. In the end America and Britain managed to produce something extraordinary. We have created nothing to compare with it since.'[36]

It is partially true that international justice has habitually been classed as a lower priority for governments than matters directly affecting the citizens of their particular states. There has been a marked reluctance, whether for financial or political reasons, to commit great resources to the pursuit and trial of alleged war criminals from other states. Even though liberal states are more motivated to support international war crimes tribunals when their own citizens have been the victims, there has also been an international conscience about the rape of Belgium in 1914, the Armenian massacres, the Holocaust or, more recently, events in the former Yugoslavia and genocide in Rwanda. In its early years the UN did encourage schemes for the creation of an international criminal court but then, in 1954, suspended its work for over 30 years until it was faced in 1993 with demands to try to deal with the conflicts arising from the collapse of Yugoslavia. The Security Council agreed, on 22 February, to establish the International Criminal Tribunal for the former Yugoslavia (ICTY), hailed by Antonio Cassese, the Tribunal's president, as 'a truly international institution. It is an expression of the entire world community, not the long arm of four powerful victors.' The following year, on 8 November 1994, the UN created the International Criminal Tribunal for Rwanda (ICTR) to prosecute those responsible for the genocide there and in 2002, in agreement with the government of Sierra Leone, it established the Special Court for Sierra Leone (SCSL). All three have helped to develop international law in respect of crimes against humanity, genocide and war crimes with the trials before the ICTY of Slobodan Milošević the former President of Serbia and of Yugoslavia, and of Radovan Karadžić former President of the Republika Srpska reinforcing the theme of the responsibility of political leadership.[37]

Such *ad hoc* tribunals emphasized the need for the permanent court the UN had been considering for many years and in 1998 a General Assembly in Rome agreed to establish the International Criminal Court which came into being on 1 July 2002. The Court is based in The Hague but may hold hearings anywhere. It is a court of last resort. Its role is to act only when national governments either cannot or will not undertake the investigation and prosecution of alleged war crimes, genocide or crimes against humanity. Its first prosecution opened in January 2009. All five of its current (2010) investigations relate to Africa – Northern Uganda, the Democratic Republic of the Congo, the Central African Republic, Darfur (Sudan) and Kenya. Over 100 states are members but China, India, Israel, Pakistan, Russia and the United States are notable exceptions, meaning that only a minority of the world's population comes within the Court's jurisdiction.

Like the League of Nations itself the developments in minority protection, disarmament and international law rested on foundations previously laid but the Paris Peace Conferences did make significant contributions in all three areas. In the field of minority protection the peacemakers strengthened the idea of group rights, which went into abeyance during the Cold War, but has returned to prominence more recently. Widening the scope of disarmament to include not simply restrictions placed on the defeated but also a commitment from the victors to pursue universal arms reduction did encourage some countries to fulfil this ambition, though the outcomes have generally been more successful when limited to particular states and targeted at specific weapons systems. The assertion of the responsibility of the political and military elites for their actions did not hold in the post-First World War trials but did pave the way for the Nuremberg and Tokyo tribunals after 1945 and helped to frame thinking about dealing with crimes against humanity. All three remain works in progress.

America's Global Reach – Soft and Hard Power

6

Ideology and the American Century

'When President Wilson left Washington he enjoyed a prestige and moral influence throughout the world unequalled in history. His bold and measured words carried to the peoples of Europe above and beyond the voices of their own politicians ... In addition to this moral influence the realities of power were in his hands. The American armies were at the height of their numbers, discipline and equipment ... Europe not only owed the United States more than she could pay; but only a large measure of further assistance could save her from starvation and bankruptcy. Never had a philosopher held such weapons wherewith to bind the princes of this world.'

John Maynard Keynes, *The Economic Consequences of the Peace,* 1919[1]

Like others, particularly in the British and American delegations at the Peace Conference, Keynes was disappointed when Wilson proved incapable of using America's moral and material might to create a settlement that conformed to his perception of the vision that the President had outlined in a remarkable series of speeches in 1918, of which the Fourteen Points of 8 January was the first and most iconic. Keynes' bitterly expressed disillusion with Wilson, whom he characterized as 'this blind and deaf Don Quixote',[2] should not obscure the two important factors he had identified: the emergence of the United States as a world leader, certainly in financial and industrial terms, backed by a growing military presence; and the centrality of Wilson's emphasis on ideology as he tried to move war aims and the eventual peace settlement to a higher moral plane.

When he sought Congressional approval for declarations of war, first against Germany in April 1917 and then in December against Austria-Hungary, Wilson however reluctantly had engaged the United States in a European conflict. This marked a further step along America's path to achieving world power and undertaking a greater involvement in international affairs, a policy enthusiastically advocated by former President Theodore Roosevelt but by few others among the country's elite. Even though the post-war period saw the United States attempt to withdraw from some of the commitments and responsibilities entailed by its participation in the war and the subsequent peace negotiations, it was apparent that a new era had dawned.

Wilson made it plain that America would build a navy capable of resisting British or German attempts to control the world's seaways or to impose their interpretations of maritime law. By 1918 the American army, little more than a force for policing the Indian reservations and the Mexican border in 1914, numbered four million men of whom two million were in France. Although American troops did undertake successful operations, most notably in the Saint-Mihiel salient in September 1918, their decisive influence on the outcome of the war rested less on their military effectiveness than on the apparently limitless reservoir of men awaiting shipment to Europe, backed by an America that produced one-third of the world's industrial output and had vast financial resources.

In 1914 the United States was the world's largest debtor,

owing some $3,700 million, by 1918 its largest creditor. The world – chiefly Britain and its allies – owed it $3,800 million; and, as Wilson made clear to his close associate Colonel Edward House in July 1917, he intended to use this leverage. 'When this war is over we can force them to our way of thinking, because by that time they [the Allies] will, among other things, be financially in our hands.'[3]

In the same year as America joined the war there were two revolutions in Russia. The first, in March, overthrew the Romanov Dynasty that had ruled for over 300 years. In the second, in November, Vladimir Lenin and the Bolsheviks seized power in Moscow and Petrograd. Lenin, the man who dominated the revolutionary movement in Russia from the moment he returned from exile in April 1917, immediately called for peace without victory, threatening to steal Wilson's lines and thunder while simultaneously advocating world revolution.

Faced with this challenge to his Gladstonian liberalism, Wilson responded on 8 January seeking to define and publicise his war aims partly for the benefit of the populations of the Central Powers but particularly in response to a perceived threat from Bolshevism and Lenin's alternative version of a new world order. Wilson's version of 'our way of thinking' emphasized democracy, self-determination and justice, advancing a vision of reformist capitalism rather than revolutionary collectivism as he struggled for the soul of the world in a long-range contest with Lenin. Wilson portrayed the United States as fighting not for any selfish motives but for the benefit of humanity, stressing that the struggle was not with the German people but against the ideas of autocracy and militarism for which their government stood.

He envisaged self-determining peoples choosing governments that would be responsible to them, and hence more responsible in their policies, particularly in international affairs, helping to create universal peace and prosperity. Making the world safe for democracy would make the world a safer place. Already a year earlier, on 22 January 1917, he had identified his policies and American values as universal: 'These are American principles, American policies. We could stand for no others. And they are also the principles and policies of forward looking men and women everywhere, of every modern nation, of every enlightened community. They are the principles of mankind and must prevail'.[4] The importance Lenin and Wilson attached to their beliefs and the rivalry between them, coupled with the need to convince public opinion on both sides of the war that theirs was the better vision for the future, revitalized ideology as a factor in international relations.

> 'These are American principles, American policies. We could stand for no others. And they are also the principles and policies of forward looking men and women everywhere, of every modern nation, of every enlightened community. They are the principles of mankind and must prevail'
> WOODROW WILSON, 1917

From the end of the Revolutionary and Napoleonic Wars until the First World War ideology was rarely, if ever, the crucial element in the conduct of international relations. States and dynasties fought and negotiated for territory, resources, thrones and material gain rather than for ideas. Liberal Britain, while convinced of the superiority of its constitutional arrangements, conducted no crusade to spread them elsewhere; it was for each state to choose its own form of governance. Britain cooperated as readily with autocratic Austria, Russia and Prussia as it did with liberal France in pursuing the balance of power; and Tsarist Russia could ally with republican France to counter the threat of Germany. Interests not ideas reigned supreme.

Nationalism was a growing phenomenon. However, for much of the 19th century it was more likely to be manipulated from above by leaders with ulterior motives than to emerge as an effective independent force from below. In the wars fought for Italian and German unification, nationalism was the product of their outcomes rather than the cause of the conflicts. Piedmont and Prussia, to some extent, cloaked their ambitions in the guise of serving the respective national causes of Italy and Germany, but Cavour and Bismarck had more tangible and particular objectives in mind. The increasing industrial capacity, military power and wealth of Bismarck's unified Germany not only disrupted Europe's political balance but also encouraged the development of national ambitions of other peoples aspiring to independence and what seemed, from the German example, the inevitable material benefits that would follow. It was in keeping with Wilson's world vision that he attributed the outbreak of war in 1914 to the frustration of these nationalist ambitions.

The horrific and persistent nature of the ensuing conflict required someone to supply convincing reasons why the sacrifices and destruction were worthwhile and could contribute to a better future world. Wilson's powerful oratory offered hope to people on both sides. His prescription for a new world order could, he said in his 4 July 1918 'Four Ends' speech, be summarized in a single sentence: 'What we seek is the reign of law, based upon the consent of the governed, and sustained by the organized opinion of mankind.'[5]

When Germany, seeking a respite to regroup, appealed

to Wilson to arrange an armistice to allow the negotiation of a peace based on his principles, he wrung grudging and resentful agreement from his major partners. This meant his prescription had now become the benchmark against which the settlement would be judged but also that not all the peacemakers believed in its efficacy. The problems arose when the aspirations that Wilson had so eloquently expressed met the reality of the national agendas of his partners, the complex interweaving of European ethnic groups, the uncertainties of actual control on the ground and the impossibly inflated expectations of peoples across the globe. Wilson's tragedy was less that, under the pressure of the need to reach agreements, he compromised his principles, rather that he failed to understand that he had done so and remained convinced that the final outcomes still broadly conformed to his vision, subject to the minor readjustments that the League of Nations could make in the future.

One of the main sources of pressure on the peacemakers was their belief that they must fill the vacuum of power in Eastern and Central Europe, caused by the collapse of the Russian, Austro-Hungarian and German Empires, before Bolshevism did so. While they did not necessarily define Bolshevism strictly in terms of Marxist-Leninist ideology, they did equate it with anarchy, lawlessness, famine and disorder; and they did identify it as one of the major threats to their task. Ray Stannard Baker, the journalist who acted as Wilson's press secretary during the Conference, wrote that 'at all times, at every turn in the negotiations there rose the spectre of chaos, like a black cloud out of the east, threatening to overwhelm and swallow up the world'. It is an exaggeration to claim, as scholars like Arno Mayer have done, that the whole process of peacemaking should be seen as an attempt to ward off the threat of revolution from the left; but as he pointed out, this was a time when ideologies emerged and clashed: '[W]hile the Peace Conference was in session in Paris, the charter meeting of the Third International was held in Moscow, the precursors of German Nazism fought Bolshevism through the Free Corps [and] Benito Mussolini scored his first fascist triumphs in Italy ...'[6] The main contest was still between Wilson and Bolshevism but was about to become more complex.

As Lenin and the Bolsheviks gradually extended Soviet control over parts of the former Tsarist empire and the USSR evolved into a credible if ambiguous state, the major European powers were faced with a dilemma that would become familiar to statesmen for much of the remainder of the century and beyond in dealing not just with the USSR but also fascist Italy, Nazi Germany, communist China and political Islam: how decisive a role did ideology play in the formulation of policy in these entities? In a sense this mirrored the debates among the Russian revolutionaries about whether their first priority was to spread world revolution or to protect the power base they had just seized. Was Russia a resource to be expended in a wider struggle or, in the first instance, should they safeguard a physical space in which to build socialism before engaging in a communist crusade? Lenin's insistence that the Soviets must surrender land to the Germans in return for peace at Brest-Litovsk so as to preserve the revolutionary base presaged his successor Joseph Stalin's doctrine of 'Socialism in one country' (an

> 'At all times, at every turn in the negotiations there rose the spectre of chaos, like a black cloud out of the east, threatening to overwhelm and swallow up the world.'
>
> **RAY STANNARD BAKER**

apparent contradiction of Marx's belief that the revolution must be universal) but was not necessarily a definitive strategic shift. Those who negotiated with the Soviets were never entirely sure whether they were dealing with a state or a revolutionary force, an ambiguity that the Soviets themselves did little to resolve, exploiting the alleged independence from the Soviet state of the revolutionary Communist Third International (the Comintern) to explain the contradiction of simultaneously seeking deals with governments that they were trying to undermine.

Lloyd George's post-war government was one of the first to experience this problem during the negotiations for an Anglo-Soviet trade agreement in 1920 and 1921, in which one of the sticking points was that the Soviets should desist from propaganda and hostile activity against the British Empire. Eventually, at Lenin's prompting, the Soviets conceded this point, on which Lord Curzon, the British Foreign Secretary and a reluctant party to the agreement, had insisted. After an embarrassing episode in 1921 when he had sent a protest note to the Soviets about their continuing campaigns against British interests which proved to be based mainly on forged German material, Curzon was determined to prove Soviet duplicity. In May 1923, armed with evidence from intercepted and deciphered Soviet messages, some of which he injudiciously cited, Curzon sent an ultimatum demanding that further hostile propaganda must cease. The Soviets agreed (though made no attempt to comply), but the main outcome was to warn them that their codes were compromised and their introduction of a new set of ciphers later that year meant that an important source of information was lost.[7]

Lloyd George was more hopeful than many of his ministers that he could wean the Soviets from their ideology and reinvigorate the USSR as an economic and trading partner. Lenin's retreat from war communism and his introduction of the New Economic Policy with some limited concessions to capitalism and free enterprise offered some evidence to support Lloyd George's aspirations for a major economic conference at Genoa in the spring of 1922. In keeping with his liberal principles he hoped that opening Russian markets would provide the stimulus to the European economy that would help Germany to pay reparations, reduce unemployment in Britain, undermine communism by increased prosperity and strengthen the post-war peace process. The conference proved a huge disappointment. The French were hostile to any arrangement that did not include the repayment of their loans to Tsarist Russia or compromised reparations. Lloyd George was convinced that they came with the intention of wrecking the whole affair but this outcome was essentially delivered to them when the Soviet and German delegations concluded a separate pact in nearby Rapallo.

The Rapallo agreement between the two pariahs of Europe offered advantages to both in terms of increased international leverage but the Soviets found themselves in a quandary after the Franco-Belgian invasion of the Ruhr in January 1923. Industrialized Germany was always a closer match for Marx's definition of a society ripe for communism than rural Russia; and this new humiliation, following closely on defeat and the disappointments of Versailles, seemed to offer a potential revolutionary opportunity, especially as inflation soared. On the other hand, the Weimar Republic represented the USSR's main partner in conventional diplomacy. Should the USSR foment revolution and undermine its ally or abandon what might be a unique opportunity to spread the gospel in favour of supporting a friendly state? In the event it pursued both policies, though its attempts to encourage revolution met with limited success while a sceptical German government, bereft of alternative allies, was forced to accept the Soviet claim that agents like Karl Radek were acting on behalf of the Comintern over which the USSR had no control.

The complications added to the conduct of international relations by the introduction of competing value systems were increased first by the advent of Mussolini's fascist government in Italy in October 1922, and then more decisively when Hitler took power in Germany in January 1933. In the ensuing clash of communist, fascist and liberal ideologies and in the aftermath of American refusal to ratify the Versailles Treaty it was Britain, rather than the United States, that found itself the pivotal representative of the western capitalist democracies. British leaders, in particular Neville Chamberlain who became Prime Minister in May 1937 but who had been an influential figure in government for much of the 1930s, found themselves facing the dictators and struggling to square the competing pressures of power politics, moral values and logistical practicalities. Like many before and since, Chamberlain found it impossible to believe that the ideology of those he faced across the negotiating table was anything more than propaganda, masking more rational and limited national objectives; or that, for the sake of it, they would endanger the safety and prosperity of their peoples by engaging in war to redress supposed grievances: 'I do not believe,' he said in November 1937, 'that such a Government anywhere exists among civilised peoples.' Unfortunately he was wrong. Nevertheless, faced with the firm advice from the Chiefs of Staff that Britain could not win simultaneous wars against three potential disturbers of the peace (Italy in the Mediterranean, Japan in the Pacific and Germany in Europe) he sought, in accordance with his own belief system, to reduce Britain's exposure by discovering and redressing their grievances, particularly those of Hitler's Germany.[8]

In pursuing this policy of appeasing Hitler, Chamberlain assumed he was dealing with a German (or, strictly speaking, an Austrian) with a finite set of demands who, once the most important of these were met, would cease to threaten the peace. He approached the negotiations rather in the manner of a trade union wage bargaining session – Hitler would demand something, Chamberlain would offer something less, they would compromise at some point between the two offers and a deal would be struck. Hitler had a different philosophy. For him Nazi ideology was real. Instead of treating the resolutions achieved in this way as final, for Hitler they simply became the base point of a new set of demands. Chamberlain's dilemma was that, if Hitler's demands were finite, it was possible to make a rational calculation about what price one was prepared to pay to satisfy them on the understanding that this would secure peace. If, however, reflecting the Nazi philosophy of endless expansion, Hitler set no limits on his ambitions, every concession made to him potentially strengthened his position and weakened that of his opponents, leading eventually to a situation where there came a stark choice between total capitulation or military resistance in less favourable circumstances than might have existed but for the attempt to resolve the problem.

It required the failure of the settlement reached in Munich in September 1938 and the Nazi seizure of Prague in March 1939 to convince the Chamberlain government that a new approach stressing deterrence rather than appeasement was needed. The problem here was that any credible backing for the British guarantees to Poland, Greece and Romania, indeed any meaningful military threat to Hitler, depended upon the cooperation of the Soviet Union. Unfortunately its ideology was, if anything, more repugnant to British and French leaders, with equally ambiguous aims and motives to those of the fascists; and its price for partnership might well equally involve the domination of Eastern Europe. Furthermore the reports of the British military attaché in Moscow suggested its military capability, in the wake of Stalin's purges, was extremely dubious. Was it sensible for Chamberlain and the French Premier Edouard Daladier to compromise their principles in return for a very uncertain return? There was also the highly pertinent unanswered question of whether Stalin wished to participate in such an alliance.

If the British had doubts about dealing with Stalin, the feeling was mutual. He distrusted Britain, a traditional rival for Russia and the main capitalist and imperial power with which the Soviets had dealings in the inter-war period. Despite the strong calls for an alliance with the USSR from Winston Churchill (still at this point a maverick isolated in the British political wilderness), Stalin knew that such an arrangement would be one of convenience only. His policies had already undergone a bewildering series of twists in the 1930s: denouncing and then embracing the idea of a Popular Front of communists, socialists and liberals to counter the threat of fascism after the Nazis did not expire in the last gasp of capitalism as Soviet doctrine predicted; joining the League of Nations, mocked by Lenin as the 'thieves' kitchen'; and entering a military alliance with France. In August 1939, in a breathtaking ideological impossibility based on ruthless *realpolitik*, Stalin concluded a deal with Hitler, turning the tables on Britain and France that he believed were weak and were seeking to divert Hitler's attention eastwards in order to engineer a Soviet-Nazi confrontation. At the worst, he calculated, the territorial gains made in Poland under the terms of the pact would protect the Soviet homeland from immediate assault should Germany eventually attack the USSR; and in the meanwhile Hitler would be free to tackle Britain and France, opening the further possibility that whichever states were defeated it might well prove fertile ground for communist revolution.

The role of the United States following its withdrawal from enforcing the peace settlements seemed to confirm Stanley Baldwin's bitter remark in 1932 that 'You will get nothing out of Washington but words ... Big words, but only words.' While this might have been true in European terms the experience of America's nearest neighbours in Latin America was very different. Here American domination was complete. It was sometimes demonstrated by military interventions as in Nicaragua in 1913 and 1926, Haiti in 1915, or Mexico in 1916. Some of which led to prolonged occupations, sometimes exercised indirectly through unsavoury dictators like Fulgencio Batista in Cuba or Raphael Trujillo in the Dominican Republic (of whom President Franklin Delano Roosevelt memorably declared in 1939, 'He may be an S.O.B. but he's our S.O.B.')

American domination sometimes rested on the power of corporations like the United Fruit Company and oil and mineral companies which controlled major parts of their economies and production. Most of Latin America's trade after the First World War was with the United States although Britain retained strong interests in Mexico and Argentina. The hope of some South American leaders was that the League of Nations would dilute American domination but this did not happen. Wilson and Roosevelt may have proclaimed that their policies were based upon principles and goodwill, promising in Roosevelt's words to act as 'good neighbors', but the United States was as determined to exercise control in its region as Britain and France were in their empires, and it enjoyed considerably more success.[9]

The Senate's rejection of the Treaty of Versailles and hence refusal to join the League meant that the United States withdrew from Treaty enforcement, leaving Britain and France as the main defenders of a settlement that Wilson's ideas and policies had played an enormous role in shaping. It did not mean, however, that America withdrew from world affairs. Although entirely out of sympathy with Wilson's idealism, President Harding did initiate a major naval disarmament conference in Washington in 1921–2; and despite its lack of military and political commitment, the United States exercised a continuing and expanding economic and cultural role in Europe even during the apparent period of 'isolation'.

America continued to be the world's banker and its attitude to Europe's war debts (succinctly summarised by President Calvin Coolidge as 'They hired the money, didn't they?') was a major factor in European calculations about reparations and their own inter-allied debts. Indeed it has been argued that America sought, in the mid-1920s, to create a new European settlement in a partnership with Britain that utilized American financial strength and British political leadership. Ultimately this failed, but despite the Mid-Western perception of the Europeans as tricksters and welchers, funds flowed into Europe through loans to Germany under the Dawes and Young Plans designed to ease the reparations problem. Although American investment fell sharply, particularly in Germany after 1929–30, some did continue.[10]

American films penetrated the European market in the

inter-war period despite the problems of language and the active hostility of authoritarian and fascist governments, but American influences were more apparent in certain features of the mass circulation press, the development of broadcasting and in jazz and dance band music, not all of which met with unanimous approval by European intellectuals. American industrial methods, often dubbed 'Fordism' after the large scale production of standardized products for a mass market by a highly-paid docile workforce pioneered by Henry Ford the automobile tycoon, also challenged traditional European approaches. 'Americanization' was seen as both an opportunity and a threat to European cultural values. This ambivalence was emphasized by the dominant position of the United States at the end of the Second World War when, once again but even more decisively than in 1918, significant American troop numbers in Europe (over three million in May 1945) were backed by an industrial base that had grown 250 per cent during the war and produced nearly half the world's manufactures, together with an overwhelming financial strength in the face of European bankruptcy.

> 'Whoever occupies a territory also imposes on it his own social system. Everyone imposes his own system as far as his army can reach. It cannot be otherwise.'
>
> **JOSEPH STALIN**

Victory brought with it the opportunity to reshape Germany and Japan into democratic societies on an American model – a new chance to deliver Wilson's vision, which Roosevelt and the British Premier Winston Churchill had reaffirmed at their ship-board meetings off Newfoundland on 9 and 10 August 1941 (even before America entered the war). Their joint statement of 14 August, later rechristened the Atlantic Charter, reduced Wilson's Fourteen Points to eight, while retaining much of their essence. In September the Soviet Union and all the governments-in-exile of the states Hitler had defeated, agreed to adhere to the Charter. With the war drawing to an end the Royal Air Force dropped leaflets seeking to reassure the German people that the defeat of Hitler would not entail a new super-Versailles but that any settlement would be based on its principles, though there were doubts as to the sincerity of the Soviet Union's commitment to such ideas. As Stalin had pointed out to the Yugoslav partisan Milovan Djilas, 'whoever occupies a territory also imposes on it his own social system. Everyone imposes his own system as far as his army can reach. It cannot be otherwise.' This suggested that two ideological systems were about to collide, though an alternative explanation of the ensuing struggle would emphasize a competition for power rather than ideas.[11]

Hitler's example suggested that his ideology did constitute a reliable indication of his ultimate goals (although he did not let it dominate every decision – he was prepared to do business with Poland in 1934, with the USSR in 1939, to recognize the Japanese as honorary Aryans and to tolerate Mussolini's rule over the German speakers of the South Tyrol). This knowledge represented an ominous warning for those who, in the post-war world, now had to assess Stalin's aims and ambitions. Once again the dilemma of judging whether they were dealing with a state or a revolutionary force arose. If the former then, given its dreadful experiences in two world wars in which Russia/the USSR had suffered over 55 million deaths, it was entitled to construct a defensive barrier in Eastern Europe against a repetition of invasion from the West. If the latter, however, that defensive barrier could become a springboard for a new revolutionary crusade at a time when defeat,

THE ATLANTIC CHARTER, 14 AUGUST 1941

[President Franklin Roosevelt of the United States and Prime Minister Winston Churchill of the United Kingdom] deem it right to make known certain common principles in the national policies of their respective countries on which they base their hopes for a better future for the world

First, their countries seek no aggrandizement, territorial or other;

Second, they desire to see no territorial changes that do not accord with the freely expressed wishes of the peoples concerned;

Third, they respect the right of all peoples to choose the form of government under which they will live; and they wish to see sovereign rights and self government restored to those who have been forcibly deprived of them;

Fourth, they will endeavor, with due respect for their existing obligations, to further the enjoyment by all States, great or small, victor or vanquished, of access, on equal terms, to the trade and to the raw materials of the world which are needed for their economic prosperity;

Fifth, they desire to bring about the fullest collaboration between all nations in the economic field with the object of securing, for all, improved labor standards, economic advancement and social security;

Sixth, after the final destruction of the Nazi tyranny, they hope to see established a peace which will afford to all nations the means of dwelling in safety within their own boundaries, and which will afford assurance that all the men in all lands may live out their lives in freedom from fear and want;

Seventh, such a peace should enable all men to traverse the high seas and oceans without hindrance;

Eighth, they believe that all of the nations of the world, for realistic as well as spiritual reasons, must come to the abandonment of the use of force. Since no future peace can be maintained if land, sea or air armaments continue to be employed by nations which threaten, or may threaten, aggression outside of their frontiers, they believe, pending the establishment of a wider and permanent system of general security, that the disarmament of such nations is essential. They will likewise aid and encourage all other practicable measures which will lighten for peace-loving peoples the crushing burden of armaments.

deprivation, destruction and disorientation, all contributing to enhanced popular support for communism in the West, would be backed by massive Soviet military forces stationed within 300 miles of the Channel ports.

Despite increasing doubts and suspicions both Roosevelt and Stalin apparently believed that the post-war world would be cooperative rather than confrontational. But whatever was left of their optimism was ill-founded. Roosevelt hoped that Britain, China, the USSR and US, acting as 'the Four Policemen', would work together to ensure world peace. Stalin mistakenly believed that Roosevelt had accepted the need for Soviet domination of Eastern Europe, while American policy rested on the delusion expressed by Secretary of State James Byrne, that it was possible to achieve 'a government [in Poland] both friendly to the Soviet Union and representative of all the democratic elements of the country'.[12] Instead, wartime suspicions resurfaced to contribute to a growing mutual animosity. Stalin's perception that the Anglo-Americans had deliberately delayed opening a second front in north-west Europe (leaving Russian forces to continue to bear the brunt of the fighting) and his resentment at the abrupt ending of American Lend-Lease shipments in August 1945 were matched by the West's knowledge of the falsehood of Soviet claims that it was the Nazis, not themselves, who were responsible for the mass Polish graves in Katyn Forest and concern about Soviet non-cooperation in 1944 with efforts to supply the Warsaw uprising. Roosevelt's death brought the less idealistic Harry Truman to power. However, the Cold War was not driven by personalities alone but more by a combination of power politics and ideological differences played out first in Poland, then Germany and on the wider world stage.

Would the United States this time rise to the challenge of world power or would the pattern of the First World War be repeated – decisive intervention followed by a retreat into isolation? It was not immediately clear. At the Yalta Conference on 5 February 1945 Roosevelt told Stalin that, 'he did not believe that American troops would stay in Europe much more than two years'; and numbers did rapidly decline from the high point of May 1945 to 391,000 by 1946, to 12 poorly equipped and trained divisions by 1948, and reaching their lowest point of the immediate post-war period of 116,000 by 1950. Yet 65 years later there were still over 80,000 American service personnel in Europe, the greatest number outside the United States apart from the war zone of Afghanistan. This military commitment matched America's earlier rapid endorsement of United Nations membership and its role in establishing the Bretton Woods post-war economic system based on the International Monetary Fund and the World Bank. Future criticisms of the United States would tend to stress its over- rather than under-involvement in world affairs, its interference rather than its isolation.[13]

At the time, the confrontation between the United States, USSR and their respective allies was presented as a clash of two monoliths. We are now aware of much greater subtleties in both their relationship with each other and in the roles played by their subordinate partners, who were often more independent in their policies than appeared to contemporary commentators. Stalin struggled to control Yugoslavia, led by Josip Broz Tito, the revolutionary commander of the communist wartime resistance movement, who maintained a fierce independence from Moscow. Anglo-American relations in the immediate post-war period were not as close as Churchill hoped. Some American officials wished to use their current superiority to undermine the financial and trading arrangements of the British Empire and sterling area which they saw as a threat to American prosperity. Lend-Lease was cancelled, collaboration in atomic research suspended and reconstruction funds came, not as a grant as Keynes had hoped, but as a loan whose terms were castigated by a British Conservative MP as 'our economic Munich ... selling the British Empire for a packet of cigarettes'. The British Foreign Secretary Ernest Bevin worked hard to maintain American commitment to Europe, but there was resentment in Britain and France at their junior roles in this partnership. Neither was necessarily convinced that cooperation with the Soviets should cease or that, failing this, there should not be some kind of middle, or third way in which the European states stood between the competing superpowers.[14]

The breakdown of the wartime alliance was not immediate; rather it was a gradual affair to which various episodes contributed. Between 1945 and 1947 in both the US and USSR the cartoon image of the other underwent a series of changes from the more benign portrayals during the war. Kindly Uncle Joe was transformed into a reborn Hitler albeit with a larger moustache, and benevolent Uncle Sam now appeared as a snarling fascist warmonger. This mirrored the increasing difficulties in their relationship, especially over the administration of their occupation zones in Germany. In February 1946 the American diplomat George Kennan sent his famous 'long telegram' from the Moscow embassy advocating the 'containment' of Soviet ambitions across the globe. In March Churchill made his 'iron curtain' speech. Confrontation in Iran followed. Important speeches from the Soviet Foreign Minister Vyacheslav Molotov in July and his American counterpart Byrne in September emphasized the ideological choices facing the German people. The key year was 1947. On 21 February Britain declared that it could no longer afford to support the governments of Greece and Turkey against implied internal and external Soviet threats. On 12 March Truman set out his doctrine backing democracy against authoritarianism declaring, 'it must be the policy of the United States to support free peoples who are resisting attempted subjugation by armed minorities or outside pressures'. His tactic of using the fears of the American public and Congress about Soviet expansion and disguising support for Greece and Turkey as a universal principle was very successful. However, the same month the Four Power meeting in Moscow to discuss a German peace treaty ended in failure.[15]

Meanwhile Western Europe faced economic ruin as its industrial weakness was compounded by extreme weather that produced poor harvests and crippled transportation. Already owing America nearly $5,000 million, it now needed to import more American grain, coal and goods but it had no money to pay for them. If the European markets collapsed the threat to the United States was three-fold: no markets for its massive agricultural and industrial surpluses, leading to unemployment at home and an increased temptation for Stalin to use the powerful communist parties in France and Italy and his massive military superiority to destabilise the situation in Europe. In June Secretary of State George Marshall offered economic assistance to '[A]ny government that is willing to assist in the task of recovery' stressing, 'Our policy is not directed against any country or doctrine but against hunger, poverty, desperation and chaos.' He warned, however, '[G]overnments, political parties, or groups which seek to perpetuate human misery in order to profit therefrom politically or otherwise will encounter the opposition of the

United States'. The message, expressed more subtly than by Truman, was the same – 'two halves of the same walnut' according to the President.[16]

Marshall demanded that European states must take the initiative and suggest ways in which they could cooperate to utilise American aid. The result, intended or otherwise, was to intensify the growing division of Europe into East and West, into Soviet and American spheres of influence. The Soviet Union, fearing for its sovereignty and the flooding of its markets by American goods, declined to participate in a conference called by Britain and France to discuss economic cooperation and dissuaded other states under its aegis, most notably Czechoslovakia, from attending.

Although Marshall's original offer had been to all European states it is interesting to speculate on the reaction of Congress if the USSR had accepted. Marshall Aid thus flowed only into the countries of Western Europe. Between 1948 and 1952 American government grants and credits totalled $13,150 million, supplemented by $500 million of private generosity. It is a matter of historical debate whether this assistance was crucial to West European recovery but few questioned at the time its contribution to a remarkable transformation. By 1951 industrial production was 43 per cent higher than pre-war and agricultural production was ten per cent better; trade between the United States and Western Europe doubled between 1947 and 1950, reaching pre-war levels in 1949. Prosperity and confidence had returned.[17]

The United States had also provided an important spur for greater West European integration. The government deemed inexpedient rather than undesirable Senator William Fulbright's attempt to amend the Marshall Aid Bill to call for the encouragement 'of the political unification of Europe'. Some made no secret of their hope to act as the Founding Fathers of a United States of Europe. In Europe Jean Monnet, the French diplomat, entrepreneur and planner, was convinced of the need to re-establish a more equal partnership with America. 'Europe,' he wrote from America in April 1948, 'cannot long afford to remain almost exclusively dependent on American credit for her production and American strength for her security, without harmful results both here and in Europe ... the countries of Europe must turn their national efforts into a truly European effort. This will be possible only through a federation of the West.' His subsequent efforts to realize this were a further illustration of the complexities and ambiguities of the post-war relationships. Monnet was a firm Atlanticist, committed to a partnership with the United States in the context of the Cold War, but believed that this required Europe to develop its own economic and political identity and to shed its client status.[18]

Truman and Marshall perceived their actions to be a defensive response to a growing Soviet threat but the Soviet perception was that these were aggressive moves designed to establish American economic hegemony since the enormous industrial advantages of the United States meant its goods would flood the free markets to which America was ideologically committed. The USSR's reaction was to tighten its grip on Eastern Europe, culminating in the dramatic overthrow of the Czech government by a communist coup in February and March 1948. Meanwhile in Germany the Anglo-American introduction of a new currency in their zone led to Stalin's attempt to isolate West Berlin by cutting the road, canal and rail links from the West in June. In response the West mounted a massive airlift to West Berlin until the Soviet blockade ended in May 1949. The United States committed itself to NATO, established 4 April 1949 and designed to protect Western Europe from Soviet attack. The Cold War was driven by such vicious circles of perceived threats, measures perceived by those taking them to be defensive and justified in the light of those threats, and the perception by their opponents that those measures instead constituted aggressive threats to themselves.

Such measures and perceived threats did not only take a military form. Those seeking to export American films to Europe claimed that 'each film ... carries important social and ideological by-products ... they serve as global showcases for American techniques, products and merchandise'. The message they carried was that social and political stability would be created by prosperity and better standards of living or, expressed simply, 'You can be like us'.

America's commitment to private enterprise, consumerism and advertising and the reactions that this provoked were encapsulated in the marketing of Coca-Cola, 'the essence of American capitalism' according to company president Robert Woodruff, as it sought to re-establish itself in Western Europe after the Second World War. Building on the foundation of 64 bottling plants created to supply American troops stationed there, the company by 1949 had bases in France, the Benelux countries and the Federal Republic of Germany. The message on the 15 May 1950 cover of *Time* magazine could not have been clearer: the globe was shown drinking Coke; the caption reading, 'World and Friend: love that piaster, that lira, that tickey and that American way of life.'

However, Coca-Cola's operations had provoked opposition in many countries on economic and cultural grounds, often led by local Communist parties. In France wine growers, Christian Democrats and Communists objected to the threat to French culture, while the Finance Ministry worried about the effect on the balance of payments. *Le Monde* declared, 'We have accepted chewing gum and Cecil B. de Mille, *Reader's Digest* and bebop. It's over soft drinks that the conflict has erupted; Coca-Cola seems to be the Danzig of European culture. After Coca-Cola, *Hola.*' The opposition to Coke only collapsed in 1953, the French disappointed in their attempt to find a compromise in this minor manifestation of American infiltration. Coca-Cola's leaders saw no middle way – to reject Coke was equivalent to siding with the Russians – while on the wider stage this episode was symbolic of America's commitment to pursue free trade and opportunities for private American companies.[19]

> 'We have accepted chewing gum and Cecil B de Mille, *Reader's Digest* and bebop. It's over soft drinks that the conflict has erupted; Coca-Cola seems to be the Danzig of European culture. After Coca-Cola, *Hola.*'
>
> **LE MONDE**

The period between the end of war and Stalin's death in March 1953 saw an early American impulse to withdraw once again into isolation transformed into a commitment to Europe and Asia in a worldwide crusade against the communists with whom Roosevelt had hoped to cooperate. The Truman Doctrine was translated by the plans and expenditure envisaged by National Security Council paper 68 (NSC 68) into an overwhelming military superiority in everything except conventional ground forces in Europe where, in September 1950, 14 NATO divisions faced 175 Soviet divisions. In 1949, after victory for Mao Zedong's communists in China, the Cold War spread to Asia as the United States extended its policy of containment to that continent, reversing its early occupation policies in Japan in favour of rebuilding the

Japanese economy and establishing a secure base to prevent the further spread of communism. In 1950 the North Korean invasion of South Korea triggered a military response from the United Nations in which the United States took the leading role, while also contributing much of the finance to fund French attempts to retain control of Indo-China in the face of Ho Chi Minh's nationalist and communist forces. At the same time America also expanded its troop numbers in Europe. Roosevelt's 'Four Policemen' of the world were reduced, at least in American eyes, to one.

Opinion polls suggested that a substantial majority of Americans approved this abandonment of isolation, believing that they had a unique mission to create a just and moral international order on a global scale; that the Soviets constituted the primary threat to world peace; that containment was the correct policy; that nuclear weapons were necessary deterrents; and that America should lead the world economy and play a major role in the United Nations. Congress agreed, giving at least 70 per cent backing for presidential initiatives in creating alliances like NATO or its South East Asian equivalent, SEATO, the Marshall Plan, defensive pacts with Formosa and South Korea and undertaking regional commitments in Cuba, the Near East and Indo-China.[20] American influence and prestige were at their height: the world allegedly liked Coke and Hollywood movies while Alexander Kortner's painting of B-52 bombers circling the earth symbolized the reach of American power.

Given America's traditional dominance of Latin America and the lack of direct Soviet involvement in the region outside Cuba, it is remarkable that it became one of the major contested areas of the Cold War. In the early post-war years the United States continued to rely on various dictatorial regimes to resist anti-American sentiments fed by resentment at the American economic and political hegemony deemed responsible for poverty, social inequality and restricted national sovereignty. America, often encouraged by would-be local political leaders, interpreted such opposition as communist-inspired. It sought to counter it by encouraging and aiding coups against elected leaders as in Guatamela in 1954 and against successful revolutionaries like Fidel Castro as in the ill-fated Bay of Pigs episode in Cuba in 1961.

In response to this latter failed attempt, Stalin's successor Nikita Khrushchev, first promised economic aid to Cuba and then offered to station nuclear missiles on the island. When American spy planes provided evidence that missile sites were being constructed in October 1962, this precipitated the greatest crisis of the Cold War as the United States prepared to prevent further Soviet missile deliveries to Cuba by imposing a naval blockade. A high stakes game of nuclear roulette ensued before President John F Kennedy's crisis team struck a deal with the Soviet ambassador whereby the USSR would withdraw its missiles from Cuba in return for America undertaking to desist from further invasions of the island and, at a later date, to decommission its missiles in Turkey.

Meanwhile Kennedy had already instigated the Alliance for Progress in August 1961, a new aid programme aimed at increasing Latin American prosperity and discouraging further communist advances. The results were less than satisfactory. There was little commitment to political reform; the dictators remained; much of the aid corruptly went into their pockets; and American businesses encouraged farmers to grow crops like coffee for export rather than much-needed food for home consumption. Discontent continued to grow, encouraging the establishment of revolutionary guerrilla

President John F Kennedy speaks to assembled Berliners in 1963

groups which were rarely able to seize power but did destabilize parts of the region. In response the United States supported military coups like those in Brazil in 1964 and Chile in 1973, undertook direct military intervention as in the Dominican Republic in 1965, engaged in covert warfare as in Nicaragua against the Sandinistas from 1979 onwards or backed right-wing opposition groups as in El Salvador in the 1980s.

Fidel Castro's Cuba remained a thorn in America's side throughout the Cold War, assisting revolutionary movements throughout Latin America and Africa. It continued to be a socialist state under his brother Raoul. However, relations with the United States improved after President Barack Obama was elected in 2009 and relaxed travel and trade restrictions for Americans. With the end of the Cold War and particularly since 9/11

'There are many people in the world who really don't understand, or say they don't, what is the great issue between the free world and the Communist world. Let them come to Berlin.'

PRESIDENT JOHN F KENNEDY, 1963

America became less focused on Latin America though it continued to be the main outlet for the region's trade, not all of which was welcome – 90 per cent of the cocaine imported into America came from Colombia; while illegal immigration, particularly from Mexico, remained a major issue. Their large neighbour to the north was still the dominant influence in the lives of the people of the region.[21]

Stalin may have transformed the USSR from a country relying on wooden ploughs to one with nuclear reactors but the cost in human terms was enormous. He was responsible for the murder of millions, imprisonment of millions more in horrific conditions, mass deportations, brutal suppression of opposition and punishment of dissent to the sometimes illogical and unsustainable orthodoxies of Soviet science. His death did bring an improved international atmosphere in Europe, marked by Soviet withdrawal from Austria in 1955 and the apparently more liberal polices of Khrushchev who denounced Stalin as a tyrant and hinted that communism need not be monolithic. This encouraged some independence in the Soviet satellite states though it became clear that there were very strict limits to Khrushchev's tolerance and that there was no respite in the ideological battle. In a remark to Western ambassadors at the Polish embassy on 18 November 1956 Khrushchev famously claimed, 'Whether you like it or not, history is on our side. We will bury you.' Nevertheless, in Berlin on 26 June 1963, President Kennedy issued a Wilsonian challenge: 'There are many people in the world who really don't understand, or say they don't, what is the great issue between the free world and the Communist world. Let them come to Berlin.'[22] In 1953 a brief workers' revolt in East Berlin was crushed while the brutal Soviet invasion of Hungary in 1956 confirmed that the USSR had no intention of abandoning its East European empire. Twelve years later the illusion of another Soviet relaxation of control was shattered by the invasion of Czechoslovakia in August 1968.

For many this reconfirmation of a Soviet menace made the argument for the continuation of an American 'empire by invitation' in Western Europe more effectively than any propagandist, though there were dissenting voices. In France General Charles de Gaulle, who returned to national politics in 1958 and dominated them for the next decade, was deeply suspicious of American power and would ideally have wished a European bloc to emerge as an arbiter between the US and USSR. President Eisenhower's reliance on nuclear weapons as a less expensive means to counter the West's inferiority in conventional forces brought a consequent fear of atomic warfare and encouraged pressure groups like the Campaign for Nuclear Disarmament (CND) to seek the removal of American weapons from European soil. CND said that its quarrel was not with America, only with its bombs and missiles; but it inevitably became associated with anti-American feeling. The public perception of its left-wing politics and its association with the broader Peace Movement meant that it was sometimes portrayed as the naïve (more rarely the deliberate) agent of Moscow.[23]

'Red' China provided another twist in the ideological confrontation. Although he had little reason to love Stalin, Mao saw no choice but to lean towards the Soviet side in the Cold War though Sino-Soviet relations were rarely as close as the Americans perceived them to be. America's attempt to roll back communism by continuing the Korean conflict into North Korea after the successful expulsion of the North Korean invaders in September 1950 provoked China to enter the conflict and pushed it closer to the USSR. Mao perceived this incursion and American support for Chiang Kai-shek, his defeated opponent in the Chinese civil war who had fled to Formosa, as evidence of America's aggressive intent. From the American perspective their policy aimed at countering what they interpreted to be an even more belligerent version of communism; though others suggested that Mao's policies might be more effectively explained in terms of Chinese nationalism and its grievances, some of which dated from the Paris Peace Conference. Fearing what they termed the 'domino effect' of communist success in one area leading to neighbouring states falling under communist control, the Americans became increasingly involved in the politics of south-east Asia and particularly in supporting South Vietnam which had been divided from Ho Chi Minh's North Vietnam under the Geneva Accords of July 1954 that ended the French war in Indo-China.

From the small beginnings of the military advisers sent to Saigon by Kennedy and escalated by President Lyndon B Johnson's authorization of America's direct involvement in the Vietnamese conflict after the Gulf of Tonkin incidents in August 1964, American troop levels in Vietnam peaked at 543,000 in 1969. They were supported by massive bombing campaigns in Vietnam itself and on targets in Laos and Cambodia in attempts to disrupt North Vietnamese supply lines. Between 1965 and 1973 America dropped three times as many bombs on Vietnam as those dropped by all sides in the Second World War. Vietnamese deaths, civilian and military on both sides, were well in excess of one million. The war cost America 58,000 lives and over $350,000 million in direct costs and subsequent pension payments – to no avail.

In January 1973, under the Paris Peace Accords, President Richard Nixon undertook to withdraw all American troops from Vietnam. Two years later Vietnam was reunited after the North's victory in the continuing war. Communist victories followed in Cambodia and Laos, suggesting that the domino theory might be correct. Nevertheless, the subsequent history of nationalist struggles, civil and international wars, genocide and outside interference revealed that the politics of Indo-China were much more complex than any monolithic ideological theory could explain. Indeed one of the cards Nixon had exploited in his negotiations to withdraw from Vietnam was the growing antagonism between the Soviet Union and China, which had come to blows along their borders in northeast Asia in March 1969. Each felt menaced by the other and feared that America might support its rival.[24]

There were mixed reactions in Europe to America's role

in the 1960s. In 1967 Jean-Jacques Servan-Schreiber, the owner of *L'Express*, a French magazine modelled on *Time* and *Newsweek*, published *Le Défi americain* (*The American Challenge*). The book, which outlined the challenge posed by America's growing investment in European businesses and suggested that Europe must respond positively by adopting the best American practices and adapting them to European traditions, was an enormous success, selling over 400,000 copies in three months. Less admiring were students on both sides of the Atlantic whose protests challenged assumptions of American ideological superiority in the light of its race relations record and its involvement in Vietnam. Even here, however, as one commentator remarked, 'The Americanization of the anti-American protest in Europe was carried out through the language of student action (sit-in, teach-in), through clothes, through music. In a certain sense, anti-Americanism became a kind of fashion which derived its mode of appearance, its forms of conduct, and even its intellectual base, from America.'[25]

In the 1970s the Cold War, in which tensions had thawed somewhat in the wake of the Cuban Missile Crisis, now threatened to refreeze. It was made more complicated by the tri-partite rivalry of the USSR, China and the US. With its attention concentrated first on South-East Asia and then, following the 1973 oil crisis, on the Middle East, America was finding the cost of European defence an increasing burden. There was a growing belief that the Europeans, whose moves towards greater integration were ideologically and politically welcome, should pull their weight in defence at a time when the European Community had become an economic rival. In the graphic 1971 phrase of Secretary of the Treasury John Connally, the Americans believed that they had 'to screw the

Europeans before they screw us'.[26] There were some positive moves to try to reduce armaments and bring about balanced force reductions; but the question of human rights complicated these discussions, threatening to bring the *realpolitik* of 'peaceful co-existence' into conflict with the ideology of individual human freedom, a cause close to the heart of President Jimmy Carter.

Carter enjoyed one great success, bringing together Egypt and Israel in the Camp David Accords in September 1978. However, failures of policy in Nicaragua and Iran, where American hostages were seized, damaged American prestige. When the USSR invaded Afghanistan in December 1979 Carter reverted to the Cold War rhetoric of the 1950s, withdrawing the US team from the 1980 Moscow Olympics to avoid a repetition of the prestige that Hitler had derived from the 1936 Berlin Olympics. The implication was that there was little difference between the totalitarianism of Nazi Germany and Soviet Communism. The suppression of the Polish Solidarity movement in 1981 seemed to confirm President Ronald Reagan's image of the USSR as 'the evil empire'. Crucially, however, the Soviets had bluffed the Polish communist leadership into acting against Solidarity, since the Politburo had decided against any invasion of Poland in the manner of 1956 or 1968.[27]

Reagan, the B movie star turned politician who hid his shrewdness behind a folksy image, began as a very firm Cold warrior. His nominee as chief arms control planner, Eugene Rostow, alarmed his listeners when he told them, 'We are living in a pre-war and not a post-war world.' Paradoxically, however, Reagan was committed to the elimination of nuclear weapons and in 1983 authorized the Strategic Defence Initiative (SDI), popularly known as 'Star Wars'. If it could be made reality, SDI would create an anti-ballistic missile system in space, upsetting the current nuclear balance of power. 'What if,' Reagan asked, 'we could intercept and destroy strategic ballistic missiles before they reached our own soil or that of our allies?' The Americans were not sure if they could build such a system but, crucially, the Soviets knew they could not, because they lacked the resources and the technology. Both sides were feeling the strain: the Soviet Union, with a smaller economy than America, was spending 50 per cent more on defence; under Reagan the US moved, within four years, from being the world's greatest creditor to being its largest debtor – a strange reversal of its experience between 1914 and 1918. American self-confidence, which had been dealt hard blows by Vietnam, Watergate and Nixon's forced resignation, was further undermined. Many believed American hegemony was doomed. Paul Kennedy's best-selling analysis of the rise and fall of great empires was eagerly studied as Americans sought to discover the signs indicating their own decline, but it was the Soviet Union that cracked.[28]

In 1988 Mikhail Gorbachev, Soviet General Secretary since 1985, walked hand-in-hand with Reagan through Red Square, symbolizing a remarkable transformation in the relations between the US and the USSR. Pursuing his new policies of *Glasnost* (transparency) and *Perestroika* (political and economic restructuring), he sought to reform the Soviet Union. Instead, unable (or unwilling) to contain the growing demands for independence from countries within the Soviet sphere and for greater freedom at home, he oversaw the dissolution, first of the Soviet Empire and then the Soviet Union itself. Reagan's successor George H Bush, in his State of the Union address in January 1992, hailed the end of the Cold War as a success of American ideals based upon the morality of liberal individualism, free enterprise and capitalism: 'For in the past 12 months, the world has known changes of almost biblical proportions… communism died this year … But the biggest thing that has happened in the world in my life – in our lives – is this: by the grace of God, America won the Cold War.' [29]

With America the one remaining world superpower and Deng Xiaoping moving China towards a socialist market economy it was possible for Francis Fukuyama, a neo-conservative with a belief in 'realistic Wilsonianism' to propose, first in an essay in 1989 and then in an expanded book form in 1992, that 'What we may be witnessing is not just the end of the Cold War, or the passing of a particular period of post-war history, but the end of history as such: that is, the end point of mankind's ideological evolution and the universalization of Western liberal democracy as the final form of human government.' [30] If one added to this the enhanced opportunities for national self-determination created by the collapse of Soviet domination then it might well be claimed that Wilson had indeed finally triumphed in his battle with Lenin (though Fukuyama did later confess that he foresaw future liberal democracy more on the model of the European Union than that of the United States). Furthermore, as Presidents Bill Clinton and George W Bush discovered, it was easier to establish the formal architecture of democracy in places like Bosnia and Afghanistan than it was to create a working democracy.

History, however, has the nasty habit of springing surprises, and the rise of political Islam as the main ideological alternative to liberal democracy and globalization in the post-Cold War world revived interest in Samuel Huntingdon's 1993 prediction that 'the fundamental source of conflict in this new world will not be primarily ideological or primarily economic; the great divisions among humankind and the dominating source of conflict will be cultural. Nation states will remain the most powerful actors in world affairs, but the principal conflicts of global politics will occur between nations and groups of different civilizations. The clash of civilizations will dominate global politics. The fault lines between civilizations will be the battle lines of the future.'[31]

There can be no doubt that the 20th century was indeed the American century or that the events of the First World War and the subsequent Peace Conference launched the United States, uncertainly at first, but with gathering momentum, on the path of world power. By 1945 it was clearly the most powerful nation on earth. Its role and influence did not rest merely upon its industrial, economic and military strength, formidable as these grew to be, but also on what came to be termed 'soft power': its ideas and cultural values. In the wake of Al-Qaeda assaults on American targets like the 1993 attempt to blow up the World Trade Center, the bombing of embassies in Kenya and Tanzania in 1998, suicide attacks on the USS *Cole* in Yemen in 2000, and on the World Trade Center and Pentagon on 11 September 2001, George W Bush proclaimed a 'War on Terror'. America's military and technological superiority in any conventional wars like those in the Gulf in 1991 and 2003 was unquestionable but how well could it cope in a new ideological battle for the hearts and minds of Muslims worldwide who believed that their co-religionists had been treated without dignity, justice and respect in the Middle East, in some of the successor states to the former Soviet Union, in north Africa and south-east Asia? There was also growing competition from China, still technically a communist state, which held the largest single portfolio of

US foreign debt, worth nearly $900,000 million at the end of 2009. Khrushchev had threatened to bury America; China might be able to buy it. Would China make more skilful use of its financial leverage than Woodrow Wilson had of his in 1919? These are interesting questions.[32]

Sir William Orpen's *A Grave in a Trench* symbolised the death and destruction of the First World War.

Conclusion

'The Peace to end Peace'

'Though there were several battles in the War, none were so terrible or costly as the Peace which was signed afterwards in the ever-memorable Chamber of Horrors at Versailles, and which was caused by the only memorable American statesmen, President Wilson and Col. White House, who insisted on a lot of Points.'

W C Sellar and R J Yeatman, *1066 And All That*, 1930[1]

Sir William Orpen's painting, *The Signing of the Peace in the Hall of Mirrors, Versailles,* which inspired this series, portrayed the occasion as a much more orderly and dignified business than it actually was. Perhaps this was ironic: he was by then very disillusioned about the Peace Conference – 'The "frocks" [politicians] had won the war. The "frocks" had signed the Peace! The Army was forgotten, some dead and forgotten, others maimed and forgotten, others alive and well – but still equally forgotten.' In contrast to the canvas his eyewitness account described first the two German delegates, Hermann Müller and Hans Bell, signing the Treaty, all the while with a hubbub of noise and movement in the hall, after which the Allied leaders penned their signatures: 'These were written without any dignity. People talked and cracked jokes to each other across tables. Lloyd George found a friend on his way up to sign his name, and as he had a story to tell him, the whole show was held up for a bit, but after all, it may have been a good story. All the "frocks" did all their tricks to perfection, President Wilson showed his back teeth; Lloyd George waved his Asquithian mane; Clemenceau whirled his grey-gloved hands about like windmills; Lansing drew his pictures and Mr Balfour slept.'[2]

Orpen proved more successful in creating order from chaos than the subjects of his painting but he had the enormous advantage of being able to portray and manipulate them to his will. He impishly included himself as the figure bent in silhouette in the arched window behind Lloyd George and Clemenceau. More symbolically, he added Orlando, who was not there; and omitted Smuts, the South African delegate who had signed the Treaty only with the greatest reluctance, who was. The peacemakers were less fortunate; their ability to control events diminished as their armies dispersed or was often non-existent in the more remote corners of Europe and the wider world where they had no means available to enforce their decisions. As Sir Henry Wilson, the British Chief of the Imperial General Staff, pointed out to Lloyd George, 'The root of evil is that the *Paris writ does not run*'.[3]

The peacemakers had to deal with a very confused and turbulent set of circumstances, especially in Eastern and Central Europe where the unprecedented, and almost certainly unrepeatable, circumstance of the near-simultaneous collapse of four empires left the area bereft of firm government or established boundaries and identities. After devoting much of the first two months of the Conference to secondary matters, they became acutely aware that, if they delayed making decisions or spent too long trying to reconcile all the conflicting aspirations of the peoples and states involved, the vacuum of power might be filled by the alternative revolutionary vision of Lenin and the Bolsheviks, creating a menace possibly even greater than that they had recently overcome from the Central Powers. With hindsight they were over-ambitious in their attempt to reshape and reorder the world at a stroke, but they found themselves in uncharted territory, as much part of a process of trial and error as they had been during the conflict itself as they struggled to adapt their states to the needs of total war. They believed that they could, indeed must, decide – 'Il faut aboutir' (We must reach conclusions) – as Clemenceau was wont to say.

They did so under huge pressure. Each faced challenges on the domestic and international stages whose interconnections were often both complex and unpredictable. The war left a bitter legacy of death, injury and destruction. This was often compounded by the disappointments of the peace terms for unsatisfied nationalists denied self-determination in Europe or the European empires; for the defeated, unconvinced, in some cases, of their defeat; and for victors for whom there was insufficient security, compensation or revenge, or all three. The peacemakers had to reassemble Europe and to seek solutions to the problems that created the war in the first place or had been compounded or supplemented by it. They had to reshape the world map to reflect the changing patterns of imperial power, taking account of new requirements of international scrutiny. All this had to be accomplished to reflect Wilson's higher moral standards for peacemaking that they had (however reluctantly in some cases) accepted. They had also to reconstruct their own countries following the changes consequent on the need to fight a total war, and, in some cases, to adjust to new boundaries and populations, aware that such domestic considerations were likely to have a greater impact on their own political futures and ambitions than peacemaking in Paris.

Under these circumstances, compounded by the organizational confusion in Paris and the impossible task of satisfying all the irreconcilable ambitions and expectations with which they were faced, exhausted, and sometimes in poor health, the peacemakers did well to create any settlements at all. Most were aware, or became aware (some more swiftly than others), that parts of those settlements but particularly aspects of that with Germany required reassessment and readjustment. Not all agreed, however. Hence the early 1920s witnessed the application by Britain and France of a self-defeating combination of conciliatory and coercive policies towards Germany, culminating in the Franco-Belgian incursion into the Ruhr in January 1923. The subsequent Dawes Plan and Locarno negotiations offered some hope that, as passions subsided and problems were overcome, it might be possible to improve on the foundations laid in Paris and build a more secure peace thus, however belatedly, achieving the reconciliation that Smuts, in particular, had sought in Paris.

One of the issues that this book has investigated is the quest for a solution to the problem of how to create structures which could accommodate Germany's legitimate aspirations without overwhelming its neighbours. Whether this was achievable in the 1920s depends much on the interpretation placed on Germany's post-war ambitions and the methods it might be prepared to employ in pursuing them. This remains one of several enormous imponderables associated with the First World War and its aftermath. But for the outbreak of war in 1914 might the Tsarist regime have avoided revolution? Might the Austro-Hungarian Empire have survived? Might the German state have reformed itself on more democratic principles? Would the implementation of the Home Rule Act have left Ireland a loyal and contented part of the United Kingdom? How might the European empires have adjusted to the nascent demands for greater self-government and imperial reform? How swiftly would America and Japan have emerged as important players on the international stage?

Gustav Stresemann was the key German figure in the mid-1920s and historical opinion is deeply divided about his role and sincerity. A J P Taylor's view was typically acerbic: 'The only question was whether the settlement would be revised and Germany become again the greatest Power in Europe, peacefully or by war. Stresemann wanted to do it peacefully. He thought this was the safer, the more certain, and the more lasting way to German predominance.'

By contrast Jonathan Wright's conclusion that, 'After 1923 he stood with increasing conviction for a democratic Germany in a democratic Europe' is more positive and sympathetic. On the one hand, Locarno suggested that, for the moment at least, Germany accepted its current western frontiers, but, on the other, there were no equivalent treaties with its eastern neighbours. We shall never know how Stresemann might have acted once Germany's international power and leverage increased because in October 1929 he died and Wall Street crashed, opening the door to another, less ambiguous, future under Hitler. It required the tragedies of a second world conflagration and the exigencies of the Cold War before a more acceptable solution to the German problem evolved.[4]

Some of Germany's grievances against the Treaty were clearly justified on the grounds of self-determination. However, this also illustrates the difficulties the peacemakers experienced in trying to reconcile that principle with the need for viable frontiers for new, or revived, states like Czecho-slovakia or Poland. Then, as now, the problems relating to self-determination remain very similar: how to reconcile the rights of peoples (whose definition itself constitutes a major area of contention) to determine their own destiny with the rights of states to enjoy territorial security and internal stability, particularly since Wilson's potentially bridging concept of civic nationalism has largely fought a losing battle with ethnic nationalism.

The Paris peace settlements created a new map of the world, sometimes only in the political sense that territories changed hands but retained their former boundaries. Nevertheless, in Europe and the Middle East they established new entities whose frontiers changed the internal configuration of their respective continents. In Africa, where many of the frontiers were the artificial creation of the imperial powers, most post-colonial states have been very careful not to open the risky question of boundary changes, though there have been indications more recently that some ambitious governments are willing to exploit or encourage civil and ethnic conflict in neighbouring states for their material advantage. The map of Asia has been more fluid partly as a result of wars and civil conflict; partly because secession has been slightly more successful there than in Africa, with East Pakistan separating from Pakistan in 1971 as the new state of Bangladesh, and East Timor leaving the former Dutch colony of Indonesia in 1999.

The 1919 map of Europe remained more or less intact (with the obvious exceptions of the frontiers of Poland and Germany after 1945) until the 1990s and the collapse of Yugoslavia and the Soviet Union. Since then 18 new states have joined the UN. It is, however, in the Middle East that the legacy of Versailles remains at its most potent today. Here ongoing problems of territorial boundaries, refugees, rights to water, terrorism and the actions of states and would-be states constitute a continuing threat to international peace and stability, as the affairs of Lebanon, Iraq and the ongoing Israeli-Palestinian quarrel have demonstrated all too clearly in recent decades.

There are other areas in which the First World War settlement succeeded in making new and, potentially, more positive contributions to future peace. Most notable of these is creating the League of Nations, but also by encouraging disarmament, extending the rights of individuals and groups, and developing international law to encompass the responsibility of political leaders for their actions. The present-day arrangements for the administration of international rivers and waterways are based on the improvements made in 1919 to those first negotiated at Vienna in 1815. Among its more aspirational goals the settlement sought to establish certain principles and rights for workers: the right to join unions, receive a reasonable wage, an 8-hour day or 48-hour week, a weekly rest day, the prohibition of child labour and the institution of proper schemes of inspection to ensure these principles were enforced.

There were a number of tentative moves towards greater gender equality proclaiming, for example, the principle that men and women should receive equal remuneration for work of equal value. Remarkably, given that three of the major powers involved did not yet allow women to vote in national elections, and Britain had only recently extended that right to certain women over the age of 30, the peacemakers specified the equal rights of men and women older than 20 to vote in the various plebiscites to be held under the Treaties. Perhaps fearing the potential complexities of multi-national families, however, they did, in the arrangements for the Upper Silesian plebiscite state that Polish and German citizens had the right to choose their nationality but that 'Option by a husband will cover his wife'. While it is true that, almost a century later, in many parts of the world such advances towards gender equality remain aspirations and not realities, this should not detract from the role of the peacemakers in emphasizing their place on the political agenda.[5]

The Paris Peace Conferences were once described, in the 1960s, as the first of the 20th century summit conferences, linking them to a style of diplomacy which was then popular, but they now seem to be more the last of the great 19th century peace congresses in the tradition of Vienna and Berlin. There was no similar attempt after either the Second World War or the Cold War to reshape world affairs in a single protracted meeting of the leaders of the major powers and it seems unlikely that such a lengthy gathering will ever recur.

There can be no doubt that the settlements they constructed were flawed and had substantial faults. It is difficult to see how this could be otherwise, given the situation at the time. Nonetheless there were positive aspects of the Treaties for which those who negotiated them should be given credit.

This present series has attempted to broaden understanding of the dilemmas facing the peacemakers and to indicate the enormity of their task. It is clear from the differing interpretations advanced by individual authors that there was never any question of imposing an editorial policy which required them to treat the settlements in a more positive and sympathetic light. The subject still has the capacity to rouse strong feelings and remains controversial, hence the diversity of approaches adopted by the contributors to this series.

What is important is that those who would continue to criti-
cize the peacemakers (even though our own generation has
not made a great hand of solving the problems of the aftermath of a Cold War and the collapse of only one empire)
should do so on the basis of greater knowledge and comprehension of the challenges and choices they confronted. The
books have also given an indication of the importance of the
role played by the smaller powers at the Conference, which
was not, *pace* Keynes, simply a matter of what three men
decided in Wilson's 'hot, dry room'.[6]

In their 'Memorable History of England', culled one sus-
pects from the unfortunate misconceptions of generations of
school examination answers, Sellars and Yeatman claimed
with some justification that after 1919, 'America was thus
clearly top nation' (though not all would concur with their
verdict that this was 'A Bad Thing'). Their assertion, however,
that then 'History came to a full stop' could certainly not
be accepted by a series which has demonstrated the significant contribution and lasting impact of the peacemakers at
the end of the First World War: the Makers of the Modern
World.[7]

Notes

Introduction

1. Cecil quoted by A Lentin, *Lloyd George and the Lost Peace: From Versailles to Hitler* (Palgrave Macmillan, 2001) p 69.
2. A Lentin, *General Smuts: South Africa* (Haus, 2010) p x.
3. They were unsuccessful in establishing one body, but the British (later Royal) Institute of International Affairs and the American organisation, the Council on Foreign Relations, were created as a result. Zimmern to Toynbee, 10.8.19, cited by G Martel, 'From *Round Table* to *New Europe:* Some Intellectual Origins of the Institute of International Affairs' in A Bosco and C Navari (eds), *Chatham House and British Foreign Policy 1919–1945* (Lothian Foundation Press, 1994) p 23. A Headlam-Morley, R Bryant and A Cienciala (eds), *Sir James Headlam-Morley: A Memoir of the Paris Peace Conference 1919* (Methuen, 1972) p 161.
4. J M Keynes, *The Economic Consequences of the Peace* (Macmillan, 1919); H Nicolson, *Peacemaking 1919* (Constable, 1933); Headlam-Morley *Memoir*; S Bonsal, *Unfinished Business* (Michael Joseph, 1944); R

Lansing, *The Peace Negotiations: A Personal Narrative* (Houghton Mifflin, 1921); Wavell quoted by D Fromkin, *A Peace to End all Peace: The Fall of the Ottoman Empire and the Creation of the Modern Middle East* (Phoenix Press, 2000 paperback ed.) Frontispiece; W S Churchill, *The Second World War: Volume I The Gathering Storm* 6 vols (Cassell and Co, 1949 ed.) p 6.

5. G F Kennan, *At a Century's Ending:Reflections 1982–1995* (W W Norton and Co, 1996) p 21; D Andelman, *A Shattered Peace: Versailles 1919 and the Price We Pay Today* (John Wiley and Sons, 2008); J Winter and B Baggett, *1914–1918: The Great War and the Shaping of the Twentieth Century* (BBC Books, 1996) p 338; *The Economist* (December 1999); H Kissinger, *Diplomacy* (Simon and Schuster, 1995 ed.) pp 218–45; D Hurd, *The Search for Peace: A Century of Peace Diplomacy* (Warner Books, 1997) p 37.

6. R Butler and J Bury (eds), *Documents on British Foreign Policy 1919–1939* (First Series, HMSO, 1954 onwards) Vol XV, pp 258–9; hereafter *DBFP.*

7. F Fischer, *Griff Nach Der Weltmacht* (Droste, 1961), translated into English with the rather feeble title of *Germany's Aims in the First World War* (Chatto and Windus, 1967), and *Krieg der Illusionen* (Droste, 1969) – English translation *The War of Illusions* (Chatto and Windus, 1975). M Trachtenberg, 'Versailles after Sixty Years', *Journal of Contemporary History,* Vol 17, No 3 (July 1982) pp 487–506; Keynes, *Economic Consequences,* p 5. Orlando is mentioned on p 27 and in a footnote on the same page which noted his poor grasp of English.

1: The Peace Settlements: Versailles, An Overview

1. M MacMillan, *Peacemakers: The Peace Conference of 1919 and Its Attempt to End War* (John Murray, 2001) p 1.

2. Quoted by D Perman, *The Shaping of the Czechoslovak State* (Brill, 1962) p 169.

3. D Watson, *Georges Clemenceau: France* (Haus, 2008) pp 156–9.

4. *DBFP,* Vol XXVII, p 315.

5. Quoted by R Debo, *Survival and Consolidation: The Foreign Policy of Soviet Russia 1918–1921* (McGill-Queen's University Press, 1992) p 145.

6. C Alston, *Piip, Meierovics & Voldemaras: Estonia, Latvia and Lithuania* (Haus, 2010); A Prazmowska, *Ignacy Paderewski: Poland* (Haus, 2009); P Neville, *Beneš, Masaryk: Czechoslovakia* (Haus, 2010); Keith Hitchin: *Ion Bratianu: Romania* (Haus, 2011).

7. B Cartledge, *Mihály Károlyi and István Bethlen: Hungary* (Haus, 2009) p 142. See also R Pearson, 'Hungary: A state truncated, a nation dismembered' in S Dunn and T G Fraser (eds), *Europe and Ethnicity: World War I and Contemporary Ethnic Conflict* (Routledge, 1996) pp 88–109.

8. J Bulloch, *Karl Renner: Austria* (Haus, 2010).

9. H Harmer, *Friedrich Ebert: Germany* (Haus, 2008).

10. Watson, *Clemenceau,* p 153.

11. See S Jeannesson, *Poincaré, La France et La Ruhr (1922–1924): Histoire d'une Occupation* (Presses Universitaires de Strasbourg, 1998).

12. Lentin, *Lloyd George and the Lost Peace,* pp 67–88.

13. Comte de Saint-Aulaire, *Confession d'un Vieux Diplomate* (Flammarion, 1953) p 53.

14. S Marks, *Paul Hymans: Belgium* (Haus, 2010).

15. S Di Scala, *Vittorio Orlando: Italy* (Haus, 2010).

16. R J Crampton, *Aleksandŭr Stamboliĭski: Bulgaria* (Haus, 2009); A Dalby, *Eleftherios Venizelos: Greece* (Haus, 2010); D Djokic, *Pašić and Trumbić: The Kingdom of the Serbs, Croats and Slovenes* (Haus, 2010).

17. A Mango, *From the Sultan to Atatürk: Turkey* (Haus, 2009).

18. R McNamara, *The Hashemites: The Dream of Arabia* (Haus, 2009).

19. D Lloyd George, *The Truth about the Peace Treaties* 2 vols (Gollancz, 1938) Vol II, p 1150.

20. T G Fraser, *Chaim Weizmann: The Zionist Dream* (Haus, 2009).

21. Lentin, *Smuts*; H Purcell, *Maharajah of Bikaner: India* (Haus, 2010); C Bridge, *William Hughes: Australia* (Haus, 2011); J Watson, *William Massey: New Zealand* (Haus, 2010).

22. J Clements, *Wellington Koo: China* (Haus, 2008).

23. J Clements, *Prince Saionji: Japan* (Haus, 2008).

24. B Morton, *Woodrow Wilson: United States* (Haus, 2008).

25. G Schulz, *Revolutions and Peace Treaties, 1917–1920* (Methuen, 1967, 1972 translation) p 223.

26. Z Steiner *The Lights that Failed: European International History 1919–1933* (Oxford, 2005); P Cohrs, *The Unfinished Peace after World War I: America, Britain and the Stabilization of Europe, 1919–1932* (Cambridge, 2006); R Boyce, *The Great Interwar Crisis and the Collapse of Globalization* (Macmillan, 2009). See also S Marks, *The Ebbing of European Ascendancy: An*

International History of the World, 1914–1945 (Arnold, 2002) which introduces a greater sense of a world aspect to these questions and the excellent chapter by C Fink, 'Revisionism' in G Martel (ed), *A Companion to Europe, 1900–1945* (Blackwell, 2006) pp 326–40.

2: The German Problem

1. Archie Thornton (1921–2004) was a D Day veteran and a distinguished historian of the British Empire who ended his career as Professor of History at the University of Toronto. Amongst his many publications his best known was his 1959 book, *The Imperial Idea and Its Enemies: A Study in British Power*. The quotation comes from a lecture he gave in the University of Ulster in May 2000.

2. Cited by A Kramer, *Dynamic of Destruction: Culture and Mass Killing in the First World War* (Oxford, 2007) p 93.

3. See the volumes in this series by Di Scala, *Orlando*; Morton, *Wilson*; A Sharp, *David Lloyd George: Great Britain* (Haus, 2008); and Watson, *Clemenceau*.

4. Nicolson, *Peacemaking,* pp 128–9.

5. A Sharp, 'Quelqu'un Nous Ecoute: French Interception of German Telegraphic and Telephonic Communications during the Paris Peace Conference, 1919' in *Intelligence and National Security,* Vol 3, No 4, October 1988, pp 124–7.

6. S Schuker, *American 'Reparations' to Germany, 1919– 1933: Implications for the Third World Debt Crisis* (Princeton, 1988) p 46.

7. R Boyce, *The Great Interwar Crisis and the Collapse of Globalization* (Palgrave Macmillan, 2009) pp 53–5.

8. See Harmer, *Ebert*, and Lentin, *Smuts*.

9. G Feldman, 'The Reparations Debate' in C Fischer and A Sharp (eds), *After the Versailles Treaty: Enforcement, Compliance, Contested Identities* (Routledge, 2008) p 70.

10. Balfour to Chamberlain, 16.12.25, R Grayson, *Austen Chamberlain and the Commitment to Europe: British Foreign Policy 1924–29* (Frank Cass, 1997) p 65.

11. H Kissinger, *Diplomacy*, p 274.

12. For overviews of these negotiations and developments see S Marks, *The Illusion of Peace: International Relations in Europe, 1918–1933* (Palgrave Macmillan, Second Edition, 2003); Steiner, *The Lights that Failed*; and Kissinger, *Diplomacy*.

13. See Steiner, *The Lights that Failed*, pp 583–7; R White, ' "Through a Glass Darkly":The Foreign Office Investigation of French Federalism, January–May 1930' in D Dutton (ed), *Statecraft and Diplomacy in the Twentieth Century* (Liverpool University Press, 1995) pp 75–97.

14. See R Henig, *The League of Nations* (Haus, 2010) pp 134–73.

15. See I Kershaw, *Fateful Choices: Ten Decisions that Changed the World 1940–1941* (Penguin, 2008) pp 382–430.

16. R Overy, *Why the Allies Won* (Norton, 1996).

17. For an overview of the early Cold War developments see J D P Dunbabin, *The Cold War: The Great Powers and Their Allies* (Longman, 1994) pp 53–105.

18. Dunbabin, *The Cold War*, p 96.

19. J Monnet, *Memoirs* transl by R Mayne (Collins, 1978) pp 433–4.

20. Monnet, *Memoirs*, p 291 and p 296.

21. For overviews of the early development of the European Union see R Mayne, *The Recovery of Europe: From Devastation to Unity* (Weidenfeld and Nicolson, 1970) and D Dinan, *Ever Closer Union: An Introduction to European Integration* (Palgrave Macmillan, Third Edition, 2005).

22. *The Times*, 9.9.09.

3: The League of Nations and the United Nations

1. Quoted by D Armstrong, *The Rise of the International Organisation: A Short History* (Macmillan, 1982) p 9.

2. Quoted by A Sharp, *The Versailles Settlement: Peacemaking after the First World War, 1919–1923* (Palgrave Macmillan, Second Edition, 2008) p 57.

3. Speech at the London Guildhall quoted by B Shaw, *Peace Conference Hints* (Constable, 1919) p 65; H W V Temperley (ed), *A History of the Paris Peace Conference* 6 vols (Oxford University Press, 1920, 1969 reprint) Vol I, pp 435, 439.

4. Armstrong, *International Organisation*, p 9; J Duroselle, *Clemenceau* (Fayard, 1988) p 738.

5. Sharp, *Versailles Settlement*, pp 42–80.

6. Henig, *League*, p 1; Salvador de Madariaga of the League Secretariat suggested, 'Everything went on as if, for lack of any common adversary, France and Britain had chosen the League as the arena in which to fight each other.' Quoted by R Henig, 'Britain, France and the League of Nations in the 1920s' in A Sharp and G Stone, *Anglo–French Relations in the Twentieth Century: Rivalry and Cooperation* (Routledge, London, 2000) pp 138–57, p 138.

7. *DBFP*, Series 1A, Vol 1, pp 847–8.

8. M Thornton, *Sir Robert Borden: Canada* (Haus 2010); *Daily News*, February 1923, quoted by Henig, *League*, pp 80–1.

9. Quoted by J P Dunbabin, 'The League of Nations' Place in the International System', *History*, Vol 78, No 254, October 1993, pp 440–1.

10. Cecil wrote to Curzon, Balfour and Lloyd George, 12 April 1920, arguing the German troop movements could be construed as contraventions of Articles 42 and 43 of the Treaty constituting a threat of war and hence the League should be summoned. Sydney Waterlow, an official in the Foreign Office, commented '… Either we must sooner or later find an occasion to promote recourse to this machinery, or we must reconcile ourselves to the Covenant becoming a dead letter …' 191340/4232/18 in F0371/3783, National Archives, Kew.

11. Hankey to D'Abernon, 2 October 1921. D'Abernon Papers, ADD MSS 48954, British Library. D'Abernon repeated the remark, 28 October 1921, ADD MSS 48953. The committee consisted of Hymans of Belgium, da Cunha from Brazil, Quinones of Spain and Koo from China. Hymans and Koo are the subjects of two of the books in this series: Marks, *Hymans*; and Clements, *Wellington Koo*.

12. See Dunbabin, 'The League of Nations' Place', pp 421–42; and Henig, *League*, pp 88–93.

13. See Henig, *League*, pp 134–53.

14. For the general European diplomatic background see S Marks, *Ebbing of European Ascendancy*, *passim* and pp 327–8; and Steiner, *The Lights that Failed*.

15. See Henig, *League*, pp 154–73.

16. Quoted by M Kennedy, *Ireland and the League of Nations 1919–1946: International Relations, Diplomacy and Politics* (Irish Academic Press, 1996) p 220.

17. Colonel Henry Pownall, CID, May 1936 quoted by Dunbabin 'The League of Nations' Place', p 441. Pownall later became Chief of the Imperial General Staff.

18. Sir Alexander Cadogan, quoted by Henig, *League*, p 182.

19. Henig, *League*, pp 182–5; S Ryan, *The United Nations and International Politics* (Macmillan, 2000) pp 7–19; P Kennedy, *The Parliament of Man: The United Nations and the Quest for World Government* (Allen Lane, 2006) pp 24–45.

20. See E Johnson, 'Britain and an International Force: The Experience of the League of Nations and the United Nations Military Staff Committee' in K Hamilton and E Johnson (eds), *Arms and Disarmament in Diplomacy* (Vallentine Mitchell 2008) pp 173–93.

21. Ryan, *United Nations*, pp 38–9, 44–5.

22. Ryan, *United* Nations, pp 39–43.

23. Ryan, *United Nations*, pp 64–7.

24. Kennedy, *Parliament of Man*, p 105.

25. Ryan, *United Nations*, pp 96–102.

26. Ryan, *United Nations,* p 110; Kennedy, *Parliament of Man*, pp 102–4. This is, of necessity, an over-simplified account of a complex set of political relationships in the US and between the US and UN. See L Murray, *Clinton, Peacekeeping and Humanitarian Interventionism; Rise and Fall of a Policy* (Routledge, 2008) for a fuller analysis.

27. A Lane, *Yugoslavia: When Ideals Collide* (Palgrave Macmillan, 2004) pp 182–94; Ryan, *United Nations*, pp 114–21; Kennedy, *Parliament of Man*, pp 97–102.

28. Kennedy, *Parliament of Man*, p 41; F Duschene, *Jean Monnet: the First Statesman of Interdependence* (Norton and Co, 1994) p 401.

4: National Self-Determination: Wilson's Troublesome Principle

1. See, for example, Prazmowska, *Paderewski*; Neville, *Beneš, Masaryk*; Alston, *Piip, Meierovics and Voldemaras*; A Dalby, *South-East Asia* (Haus, 2010); Purcell, *Bikaner*.

2. D P Moynihan, *Pandaemonium: Ethnicity in International Politics* (Oxford University Press, 1994) p 81.

3. Lloyd George's speech, 5 January 1918, D Lloyd George, *War Memoirs* 2 vols (Odhams, 1938) Vol II, p 515; Wilson's speech, 11 February 1918, Temperley, *History*, Vol I, pp 438–9.

4. Temperley, *History*, Vol IV, p 429.

5. Temperley, *History*, Vol I, p 438.

6. See E Manela, *The Wilsonian Moment: Self-Determination and the International Origins of Anticolonial Nationalism* (Oxford, 2007) pp 60–1; Lansing's note of 30 December 1918, Lansing, *The Peace Negotiations*, pp 97–8.

7. See T G Fraser, 'Germany and Indian Revolution, 1914–1918', *Journal of Contemporary History*, 1977, 12, pp 255–72.

8. See McNamara, *The Hashemites*.

9. Fraser, *Weizmann*.

10. Sharp, *The Versailles Settlement*, pp 186–94.

11. G Clemenceau, *Grandeur and Misery of Victory* (Harrap, 1930) p 180.

12. S H Thompson, *Czechoslovakia in European History* (Frank Cass, 1965) p 326.

13. Correspondence with the German delegation. *Papers relating to the Foreign Relations of the United States Paris Peace Conference 1919* (13 vols), Vol VI, p 939; hereafter *FRUS*.

14. Lord Hardinge, Minute, *c*.10 March 1919, in Fo608/51 in the National Archives, Kew; Temperley, *History*, Vol VI, p 556; Headlam-Morley letter, 5 March 1919, in Headlam-Morley, *Memoir*, p 44.

15. Stephen Tallents (Private Secretary to the Lord-Lieutenant of Ireland) reporting Churchill's words at a meeting, 13 April 1922 (Tallents Papers in the family hands).

16. Lloyd George, *The Truth About the Peace Treaties*, Vol II, p 1150.

17. K Bourne and D C Watt (eds), *British Documents on Foreign Affairs: Reports and Papers from the Foreign Office Confidential Print: The Paris Peace Conference of 1919* 7 vols (University Publications of America, 1989) Vol II, p 264.

18. See Purcell, *Bikaner.* A Best, J Hanhimaki, J Maiolo, K Schulze, *International History of the Twentieth Century* (Routledge, 2004) pp 94–7. J Darwin, *Britain and Decolonisation* (Macmillan, 1988) pp 79–85.

19. See R Betts, *France and Decolonisation, 1900–1960* (Macmillan, 1991) pp 22–32.

20. Marks, *Ebbing of European Ascendancy*, pp 143–6.

21. C Andrew and A Kany-Forstner, *France Overseas: The Great War and the Climax of French Imperial Expansion* (Thames and Hudson, 1981) p 242.

22. A Adamthwaite, *The Making of the Second World War* (Allen and Unwin, 1977) p 184.

23. P Wandycz, *The Price of Freedom: A History of East Central Europe from the Middle Ages to the Present* (Routledge, 1992) pp 238–40; S Horak et al, *Eastern European National Minorities, 1919–1980: A Handbook* (Littleton, 1980) pp 2–4; D Kaiser, *Politics and War: European Conflict from Philip II to Hitler* (Tauris, 1990) pp 392–410.

24. T G Fraser, *The Arab-Israeli Conflict* (Third Edition, Palgrave Macmillan, 2008) pp 23–58 and *passim*.

25. Darwin, *Britain and Decolonisation*, pp 67–106

26. N Nicolson (ed), *Vita and Harold: The Letters of Vita Sackville-West and Harold Nicolson* (Putnam, 1992) p 83; Darwin, *Britain and Decolonisation*, pp 107–10, 155–8, 202–4.

27. Betts, *France and Decolonisation*, pp 78–114.

28. Darwin, *Britain and Decolonisation*, pp 208–14; K Kyle, *Suez* (Weidenfeld and Nicolson, 1991) *passim*.

29. Ryan, *United Nations*, pp 78–9.

30. P Bell, *The World Since 1945* (Arnold, 2001) pp 235–8, 448–51, 453–5; Best *et al*, *International History*, pp 389–90.

31. Best et al, *International History*, pp 474–5.

32. Ryan, *United Nations*, p 78.

33. Quoted in D Heater, *National Self-Determination: Woodrow Wilson and his Legacy* (Macmillan, 1994) pp 207–8.

34. Quoted in A Roberts in his preface to Moynihan, *Pandaemonium*, p xvi.

35. M Howard, 'The Legacy of the First World War' in R Boyce and E M Roberston (eds), *Paths to War: New Essays on the Origins of the Second World War* (St Martin's Press, 1989) p 50.

36. E Hobsbawm, *Age of Extremes; The Short Twentieth Century 1914–1991* (Michael Joseph, 1994) p 31.

37. Pearson, 'Hungary' in Dunn and Fraser (eds), *Europe and Ethnicity*, pp 104–7.

38. K Meyer, *New York Times* and Lansing 20 and 30 December 1918, both cited by Moynihan, *Pandaemonium*, pp 80, 82–3.

5: Minority Protection, Disarmament and International Law

1. Quoted by C Kitching, *Britain and the Problem of International Disarmament 1919–1934* (Routledge, 1999) p 9.

2. See C Fink, 'The Minorities Question at the Paris Peace Conference' in Boemeke *et al*, *The Treaty of Versailles*, pp 249–74; J J Preece, 'Minority Rights in Europe: from Westphalia to Helsinki', *Review of International Studies* (1997) No 23, pp 75–92; A Sharp, 'Britain and the Protection of Minorities at the Paris Peace Conference, 1919' in A C Hepburn (ed), *Minorities in History* (Edward Arnold, 1978) pp 170–88; P de Azcárate, *The League of Nations and National Minorities: An Experiment* (Carnegie Endowment, 1945) *passim*.

3. C A Macartney, *National States and National Minorities* (Oxford, 1934) p 4.

4. Fink, 'Minorities Question,' pp 256–9. Later attempts to generalize the system, for example by Lithuania in 1925, also failed – see A Alcock, *A History of the Protection of Regional Cultural Minorities in Europe: From the Edict of Nantes to the Present Day* (Macmillan, 2000) p 82.

5. Sharp, 'Britain and the Protection of Minorities', pp 173–5; Preece, 'Minority Rights', pp 81–2. Eighth Plenary Session of the Conference, 31.5.19, *FRUS*, Vol. III, pp 395–7, 406.

6. League of Nations Official Journal (1926) p 144.

7. Alcock, *History*, p 85.

8. Minutes of 12 and 14.4.19 in F0608/6.

9. Minute by C M Palairet, 19.3.20 in F0371/4385; Alcock, *History*, pp 52–5.

10. The League minority protection system was not formally pronounced extinct by the UN until 1950. Preece, 'Minority Rights', pp 83–4; Alcock, *History*, pp 81–7.

11. Preece, 'Minority Rights', pp 84–8; M N Shaw, *International Law* (Cambridge University Press, Third Edition, 1994) pp 221–33.

12. Shaw, *International Law*, pp 233–38, 176–8.

13. Alcock, *History*, pp 135–213 covers many of these issues in greater detail; Preece, 'Minority Rights', pp 88–91; T Benedikter, *Legal Instruments of Minority Protection in Europe – An Overview* (Bolzano/Bozen, 2006); http://www.gfbv.it/3dossier/eu-min/autonomy-eu.html, accessed 28 April 2010) pp 1–36.

14. Benedikter, *Legal Instruments*, p 15 and pp 20–7.

15. Inge was a theologian and popular commentator. The quotation comes from 'Patriotism' in *Outspoken Essays* (Longmans, 1919) pp 42–3.

16. P Towle, *Enforced Disarmament: From the Napoleonic Campaigns to the Gulf War* (Oxford, 1997) p 1; Temperley, *History*, Vol I, p 433.

17. D Stevenson, 'Britain, France and the Origins of German Disarmament, 1916–1919', *Journal of Strategic Studies* Vol 29, No 6, April 2006, p 196. The articles in this special issue reflect a new interest in the subject of disarmament since the two Gulf Wars.

18. A Barros, 'Disarmament as a Weapon: Anglo-French Relations and the Problems of Enforcing German Disarmament' and P Jackson 'France and the Problem of Security and International Disarmament after the First World War', both in *Journal of Strategic Studies* Vol 29, No 6, April 2006, pp 301–21, 247–80. A Sharp, 'Mission Accomplished? Britain and the Disarmament of Germany, 1918–1923' in K Hamilton and E Johnson (eds), *Arms and Disarmament in Diplomacy* (Vallentine Mitchell, 2008) pp 73–90.

19. Boyce, *The Great Interwar Crisis*, pp 25–35.

20. J H Morgan, *Assize of Arms* (Methuen, 1945) pp xi–xvii; R Recouly, *Où en est l'Allemagne: Comment La Faire Payer* (Hachette, 1922), p 154.

21. *Papers Respecting Negotiations for an Anglo-French Pact*, Cmd 2169 (HMSO, 1924) p 82; quoted in Henig, *League*, p 109; *The Treaty of Versailles and After: Annotations of the Text of the Treaty* (Greenwood reprint, 1968, of original US Government Printing Office, 1944) pp 309, 82.

22. Notes by Crowe, 12 October 1916, quoted in Henig, *League*, p 111.

23. Quoted in Boyce, *The Great Interwar Crisis*, p 115.

24. For the League's initiatives in disarmament see Henig, *League*, pp 112–33.

25. Henig, *League*, pp 116–17.

26. Best *et al*, *International History of the Twentieth Century*, p 269.

27. Best *et al*, *International History of the Twentieth Century*, pp 450–1.

28. http://www.icomos.org/unesco/unesco_constitution. html (accessed 18 May 2010).

29. Quoted by J Willis, *Prologue to Nuremberg: The Politics and Diplomacy of Punishing War Criminals of the First World War* (Greenwood, 1982) p 61.

30. *Treaty*, pp 376–9; Willis, *Prologue*, p 26.

31. Willis, *Prologue*, pp 4–6, 47–62.

32. Willis, *Prologue*, pp 65–82, 98–112.

33. Willis, *Prologue*, pp 126–47.

34. G Bass, *Stay the Hand of Vengeance: The Politics of War Crimes Tribunals* (Princeton, 2002 ed.) pp 106–30.

35. Bass, *Stay the Hand*, pp 130–46.

36. Willis, *Prologue*, pp 164–76; Bass, *Stay the Hand*, pp 147–205. The quotations are on pp 202 and 205.

37. W Schabas, *The UN International Criminal Tribunals: The Former Yugoslavia, Rwanda and Sierra Leone* (Cambridge, 2006) pp 3–6; Bass, *Stay the Hand*, p 282.

6: Ideology and the American Century

1. Keynes, *Economic Consequences*, p 38.

2. Keynes, *Economic Consequences*, p 41.

3. D Fromkin, *In The Time of the Americans: The Generation That Changed America's Role in the World* (Papermac, 1995) pp 95, 179, 81; G J Ickenberry, *After Victory: Institutions, Strategic Restraint, and the Rebuilding of Order After Major Wars* (Princeton, 2001) p 122.

4. Wilson's speech to the Senate, 22 January 1917 http://millercenter.org/scripps/archive/speeches/detail/3797 (accessed 21 June 2010).

5. Temperley, *History*, Vol 1, p 444.

6. R S Baker, *Woodrow Wilson and World Settlement* 3 vols (Doubleday Page, 1923) Vol 1, p 102; A J Mayer, *Politics and Diplomacy of Peacemaking: Containment and Counter-Revolution at Versailles 1918–1919* (Weidenfeld and Nicolson, 1968) p 30.

7. C Andrew, *Secret Service: The Making of the British Intelligence Community* (Heinemann, 1985) pp 259–92.

8. N Chamberlain, *The Struggle for Peace* (Hutchinson, 1940) p 50; M Howard, *The Continental Commitment: The Dilemma of British Defence Policy in the Era of Two World Wars* (Pelican, 1974) pp 123–49.

9. Baldwin quoted by Henig, *League*, p 146; M Streeter, *South America* (Haus, 2010); Best *et al*, *International History*, pp 129–50; Marks, *Ebbing of European Ascendancy*, pp 225–52.

10. P Cohrs, *The Unfinished Peace after World War I: America, Britain and the Stabilisation of Europe 1919–1932* (Cambridge, 2006) *passim*.

11. Quoted by W Hitchcock, *The Struggle for Europe: The History of the Continent since 1945* (Profile Books, 2004) p 26.

12. Quoted by S Ambrose, *The Rise to Globalism: American Foreign Policy, 1938–1970* (Penguin, 1971) p 104.

13. Roosevelt quoted by H Feis, *Churchill, Roosevelt, Stalin: The War They Waged and The Peace They Sought* (Princeton, 1957) p 531. Figures from US General Accounting Office, *Military Presence: United States Personnel in NATO* (October 1989) and http://siadapp. dmdc.osd.mil/personnel/MILITARY/history/hst0709. pdf (accessed 14 June 2010).

14. D Watt, *Succeeding John Bull: America in Britain's Place* (Cambridge University Press, 1984) pp 106–7; W Loth, *The Division of the World 1945–1951* (Routledge, 1988) p 25.

15. R Mayne, *The Recovery of Europe: From Devastation to Unity* (Weidenfeld and Nicolson, 1970) pp 93–4; Loth, *Division*, p 142.

16. Mayne, *Recovery*, pp 99, 103–4.

17. C Mee, *The Marshall Plan* (Simon and Schuster, 1984) pp 246–52; Mayne, *Recovery*, p 117.

18. M Beloff, *The United States and the Unity of Europe* (Faber, 1963) pp 27–8; Monnet, *Memoirs*, pp 272–3.

19. A Sharp and K Ward, 'The United States and Europe, 1945 to 1991' in B Waites (ed), *Europe and the Wider World* (Open University, 1993) pp 119–64, 139–41; R Willett, *The Americanization of Germany, 1945–1949* (Routledge, 1989) p 103; R Kuisel, 'Coca-Cola and the Cold War: the French Face Americanization, 1948–1953', *French Historical Studies*, Spring 1991, pp 96–116.

20. R Mellanson, *Reconstructing Consensus: American Foreign Policy Since the Vietnam War* (St Martin's Press, 1991) pp 4–10.

21. Streeter, *South America*; Best *et al*, *International History*, pp 362–80; P Bell, *The World Since 1945: An International History* (Arnold 2001) pp 470–93.

22. http://www.time.com/time/magazine/article/0,9171,867329,00.html; http://www.historyplace.com/speeches/berliner.htm (accessed 21 June 2010).

23. R J Barnett, *Allies: America, Europe, Japan since the War* (Jonathan Cape, 1984) pp 416–23.

24. Best *et al*, *International History*, pp 288–304; M MacMillan, *Nixon and Mao: The Week That Changed the World* (Random House, 2007) *passim*.

25. J Servan-Schreiber, *The American Challenge* (Penguin, 1969), originally published as *Le Défi American* (1967) *passim*; A Grosser, *The Western Alliance: European-American Relations since 1945* (Continuum, 1980) p 247.

26. Quoted by M Smith, ' "The devil you know": The United States and a Changing European Community' *International Affairs*, Vol 68, January 1993, pp 103–20, p 110.

27. J L Gaddis, *The Cold War* (Allen Lane, 2005) p 221.

28. Sharp and Ward, 'United States and Europe', pp 153–61; Reagan quoted by Gaddis, *The Cold War*, pp 225–6; P Kennedy, *The Rise and Fall of the Great Powers: economic change and military conflict from 1500–2000* (Fontana, 1988).

29. President Bush, State of the Union Address, 28 January 1992 http://www.fas.org/spp/starwars/offdocs/union92.htm (accessed 1 July 2010).

30. F Fukuyama, 'The End of History?', *The National Interest* (1989) reprinted in G Ó Tuathail, S Dalby, P Routledge (eds), *The Geopolitics Reader* (Routledge, Second Edition, 2006) pp 107–114, p 107; 'The History at the End of History', *The Guardian*, 3 April 2007, http://www.guardian.co.uk/commentisfree/2007/apr/03/ thehistoryattheendofhist (accessed 20 June 2010).

31. S Huntington, 'The Clash of Civilizations', *Foreign Affairs*, 72, July/August 1993, pp 22–49.

32. Best *et al*, *International History*, pp 421–42; 'US Federal deficit: who owns America's debt?', *The Guardian*, 9 March 2010 http://www.guardian.co.uk/news/ datablog/2010/mar/09/china-federal-deficit-us-america-debt (accessed 20 June 2010).

Conclusion: 'The Peace to end Peace'

1. W C Sellar and R J Yeatman, *1066 And All That* (Penguin reprint, 1960, originally published by Methuen, 1930) p 122.

2. Sir W Orpen, *An Onlooker in France 1917–1919* (Dodo Press reprint of the original Williams and Norgate publication, 1921) pp 125–6.

3. MacMillan, *Peacemakers*, p 7.

4. N Ferguson (ed), *Virtual History: Alternatives and Counterfactuals* (Picador, 1997) investigates some of these possibilities. A J P Taylor, *The Origins of the Second World War* (Penguin, 1964) p 79; J Wright, *Gustav Stresemann: Weimar's Greatest Statesman* (Oxford, 2002) p 523.

5. See Articles 331–64; Article 427; Article 34 of the Annex relating to the Saar plebiscite and Article 91 of

that relating to the Upper Silesian plebiscite. *Treaty*
pp 655–79; 718–9, 190 and 221.

6. K Eubank, *The Summit Conferences 1919–1960*
(Oklahoma University Press, 1966).

7. Sellar and Yeatman, *1066*, p 123.

Chronology

YEAR	INTERNATIONAL DIPLOMATIC HISTORY
1648	Treaty of Westphalia: ended Thirty Years' War (1618–1648) in Holy Roman Empire, and Eighty Years' War (1568–1648) between Spain and Dutch Republic; established concept of sovereign state, territorial sovereignty.
1713	Treaty of Utrecht: series of peace treaties, between several European states, including Britain, France, Spain, Savoy, and Dutch Republic, helped end War of Spanish Succession; preserved the European system based on balance of power.
1814–15	Congress of Vienna: conference of ambassadors of European states chaired by Austrian statesman Klemens Wenzel von Metternich to settle issues arising from French Revolutionary Wars, Napoleonic Wars, and dissolution of Holy Roman Empire; resulted in redrawing of continent's political map, and creation of spheres of influence through which France, Austria, Russia and Britain brokered local and regional problems; established Congress System (which developed into Concert of Europe), a voluntary great power consultation process which contributed to ideas for the League of Nations Treaty of Ghent: ends British American war

YEAR	HISTORY	CULTURE
1648	English Civil War: Parliament votes to bring King Charles I to trial.	Rembrandt, *The Pilgrims at Emmaus*.
	George Fox founds Society of Friends (Quakers).	
	Population of Germany sinks to 8 million from 17 million in 1618 due to war, famine and plague.	
1713	Pragmatic Sanction issued by Emperor Charles VI: female right of succession in Habsburg domains.	Abbé St Pierre, *Projet pour la paix perpétuelle*.
		School of Dance established at Paris Opera.
	Witch trials abolished in Prussia in following year.	Board of Longitude established in England.
1814–15	Napoleon abdicates, banished to Elba	Jane Austen, *Mansfield Park*.
		Lord Byron, *The Corsair*.
	Cape Province becomes British colony.	Dulwich Gallery, London, opens.
	George Stephenson constructs first practical steam locomotive.	J N Maelzel invents metronome in Vienna.
	Napoleon leaves Elba, lands in France, allies defeat Napoleon at Waterloo, Napoleon abdicates second time, banished to St Helena.	Francis Scott Key, *Defense of Fort McHenry* (later becomes US national anthem, *The Star Spangled Banner*).

YEAR	INTERNATIONAL DIPLOMATIC HISTORY
1839	Treaty of London: between European great powers, Netherlands and Belgium; European powers recognise/ guarantee independence/ neutrality of Belgium, confirm independence of German speaking part of Luxembourg; Article VII requires Belgium to remain perpetually neutral, commits signatory powers to guard that neutrality in event of invasion.
1864	Austro-Prussian Peace of Prague: treaty between Austria and Prussia, Schleswig promised plebiscite within six years on whether to return to Danish rule or remain Prussian promised by Bismarck; promised unfulfilled until 1920. Geneva Convention: Protection of medical personnel and facilities in wartime.
1878	Congress of Berlin: led by Otto von Bismarck of European Great Powers and Ottoman Empire's leading statesmen after Russo-Turkish War (1877–78) to reorganize Balkans countries to balance distinct interests of United Kingdom, Russia and Austria-Hungary; as consequence, differences between Russia and Austria-Hungary intensified, as did nationality question in Balkans; Congress revised Treaty of San Stefano and kept Constantinople in Ottoman hands, effectively disavowing Russia's victory over Ottomans in Russo-Turkish War; formally recognized independence of *de facto* sovereign states of Montenegro, Serbia and Romania, as 27th-29th free states of world.

YEAR	HISTORY	CULTURE
1839	Uruguay declares war on Argentina.	Edgar Allen Poe, *The Fall of the House of Usher*.
	First Opium War between Great Britain and China begins.	First baseball game in US.
		First Grand National horserace held at Aintree.
	Charles Goodyear's 'vulcanisation' process allows commercial use of rubber.	
1864	Archduke Maximilian of Austria crowned Emperor of Mexico.	Charles Dickens, *Our Mutual Friend*.
	US Civil War (1861–1865) General Ulysses S Grant made Commander-in-Chief of Union Army, General William Sherman marches through Georgia.	Leo Tolstoy, *War and Peace* (-1869).
	Abraham Lincoln re-elected US President.	
1878	Electric street lighting introduced in London.	Thomas Hardy, *The Return of the Native*.
	British fleet arrives off Constantinople.	Algernon Charles Swinburne, *Poems and Ballads*.
	CID, New Scotland Yard established in London.	Ruskin-Whistler libel case.
	Attempt to assassinate Kaiser Wilhelm I of Germany.	

YEAR	INTERNATIONAL DIPLOMATIC HISTORY
1885	Indian National Congress formed
1914	Outbreak of World War I following Archduke Franz Ferdinand's assassination
1915	Treaty of London: secret pact between Italy and Triple Entente (United Kingdom, France and Russia) requiring Italy to leave the Triple Alliance (Germany, Austria-Hungary, Italy) and join Triple Entente in exchange for Italian territorial gainsat the end of the War.

YEAR	HISTORY	CULTURE
1885	General Charles G Gordon killed in fall of Khartoum to the Mahdi. Britain establishes protectorate over North Bechuanaland, Niger River region, South New Guinea; occupy Port Hamilton, Korea. The Congo becomes personal possession of King Léopold II of Belgium. Germany annexes Tanganyika and Zanzibar.	Guy de Maupassant, *Bel Ami*. H Rider Haggard, *King Solomon's Mines*. W S Gilbert and Arthur Sullivan, *The Mikado*.
1914	First World War begins: Battles of Mons, the Marne and First Ypres; trench warfare on Western Front; Russians defeated in Battles of Tannenberg and Masurian Lakes.	James Joyce, *Dubliners*. Gustav Holst, *The Planets*. Matisse, *The Red Studio*. Film: Charlie Chaplin in *Making a Living*.
1915	First World War: German U Boat sinks liner *Lusitania*, killing 1,195 people including 123 Americans. Battles of Neuve Chapelle and Loos, 'Shells Scandal', Gallipoli campaign; Germans execute British nurse Edith Cavell in Brussels for harbouring British prisoners.	John Buchan, *The Thirty-Nine Steps*. Ezra Pound, *Cathay*. Marcel Duchamp, *The Large Glass*. Pablo Picasso, *Harlequin*. Marc Chagall, *The Birthday*. Max Reger, *Mozart Variations*. Film: *The Birth of a Nation*.

YEAR	INTERNATIONAL DIPLOMATIC HISTORY
1916	Treaty of Bucharest: between Romania and Entente; Romania to declare war on Austria-Hungary in exchange for territorial gains.
1917	US declares war on Germany and Austria-Hungary.
	Arthur Balfour pledges support for Jewish National Home in Palestine.
1918	US President Woodrow Wilson makes "Fourteen Points" speech.
	Peace Treaty of Brest-Litovsk signed between Russia and Central Powers.
	Peace of Bucharest signed between Romania and Germany and Austria-Hungary
	Armistices signed between Allies and Bulgaria, Austria-Hungary, the Ottomans and Germany.

YEAR	HISTORY	CULTURE
1916	First World War: Battles of Verdun, Jutland and the Somme.	Lionel Curtis, *The Commonwealth of Nations.*
	Development and use of first effective tanks.	James Joyce, *Portrait of an Artist as a Young Man.*
	US President Woodrow Wilson re-elected; issues Peace Note to belligerents in European war.	Claude Monet, *Waterlilies.*
		'Dada' movement produces iconoclastic 'anti-art'.
	David Lloyd George becomes British Prime Minister.	Richard Strauss, *Ariadne auf Naxos.*
1917	First World War: Battle of Passchendaele (Third Ypres); British and Imperial forces take Jerusalem;; China declares war on Germany and Austria-Hungary.	P G Wodehouse, *The Man With Two Left Feet.*
		Piet Mondrian launches *De Stijl* magazine in Holland.
	February Revolution in Russia, Romanov dynasty overthrown; Lenin and Bolsheviks seize power in Moscow and Petrograd.	Pablo Picasso designs 'surrealist' costumes, set for Erik Satie's *Parade.*
1918	First World War: German Spring offensives on Western Front fail; German Fleet surrenders.	Luigi Pirandello, *Six Characters in Search of an Author.*
	Ex-Tsar Nicholas II and family murdered	Bela Bartok, *Bluebeard's Castle.*
	Kaiser Wilhelm II of Germany abdicates.	Giacomo Puccini, *Il Trittico.*
		Oskar Kokoshka, *Friends* and *Saxonian Landscape.*
	Women over 30 get right to vote in Britain.	Edvard Munch, *Bathing Man.*
	Worldwide influenza epidemic strikes; by 1920 nearly 22 million dead.	

YEAR	INTERNATIONAL DIPLOMATIC HISTORY
1919	Amritsar Massacre in India
	Draft treaty submitted to German delegates.
	Paris Peace Treaties signed (Versailles with Germany, St Germain with Austria, Neuilly with Bulgaria).
	US Senate refuses to ratify Treaty: leaves US outside League of Nations.
	League of Nations established.
	John Maynard Keynes publishes *Economic Consequences of Peace*: attacks results of Paris settlement.
1920	Inaugural League of Nations General Assembly meeting.
	US Senate again refuses to ratify Treaty.
	Further Paris Peace Treaties signed (Trianon with Hungary, Sèvres with Ottoman Empire).
	Russo-Polish War
	Treaties of Tartu: peace treaties between Russia and newly independent Estonia and Finland after Civil War in Finland and after war between Bolshevik Russia and Estonia; recognizes independence of Estonia; solved disputes and issues connected with delineation of borders and transfer of property.
	Åaland Island dispute.
1921	Anglo-Russian Trade Treaty.
	Feisal becomes King of Mesopotamia (Iraq).
	Paris Conference of wartime allies fixes Germany's reparation payments.
	Peace treaty signed between USA and Germany.
	Washington Naval Treaty signed: limits naval armaments of its five signatories (USA, Britain, Japan, France, Italy).

YEAR	HISTORY	CULTURE
1919	Communist Revolt in Berlin. Orlando government falls. Benito Mussolini founds Fascist movement in Italy. Irish War of Independence begins. Lady Astor is first British woman to sit as MP.	Bauhaus movement founded by Walter Gropius. Herman Hesse, *Demian*. George Bernard Shaw, *Heartbreak House*. Edward Elgar, *Concerto in E Minor for Cello*.
1920	Kapp Putsch: right wing coup d'état attempted to overthrow fledgling Weimar Republic. US Constitutional Amendments: 18th (Prohibition) goes into effect, 19th gives women right to vote. Government of Ireland Act passed: Ireland divided into two territories. Bolsheviks win Russian Civil War	F Scott Fitzgerald, *This Side of Paradise*. Franz Kafka, *The Country Doctor*. Katherine Mansfield, *Bliss*. Rambert School of Ballet formed in London. Lyonel Feininger, *Church*. Maurice Ravel, *La Valse*.
1921	Irish Free State established. State of Emergency proclaimed in Germany in face of economic crisis. Abdullah becomes Emir of Transjordan	Georges Braque, *Still Life with Guitar*. Aldous Huxley, *Chrome Yellow*. D H Lawrence, *Women in Love*. John Dos Passos, *Three Soldiers*. Salzburg Festival established. Sergei Prokofiev, *The Love for Three Oranges*.

YEAR	INTERNATIONAL DIPLOMATIC HISTORY
1922	Treaty of Rapallo: Russia-Germany Peace Treaty
	Britain accepts Mandate for Palestine.
	Benito Mussolini comes to power in Italy.
1923	French occupy Ruhr when Germany fails to make reparation payments
	Treaty of Lausanne: Treaty with Turkey.
	.
1924	Hussein declares himself Caliph: Ibn Saud conquers Hejaz, Hussein exiled.

YEAR	HISTORY	CULTURE
1922	Britain recognises Kingdom of Egypt under Fuad I.	James Joyce, *Ulysses.*
	Mahatma Gandhi sentenced to six years in prison for civil disobedience.	F Scott Fitzgerald, *The Beautiful and Damned.* Hermann Hesse, *Siddartha.*
	Election in Irish Free State gives majority to Pro-Treaty candidates: IRA takes large areas under its control.	Clive Bell, *Since Cezanne.* Irving Berlin, *April Showers.* British Broadcasting Company (later Corporation) (BBC) founded: first radio broadcasts.
	Lloyd George resigns as pm	
1923	USSR formally comes into existence.	François Mauriac, *Genitrix.*
	Severe earthquake in Japan destroys all of Yokohama.	P G Wodehouse, *The Inimitable Jeeves.*
	British Mandate in Palestine begins.	Martin Buber, *I and Thou.* Sigmund Freud, *The Ego and the Id.*
	Miguel Primo de Rivera assumes dictatorship of Spain.	George Gershwin, *Rhapsody in Blue.*
	State of Emergency declared in Germany; Adolf Hitler's *coup d'état* (Beer Hall Putsch) fails.	Bela Bartok, *Dance Suite.*
1924	Lenin dies.	Noel Coward, *The Vortex.*
	Turkish National Assembly expels Ottoman dynasty.	E M Forster, *A Passage to India.*
	Greece proclaimed republic.	Thomas Mann, *The Magic Mountain.*
	German Nazi Party enters Reichstag with 32 seats for first time after elections.	George Bernard Shaw, *St Joan.*
		'The Blue Four' expressionist group is formed.

YEAR	INTERNATIONAL DIPLOMATIC HISTORY
1925	Locarno Agreements: France, Germany, Belgium non-aggression pact, Germany to enter League of Nations.
1927	Briand becomes president of Pan-European Union: sees value in federalised Europe.
1929	Briand speaks to League Assembly about federal Europe.

YEAR	HISTORY	CULTURE
1925	Christiania, Norwegian capital, renamed Oslo. Mussolini announces he will take dictatorial powers in Italy. British Pound Sterling returns to Gold Standard. Paul von Hindenburg elected President of Germany. Hitler reorganises Nazi Party in Germany.	Noel Coward, *Hay Fever*. Franz Kafka, *The Trial*. Virginia Woolf, *Mrs Dalloway*. Pablo Picasso, *Three Dancers*. Marc Chagall, *The Drinking Green Pig*. Lyonel Feininger, *Tower*. Alban Berg, *Wozzek*. Ferruccio Busconi, *Doctor Faust*. Film: *Battleship Potemkin*.
1927	Inter-Allied military control of Germany ends. Britain recognises rule of Ibn Saud in the Hejaz. President Paul von Hindenburg repudiates Germany's responsibility for First World War. Britain recognises Iraq's independence, promises to support its League of Nations membership application .	Marcel Proust, *Le Temps Retrouvé*. Virginia Woolf, *To the Lighthouse*. Hermann Hesse, *Steppenwolf*. Adolf Hitler, *Mein Kampf*. Martin Heidegger, *Sein und Zeit*. Edward Hopper, *Manhattan Bridge*. Film: *The Jazz Singer*.
1929	Dictatorship established in Yugoslavia under King Alexander I. Germany accepts Young Plan at Reparations Conference in the Hague: Allies agree to evacuate Rhineland. Arabs attack Jews in Palestine following dispute over Jewish use of Wailing Wall. Wall Street Crash: world economic crisis begins; Cessation of loans to Europe.	Ernest Hemingway, *A Farewell to Arms*. Erich Maria Remarque, *All Quiet on the Western Front*. Piet Mondrian, *Composition with Yellow and Blue*. Museum of Modern Art New York opens. Martin Heidegger, *What is Philosophy?*

YEAR	INTERNATIONAL DIPLOMATIC HISTORY
1931	Japanese invade Manchuria.
1932	Ibn Saud combines Hejaz and Nejd into Saudi Arabia.
	Chancellor Heinrich Brüning declares Germany cannot and will not resume reparation payments.
	Germany withdraws temporarily from Geneva Disarmament Conference demanding permission for armaments equal to those of other powers.
	Britain, France, Germany and Italy make 'No Force Declaration' renouncing use of force for settling differences.
1933	Hitler appointed German Chancellor.
	Japan withdraws from League of Nations.
	Germany withdraws from League of Nations and Disarmament Conference.
	Anglo-German Trade Agreement.
	Britain, France, Germany and Italy sign diluted version of Mussolini's proposed Four-Power Pact.
	Japan announces it will leave League of Nations.
	Geneva Disarmament Conference collapses.

YEAR	HISTORY	CULTURE
1931	Delhi Pact between Viceroy of India and Mahatma Gandhi suspends civil disobedience campaign. Austrian Credit-Anstalt bankruptcy begins Central Europe's financial collapse. National Government formed in Britain; abandons Gold Standard. Bankruptcy of German Danatbank leads to closure of all German banks.	Noel Coward, *Cavalcade.* William Faulkner, *Sanctuary.* George and Ira Gershwin, *Of Thee I Sing.* George Dyson, *The Canterbury Pilgrims Oratorio.* Salvador Dali, *The Persistence of Memory.* Max Beckmann, *Still Life with Studio Window.* Architecture: Empire State Building, New York.
1932	Oswald Mosley founds British Union of Fascists. Mahatma Gandhi returns to India: later arrested. Franklin D Roosevelt wins US Presidential election. German Chancellor Kurt von Schleicher attempts to unify Centre and Left.	Bertholt Brecht, *St Joan of the Slaughterhouses.* Aldous Huxley, *Brave New World.* Pablo Picasso, *Head of a Woman.* Samuel Barber, *Overture to School for Scandal.* Films: *Grand Hotel. Tarzan the Ape Man.*
1933	Adolf Hitler appointed Chancellor of Germany; fire destroys Reichstag in Berlin; Enabling Act gives Hitler dictatorial powers; concentration camps opened for enemies of Nazi regime: start of official persecution of Jews. In US, 21st Amendment repeals 18th Amendment: Prohibition ends.	All books by non-Nazi and Jewish authors burned in Germany. André Malraux, *La condition humaine.* George Orwell, *Down and Out in Paris and London.* All modernist German art suppressed. Duke Ellington's Orchestra debuts in Britain.

YEAR	INTERNATIONAL DIPLOMATIC HISTORY
1934	German-Polish non-aggression pact.
	Anglo-Russian trade agreement.
	USSR admitted to League of Nations.
	Japan repudiates Washington Treaties of 1922 and 1930.
1935	Italian-French-Anglo Stresa meeting: Attempt to form anti-Germany bloc.
	Germany rearms: reintroduces conscription and reveals air force; Prime Ministers of Italy, France and Britain issue protest, agree to act together against Germany.
	Italy invades Abyssinia: League of Nations imposes sanctions against Italy.
	Hoare-Laval Pact.
1938	Austrian Anschluss: Germany annexes Austria
	Japanese puppet government of China at Nanjing.

YEAR	HISTORY	CULTURE
1934	General strike staged in France. Germany: 'Night of the Long Knives'; role of German President and Chancellor merged, Hitler becomes *Führer* after German President Paul von Hindenburg dies. Austrian Chancellor Dollfuss murdered. Kirov assassinated in USSR.	F Scott Fitzgerald, *Tender Is the Night.* Robert Graves, *I, Claudius.* Dmitri Shostakovich, *Lady Macbeth of Mtsensk.* Sergei Rakhmaninov, *Rhapsody on a Theme of Paganini.* Films: *David Copperfield.*
1935	Anglo-Indian trade pact signed. Saarland incorporated into Germany following plebiscite. British King George V's Silver Jubilee. Hitler announces anti-Jewish 'Nuremberg Laws'; Swastika becomes Germany's official flag.	Karl Barth, *Credo.* *Brockhaus Encyclopaedia* completed. George Gershwin, *Porgy and Bess.* Richard Strauss, *Die Schweigsame Frau.* T S Eliot, *Murder in the Cathedral.* Films: *The 39 Steps. Top Hat.*
1938	Neville Chamberlain, on third trip to Germany for talks to avert war, signs Munich Agreement hands Sudetenland to Germany: Returns to declare 'Peace in our time.') Kristallnacht in Germany: two day attack on Jewish businesses, houses, synagogues and schools. Nuclear fission discovered in Germany.	Frank Lloyd Wright, Taliesen West, Phoenix, USA. Graham Greene, *Brighton Rock.* Evelyn Waugh, *Scoop.* Ballpoint pen patented in Hungary. *Picture Post* founded in Britain. Films: *Pygmalion. Alexander Nevsky.*

YEAR	INTERNATIONAL DIPLOMATIC HISTORY
1939	Germany invades Czechoslovakia.
	Italy invades Albania.
	Germany demands Danzig and Polish Corridor: Poland refuses; Chamberlain guarantees Polish sovereignty.
	Hitler and Mussolini sign Pact of Steel.
	Nazi-Soviet Non-Aggression Pact (Molotov–Ribbentrop Pact): agrees no fighting, partition of Poland; Japanese withdraw from Anti-Comintern Pact in protest.
	Second World War begins: Germany invades Poland: Britain and France forced by treaty to declare war.
	Soviets invade Finland.
1941	Germany attacks USSR.
	Roosevelt and Churchill issue Atlantic Charter: established vision for post-World War II, its 8 points echoing many of Wilson's 14 points.
	Japan attacks US at Pearl Harbor.
	Hitler declares war on US.
	US enters World War Two.

YEAR	HISTORY	CULTURE
1939	Spanish Civil War ends as Nationalists take Madrid. Japanese-Soviet clashes in Manchuria.	Bela Bartok, *String Quartet No. 6.* James Joyce, *Finnegan's Wake.* Thomas Mann, *Lotte in Weimar.* John Steinbeck, *The Grapes of Wrath.* Films: *Gone with the Wind. Goodbye Mr Chips. The Wizard of Oz.*
1941	Second World War: British troops evacuate Greece, Crete falls. Japanese troops occupy Indochina. Germans besiege Leningrad and Moscow. Soviets counter attack at Moscow. Atomic bomb development begins in USA.	Etienne Gilson, *God and Philosophy.* Bertold Brecht, *Mother Courage and Her Children.* Noel Coward, *Blithe Spirit.* British communist paper, *The Daily Worker,* suppressed. Films: *Citizen Kane. Dumbo. The Maltese Falcon.*

YEAR	INTERNATIONAL DIPLOMATIC HISTORY
1945	Yalta Conference: creates four power military post-war occupation of Germany.
	US ratifies UN Charter: First nation to do so.
	US drops atomic bombs on Japan: forces end of World War II.
	UN Charter enters into force.
	Nuremberg War Crimes Tribunal set up.

YEAR	HISTORY	CULTURE
1945	Second World War: British troops invade Burma; Soviet Army takes Vienna and advances to Berlin; Mussolini shot; Germans surrender on Italian front; Hitler commits suicide in Berlin; unconditional German surrender.	Karl Popper, *The Open Society and its Enemies.*
		Benjamin Britten, *Peter Grimes.*
		Richard Strauss, *Metamorphosen.*
		Arts Council of Great Britain established.
	US President Franklin D Roosevelt dies, Harry S Truman becomes President.	George Orwell, *Animal Farm.*
		Jean-Paul Sartre, *The Age of Reason.*
	Labour Party wins landslide victory in British general election.	Evelyn Waugh, *Brideshead Revisited.*
		Films: *Brief Encounter. The Way to the Stars.*
	Korea placed under US and Soviet occupation, Outer Mongolia under Soviet control.	
	French refuse to recognise Ho Chi Minh's proclamation of Democratic Republic of Vietnam.	
	Chinese Nationalists under Chiang Kai-Shek fight Communists under Mao Zedong for control of Manchuria.	
	Josip Tito's National Front wins elections to Yugoslav constituent assembly.	
	Charles de Gaulle becomes prime minister of France.	

YEAR	INTERNATIONAL DIPLOMATIC HISTORY
1946	UN General Assembly opens in London Trygve Lie first Secretary-General
	League of Nations ceases to exist: many League bodies, such as International Labour Organization, continue to function and eventually become affiliated with UN.
	George Kennan sends 'long telegram' from Moscow: argues Soviet regime inherently expansionist; inspires Truman Doctrine and US foreign policy of Soviet containment.
	Churchill delivers 'Iron Curtain' speech at Fulton, Missouri.
	.Nuremberg establishes guilty verdicts for war crimes.
1947	Truman announces 'Truman Doctrine': pledges support to 'free peoples resisting subjugation by armed minorities or outside pressures', beginning of Cold War.
	Announcement of European Recovery Programme (Marshall Plan).
	India and Pakistan gain independence.
1948	Burma and Ceylon gain independence .
	Britain, France, Belgium, Netherlands, and Luxemburg sign Brussels Treaty: 50-year alliance for military, economic and social cooperation.
	State of Israel proclaimed: immediately recognised by US and USSR; neighbour states declare war on Israel.
	Start of Berlin blockade: Soviet response to Western Allies currency reform in their zones of occupation; Berlin Airlift ensues.
	Universal Declaration of Human Rights.

YEAR	HISTORY	CULTURE
1946	NHS and Welfare State founded in Britain.	Bertrand Russell, *History of Western Philosophy*.
	Yugoslav constitution creates six constituent republics.	Jean-Paul Sartre, *Existentialism and Humanism*.
	France recognises Vietnam as Democratic Republic within Indochinese Federation.	Jacques Prevert, *Paroles*.
		Eugene O'Neill, *The Iceman Cometh*.
	US President Harry Truman signs $3.75 billion bill of credit for Britain.	Films: *Great Expectations*. *It's a Wonderful Life*.
	US Supreme Court rules segregation on buses unconstitutional.	
	Greek Civil War begins.	
1947	Hungary reassigned its 1938 frontiers.	Edinburgh Festival is founded.
		Albert Camus, *The Plague*.
	Moscow Conference fails over problem of Germany.	Anne Frank, *The Diary of Anne Frank*.
	Indonesian independence movement rises against Dutch troops: UN Security Council calls for ceasefire.	Tennessee Williams, *A Streetcar Named Desire*.
		Le Corbusier, Unité d'Habitation Marseille, France.
	Communists win Hungarian election.	Films: *Monsieur Verdoux*. *Black Narcissus*.
	New Japanese constitution renounces use of war.	
1948	Gandhi assassinated in India: last British troops leave.	Jackson Pollock, *Composition NO.1*.
	US Congress passes Marshall Aid Act: contributes $5.3 billion to European recovery.	Columbia Record Company releases first LP.
		Graham Greene, *The Heart of the Matter*.
	South African Nationalists and Afrikaner Party win election, advocate Apartheid.	Christopher Fry, *The Lady's Not for Turning*.
	USSR expels Yugoslavia from Cominform.	Film: *The Fallen Idol*. *Hamlet*. *Whisky Galore*.

YEAR	INTERNATIONAL DIPLOMATIC HISTORY
1949	NATO established. GDR and FRG created: East and West Germany. Council of Europe Statute signed in London. Berlin Blockade lifted.
1950	European Convention on Human Rights signed. North Korea invades South, start of Korean 'Police Action'. USSR and China sign 30-year Treaty of Friendship.
1951	Treaty of Paris: creates European Coal and Steel Community. Peace Treaty with Japan signed by 49 powers, though not USSR.

YEAR	HISTORY	CULTURE
1949	Chiang Kai-Shek withdraws Nationalists to Formosa (Taiwan); Mao Zedong establishes People's Republic of China. Greek Civil War ends. South Africa begins legislated Apartheid. USSR tests its first atomic bomb.	Simone de Beauvoir, *The Second Sex*. Richard Rogers and Oscar Hammerstein, *South Pacific*. George Orwell, *Nineteen Eighty-Four*. Arthur Miller, *Death of a Salesman*. Film: *The Third Man*.
1950	France announces Schuman Plan. West Germany joins Council of Europe.	Pablo Neruda, *General Song*. Ezra Pound, *Seventy Cantos*. Films: *Orphée*. *Rashomon*. *Sunset Boulevard*.
1951	Korean War: Chinese forces take Seoul. French elections cause Ministerial crisis: René Pleven forms Coalition of the Centre. Juan Peron re-elected President of Argentina. Adib al-Shishakli leads Syrian coup. Libya becomes independent federation. Electric power produced from atomic energy in US. King Farouk of Egypt deposed.	Henry Moore, *Reclining Figure*. Benjamin Britten, *Billy Budd*. Igor Stravinsky, *The Rake's Progress*. Isaac Asimov, *Foundation*. J D Salinger, *The Catcher in the Rye*. Herman Wouk, *The Caine Mutiny*. Jean-Paul Sartre, *Le Diable et le Bon Dieux*.

YEAR	INTERNATIONAL DIPLOMATIC HISTORY
1953	Korean conflict armistice.
	European Convention on Human Rights comes into force.
	Arab League Security Pact comes into force.
	Iran breaks diplomatic relations with Britain over oil dispute.
1954	French fight and lose Battle of Dien Bien Phu in Vietnam.
	European Defence and Political Community Constitutions drafted, later rejected.
1955	FRG joins NATO.
	Warsaw Pact formed: Mutual defense treaty between USSR and 8 satellite states.
	USSR withdraws from Austria.

YEAR	HISTORY	CULTURE
1953	Stalin dies Nikita Khrushchev appointed First Secretary of Communist Party Central Committee. USA explodes first hydrogen bomb in Pacific.	Ludwig Wittgenstein, *Philosophical Investigations*. Benjamin Britten, *Gloriana*. Dmitri Shostakovich, *Symphony No. 10*. Arthur Miller, *The Crucible*.
1954	Yugoslav National Assembly adopts new constitution; Josip Tito elected first President of Yugoslav Republic. Anglo-Egyptian Agreement for British withdrawal from Canal Zone signed. Konrad Adenauer forms new government in West Germany.	Kingsley Amis, *Lucky Jim*. William Golding, *Lord of the Flies*. J R R Tolkein, *The Lord of the Rings I, II*. (*III* in 1955) Tennessee Williams, *Cat on a Hot Tin Roof*. Films: *On the Waterfront. Rear Window. The Seven Samurai*.
1955	USSR declares end of war with Germany. Winston Churchill resigns as British Prime Minister: replaced by Anthony Eden. Armistice for Indochina signed: France evacuates North Vietnam; Ho Chi Minh forms government.	Graham Greene, *The Quiet American*. Vladimir Nabokov, *Lolita*. Samuel Beckett, *Waiting for Godot*. Films: *The Seven Year Itch. Rebel Without A Cause. The Ladykillers*.

YEAR	INTERNATIONAL DIPLOMATIC HISTORY
1956	Suez Crisis: Last British troops leave Canal Zone under 1954 agreement; US abandons support of Aswan Dam project; Nasser nationalises Suez Canal; Sévres Protocol - Britain, France and Israel agree plan for invasion of Egypt; French and British troops land in Egypt; US pressure on sterling forces cease-fire; UN forces Britain to withdraw from Suez.
1957	Treaty of Rome: creates European Economic Community (Common Market).
	US, Britain, France and West Germany issue declaration on principles for German reunification: call for free elections; sweeping victory for Konrad Adenauer in West German elections.
1961	Kennedy initiates Alliance for Progress.
	USSR's Nikita Khrushchev proposes German peace conference to US President John F Kennedy.
	US and USSR begin disarmament talks in Washington, DC.
	Soviets build Berlin Wall: attempt to halt 'brain drain' from East Berlin and eastern zone of occupation.
	Dag Hammarskjold dies in plane crash, U Thant becomes third UN Secretary General.
	Bay of Pigs: US attempt to invade Cuba to unseat Fidel Castro.

YEAR	HISTORY	CULTURE
1956	Soviet General Secretary Nikita Khrushchev denounces Joseph Stalin's policies. UN obtains ceasefire agreements from Israel and Jordan, Lebanon, Syria. New government, including non-communists, formed in Hungary: renounces Warsaw Treaty; Soviet forces attack Budapest. Fidel Castro lands in Cuba.	First computer-programming language invented in US. A J Ayer, *The Problem of Knowledge*. Benjamin Britten, *The Prince of the Pagodas*. Alan J Lerner and Frederick Lowe, *My Fair Lady*. Rock'n'Roll dominates dance floors. John Osborne, *Look Back in Anger*.
1957	Malaya becomes independent Space Age begins: Soviets launch Sputnik, first man-made object, into space.	Patrick White, *Voss*. Samuel Beckett, *Endgame*. Leonard Bernstein, *West Side Story*. Francis Poulenc, *Les Dialogues des Carmelites*. Francis Bacon, *Screaming Nurse*. Films: *The Bridge on the River Kwai*.
1961	Britain applies for membership to European Economic Community. Space Race: Soviet cosmonaut Yuri Gargarin becomes first man to orbit Earth aboard Vostok I; American astronaut Alan Shephard follows into space less than one month later; Kennedy initiates 'space race' by issuing challenge to land man on Moon and return him safely by end of decade.	Jean Anouilh, *Becket*. John Osborne, *Luther*. Philip Hardwick's neo-classical arch at Euston Station demolished in London. Henry Mancini, *Moon River*. Elvis Presley, *Are you lonesome tonight?* The Beatles debut in Liverpool. Films: *Breakfast at Tiffany's*. *West Side Story*.

YEAR	INTERNATIONAL DIPLOMATIC HISTORY
1962	Cuban Missile Crisis: Confrontation between US and USSR over Soviets' building missile bases on Cuba.
1963	Geneva Conference on General Agreement on Tariffs and Trade begins 'Kennedy Round' of negotiations for tariff cuts.
	Partial Test Ban Treaty: Prohibits all but underground nuclear testing.
	Britain and US sign Polaris missile agreement.
1964	Gulf of Tonkin Incidents: leads to passage by US Congress of Resolution granting President Lyndon B. Johnson authority to assist any Southeast Asian country considered to be jeopardized by 'communist aggression'; resolution serves as legal justification for deploying US forces and commencement of open warfare against North Vietnam.

YEAR	HISTORY	CULTURE
1962	France proclaims independence of Algeria.	Edward Albee, *Who's afraid of Virginia Woolf?*
	USSR agrees to send arms to Cuba.	Benjamin Britten, *War Requiem.*
	John Glenn becomes first US astronaut to orbit Earth, aboard Friendship 7.	Michael Tippet, *King Priam.*
		Bob Dylan, *Blowing in the Wind.*
		The Beatles, *Love Me Do.*
		Films: *The Birds. Lawrence of Arabia. Lolita. The Loneliness of the Long Distance Runner.*
1963	Charles de Gaulle states objections to Britain joining EEC; Britain denied entry.	Eugene Ionesco, *Exit the King.*
	US President John F Kennedy visits West Berlin; gives 'Ich bin ein Berliner' speech.	John Le Carré, *The Spy Who Came in from the Cold.*
	Martin Luther King Jr: 'I have a dream ... ',	Le Corbusier designs Carpenter Center Harvard.
	Lee Harvey Oswald assassinates Kennedy in Dallas, Texas.	Gerry and the Pacemakers, *You'll Never Walk Alone.*
		The Beatles, *Please Please Me. She Loves You. I Want to Hold Your Hand.*
		Films: *The Great Escape. Cleopatra. Tom Jones.*
1964	Anti-US riots in Panama lead to break in diplomatic relations.	Op-art emerges.
	Nelson Mandela sentenced to life in prison in South Africa.	Sheldon Harnick and Jerry Bock, *Fiddler on the Roof.*
	Martin Luther King awarded Nobel Peace Prize.	Saul Bellow, *Herzog.*
	Leonid Brezhnev replaces Nikita Khrushchev as Soviet Communist Party First Secretary.	Philip Larkin, *The Whitsun Weddings.*
		Jean-Paul Sartre, *Les Mots.*
		Peter Shaffer, *The Royal Hunt of the Sun.*
	China explodes atomic bomb.	Films: *Mary Poppins. A Hard Day's Night.*

YEAR	INTERNATIONAL DIPLOMATIC HISTORY
1968	Nuclear Non-Proliferation Treaty.
1969	American Convention on Human Rights agreed by OAS.
1971	Indo-Pakistan War: East Pakistan becomes Bangladesh.

YEAR	HISTORY	CULTURE
1968	Vietnam Conflict: Vietcong launch Tet Offensive.	Jurgen Habermas, *Knowledge and Human Interests*.
	US: Martin Luther King and Senator Robert Kennedy assassinated.	Richard Hamilton, *Swinging London*.
		Sol Lewitt, *Untitled Cube (6)*.
	Enoch Powell's 'Rivers of Blood' speech.	Paul Simon and Art Garfunkel, *Mrs Robinson*.
	Sectarian violence erupts in Northern Ireland.	Theatre censorship in Britain abolished.
	Student riots in Paris.	Rupert Murdoch beats Robert Maxwell to ownership of *The News of the World*.
	'Prague Spring': Political liberalisation ends when Soviet forces invade Czechoslovakia.	Films: *Butch Cassidy and the Sundance Kid. The Graduate. If... 2001, A Space Odyssey*.
	Vatican bans contraception.	
	Apollo 8 crew orbit Moon.	
1969	British Army assumes responsibility for security in Northern Ireland.	Isaiah Berlin, *Four Essays on Liberty*.
		Kenneth Clark, *Civilisation*.
	PLO elects Yasser Arafat as Chairman.	Woodstock Music and Arts Fair.
	Charles de Gaulle resigns.	John Fowles, *The French Lieutenant's Woman*.
	Vietnam Conflict: President Nixon suggests withdrawal; millions demonstrate against Vietnam War in US.	Mario Puzo, *The Godfather*.
		Rupert Murdoch buys *The Sun*.
	'One Small Step...': Neil Armstrong first man to walk on Moon.	Films: *Easy Rider. Oh! What a Lovely War*.
1971	Idi Amin seizes power in Uganda.	Dmitri Shostakovich, *Symphony No. 15*.
	US ends trade embargo with China.	Films. *A Clockwork Orange. Death in Venice. Sunday, Bloody Sunday*.

YEAR	INTERNATIONAL DIPLOMATIC HISTORY
1972	Kurt Waldheim becomes fourth UN Secretary-General
	Strategic Arms Limitation Treaty (SALT I).
1975	Helsinki Final Act: signed by 35 states, including USA, USSR, Canada, and all European states except Albania and Andorra, reduces Cold War tensions, seen as major diplomatic boost for Soviet Union, due to its clauses on inviolability of national borders and respect for territorial integrity, seen to consolidate USSR's territorial gains in Eastern Europe following Second World War.
1978	American Convention on Human Rights comes into force.
	Camp David Accords: brokered by US President Jimmy Carter, signed by Egyptian President Anwar El Sadat and Israeli Prime Minister Menachem Begin, led directly to 1979 Israel-Egypt Peace Treaty; resulted in Sadat and Begin sharing 1978 Nobel Peace Prize.

YEAR	HISTORY	CULTURE
1972	Britain joins EEC. 'Bloody Sunday' in Northern Ireland: British impose direct rule. Richard Nixon first US President to visit USSR and China. Watergate scandal begins. Arab terrorists murder 11 Israeli athletes at Munich Olympics.	Jim Jacobs and Warren Casey, *Grease*. Roxy Music, *Roxy Music*. Frederick Forsyth, *The Day of the Jackal*. V S Naipaul, *In a Free State*. Films: *Deliverance. The Godfather. Cabaret*.
1975	British vote 'Yes' in referendum on EEC membership. Vietnam Conflict: Khmer Rouge revolutionaries capture Phnom Penh, Cambodia; last US personnel flee Saigon by helicopter from US embassy; Saigon surrenders to communist forces; communist forces take control of Laos. Indira Gandhi declares state of emergency in India. General Franco dies in Spain.	Michel Foucault, *Discipline and Punish*. Queen, *Bohemian Rhapsody*. Bruce Springsteen, *Born to Run*. Saul Bellow, *Humboldt's Gift*. Primo Levi, *The Periodic Table*. Films: *Jaws. One Flew Over the Cuckoo's Nest. The Rocky Horror Picture Show*.
1978	Communist and Islamic forces take power in Afghanistan. Pope Paul VI dies: succeeded by John Paul I and then John Paul II	Tim Rice and Andrew Lloyd Webber, *Evita*. Graham Greene, *The Human Factor*. John Irving, *The World According to Garp*. Harold Pinter, *Betrayal*. Films: *The Deer Hunter. Midnight Express. Superman*.

YEAR	INTERNATIONAL DIPLOMATIC HISTORY
1979	US President Jimmy Carter and Soviet Premier Leonid Brezhnev sign SALT II limiting nuclear weapons.
1981	Banjul Charter on Human and Peoples' Rights adopted for Africa Javier Perez de Cuéllar elected fifth UN Secretary-General, takes office 1.1.1982
1983	Reagan authorizes Strategic Defence Initiative ('Star Wars').

YEAR	HISTORY	CULTURE
1979	Margaret Thatcher wins British general election.	The Clash, *London Calling*.
	US and China open diplomatic relations.	Boomtown Rats, *I Don't Like Mondays*.
	Khmer Rouge regime ousted.	Italo Calvino, *If on a Winter's Night a Traveller*.
	Shah flees Iran with family.	Peter Schaffer, *Amadeus*.
	European Monetary System becomes operational.	Martin Sherman, *Bent*.
	Ayatollah Khomeini declares Iran an Islamic Republic; Iran Hostage Crisis.	Films: *Alien. Mad Max. Manhattan*.
	Soviets invade Afghanistan.	
1981	Iran Hostage Crisis: remaining 55 US hostages released minutes after US President Ronald Reagan's inauguration.	Alisdair MacIntyre, *After Virtue*.
		Bucks Fizz win Eurovision Song Contest for Britain.
	Greece becomes tenth member of EC.	Films: *Mommie Dearest. The Postman Always Rings Twice. On Golden Pond*.
	François Mitterrand becomes first socialist President of France.	
	Assassination attempt on Pope John Paul II.	
	Israel formally annexes Golan Heights, occupied since 1967.	
1983	US invades Grenada.	Alice Walker, *The Colour Purple*.
	IBM produces first PC with inbuilt hard disk.	Gabriel Garcia Marquez, *Chronicle of a Death Foretold*.
	HIV virus isolated.	Michael Jackson, *Beat It. Billie Jean*.
		Films: *The Dresser. Zelig*.

YEAR	INTERNATIONAL DIPLOMATIC HISTORY
1986	Banjul Charter on Human and Peoples' Rights comes into force
	Anglo-US Summit at Camp David: Margaret Thatcher and Ronald Reagan issue arms control statement.
	Seven major Western economic powers hold summit in Tokyo.
	Reykjavik Summit (Reagan-Gorbachev): talk of abolishing nuclear weapons.
1989	Fall of Berlin Wall: Symbolic end of Cold War
1990	Germany reunited.

YEAR	HISTORY	CULTURE
1986	US air raids on Libya.	Kingsley Amis, *The Old Devils.*
	Portugal and Spain enter European Community.	Larry McMurtry, *Lonesome Dove.*
	Major accident at Chernobyl nuclear power station near Kiev announced.	Musee D'Orsay, Paris, opened.
		Lucien Freud, *Painter and Model.*
	US Space Shuttle Challenger breaks up 73 seconds into flight, killing all 7 crew members.	Andrew Lloyd Webber, *The Phantom of the Opera.*
		Paul Simon, *Graceland.*
	Work on 'Chunnel' (Channel Tunnel) begins.	
1989	Iran's Ayatollah Khomeini issues *fatwa* against Salman Rushdie for *Satanic Verses.*	Kazuo Ishiguro, *The Remains of the Day.*
		Anne Tyler, *Breathing Lessons.*
	Tiananmen Square massacre in Beijing.	William Nicholson, *Shadowlands.*
	Disintegration of Soviet Influence: East Germany announces opening of borders with West Germany; Communist rule in Czechoslovakia ends, Havel made President; Romanian dictator Ceausescu overthrown and killed.	I M Pei, *Pyramid* outside Louvre, Paris.
		John Cage, *Europera III/IV.*
		Films: *Batman. When Harry Met Sally. Dead Poets' Society.*
1990	General Noriega surrenders to US authorities.	Karl Popper, *A World of Propensities.*
	President Frederick de Klerk ends 30-year ban on ANC in South Africa: Nelson Mandela released after 27 years in prison.	Martin Amis, *London Fields.*
		Patricia Cornwell, *Post Mortem.*
		Ian McEwan, *The Innocent.*
	Boris Yeltsin elected President of Russian SFSR, defeating Gorbachev's candidate.	Derek Wolcott, *Remembrance.*
		Jeff Koons, *Jeff and Ilona.*
		Damian Hirst, *My Way.*
	First Gulf War begins: Iraq invades Kuwait.	

YEAR	INTERNATIONAL DIPLOMATIC HISTORY
1991	George H Bush and Mikhail Gorbachev sign Strategic Arms Reduction Treaty (START I)
1992	Boutros Boutros-Ghali becomes sixth UN Secretary-General
	Chemical Weapons Convention: 188 nations have signed to date.
	Maastricht Treaty signed: creates directly elected European Parliament, rebrands itself EU.
1993	International Criminal Tribunal for former Yugoslavia (ICTY).
	START II: Never agreed.
	Israel and PLO sign peace agreement in Washington DC.

YEAR	HISTORY	CULTURE
1991	First Gulf War ends: Coalition forces liberate Kuwait.	Michael Dummett, *The Logical Basis for Metaphysics*.
	Warsaw Pact military structure dissolved; Boris Yeltsin becomes President of Russian Federation; Gorbachev resigns as President of USSR; USSR officially ceases to exist.	Brett Easton Ellis, *American Psycho*. John Grisham, *The Firm*. Madonna, *Sex*. John Updike, *Rabbit at Rest*.
	Peace accord ends 11-year civil war in El Salvador.	Ariel Dorfman, *Death and the Maiden*.
	South African legal framework for Apartheid destroyed.	Films: *JFK. Silence of the Lambs. Thelma and Louise*.
1992	Bosnian Conflict: EC recognises Croatia and Slovenia as independent republics; Serb and federal army forces begin Sarajevo bombardment after fighting escalates; UN condemns Serbs' 'ethnic cleansing' as war crime; first British troops deployed to Bosnia.	J K Galbraith, *The Culture of Contentment*. Jung Chang, *Wild Swans*. Ian McEwan, *Black Dogs*. Michael Ondaatje, *The English Patient*. Damien Hirst, *The Physical Impossibility of Death in the Mind of Someone Living*.
	'Black Wednesday': Britain drops out of European Exchange Rate Mechanism.	Films: *Howard's End. Orlando*.
1993	Terrorists bomb World Trade Center in New York.	Andrew Motion, *Philip Larkin, A Writer's Life*.
	Bosnian Conflict: UN Security Council declares 'safe areas' in Sarajevo, Tuzla, Zepa, Goradze, Bihac and Srebrenica in Bosnia-Herzegovina; Serbs attack Srebrenica and Goradze.	Isabel Allende, *The Infinite Plain*. Roddy Doyle, *Paddy Clarke Ha Ha Ha*. Harold Pinter, *Moonlight*. Take That, *Take That and Party. Everything Changes*.
	Joint British-Irish declaration to encourage peace talks in Northern Ireland.	U2, *Zooropa*.

YEAR	INTERNATIONAL DIPLOMATIC HISTORY
1994	International Criminal Tribunal for Rwanda (ICTR).
1996	Comprehensive Test Ban Treaty.
	Kofi Annan elected seventh UN Secretary-General, takes office 1.1.1997
1999	East Timor separates from Indonesia to become new nation
	Euro currency introduced.

YEAR	HISTORY	CULTURE
1994	Nelson Mandela sworn in as President of South Africa. Israel withdraws military forces from Jericho area of West Bank: Israel and Jordan formally end their conflict. Russian forces invade Chechnya. US Space Shuttle visits Russian Mir Space Station. British Queen and French President open Channel Tunnel.	Eric Hobsbawm, *Age of Extremes, The Short Twentieth Century.* V S Naipaul, *A Way in the World.* Arthur Miller, *Broken Glass.* Sistine Chapel's cleaning completed. Films: *Forrest Gump. The Madness of King George. Pulp Fiction.*
1996	Yasser Arafat elected President in first Palestinian general elections. Boris Yeltsin inaugurated as Russian President after re-election. Taliban take over Kabul, impose Islamic law in Afghanistan. Bill Clinton re-elected US President.	Daniel Goldhagen, *Hitler's Willing Executioners.* T S Eliot, *Inventions of the March Hare, Poems.* Films: *William Shakespeare's Romeo and Juliet. Trainspotting.*
1999	Bosnian Conflict: NATO begins bombing Yugoslavia, Serbian President Slobodan Milosevic agrees terms on Kosovo. US President Bill Clinton acquitted in impeachment trial. Hungary, Poland and Czech Republic join NATO. First major anti-globalisation demonstrations at WTO meeting in Seattle.	Anthony Beevor, *Stalingrad.* J M Coetzee, *Disgrace.* Joanne Harris, *Chocolat.* Frank McCourt, *'Tis.* J K Rowling, *Harry Potter and the Prisoner of Azkaban.* Cher, *Believe.* Films: *The Matrix. The Sixth Sense. Three Kings. Star Wars.*

YEAR	INTERNATIONAL DIPLOMATIC HISTORY
2001	September 11: Hijacked airliners crash into World Trade Center in New York and Pentagon near Washington, DC; some 3,000 killed; President George W Bush declares 'War on Terror'.
2002	International Criminal Court created. Strategic Offensive Reductions Treaty (SORT). Special Court for Sierra Leone.
2003	Start of Operation Iraqi Freedom. Draft of European Constitution revealed.

YEAR	HISTORY	CULTURE
2001	US and British warplanes attack targets in Iraq. Serbia's Slobodan Milosevic surrenders to police to face trial for war crimes. Afghanistan: US/NATO and Northern Alliance forces attack Taliban, who abandon Kabul. Russia takes Mir Space Station out of orbit.	Umberto Eco, *Baudolino*. John Le Carré, *The Constant Gardener*. Michael Moore, *Stupid White Men*. W G Sebald, *Austerlitz*. Films: *Bridget Jones's Diary. Harry Potter and the Philosopher's Stone. Lord of the Rings: The Fellowship of the Ring*.
2002	War on Terror: US President George W Bush names Iran, Iraq and North Korea as 'Axis of Evil' in State of the Union Address to Congress; Bali bombings, 202 killed. Iraq War: US President warns UN to take action against threat of Iraq's weapons of mass destruction or stand aside while US does; Iraq's response to UN weapons resolution seen as incomplete.	Iain Banks, *Dead Air*. Ian McEwen, *Atonement*. Donna Tartt, *The Little Friend*. Films: *The Lord of the Rings: The Two Towers. Star Wars Episode II: Attack of the Clones*.
2003	War on Terror: US Department of Homeland Security formed. Iraq War: Mass worldwide anti-war protests; US and British forces invade Iraq, Baghdad falls a month later; Saddam Hussein captured by US forces. US Space Shuttle Columbia breaks up on re-entry. Last commercial flight of Concorde.	Dan Brown, *The Da Vinci Code*. Mark Haddon, *The Curious Incident of the Dog in the Night-Time: A Novel*. Lynn Truss, *Eats, Shoots & Leaves*. Films: *The Lord of the Rings: The Return of the King. Pirates of the Caribbean: The Curse of the Black Pearl*.

YEAR	INTERNATIONAL DIPLOMATIC HISTORY
2007	Ban Ki-moon becomes eight UN Secretary-General
	Lisbon Treaty: creates posts of European President and Foreign Minister.
2010	New START Treaty signed by Russia and US.

YEAR	HISTORY	CULTURE
2007	Bulgaria and Romania join EU. Iraq War: US announces 'troop surge' in Iraq; British troops withdraw from Basra. North Korea agrees to shut down nuclear facilities in return for energy aid. Tony Blair resigns as British Prime Minister: succeeded by Gordon Brown.	Alan Bennett, *The Uncommon Reader*. Don DeLillo, *Falling Man*. J K Rowling, *Harry Potter and the Deathly Hallows*. Films: *Spider Man 3. Ratatouille*.
2010	Ash from Iceland volcano disrupts European air travel. UK has coalition government for first time since World War II, David Cameron (Conservative) PM and Nick Clegg (Liberal Democrat) Deputy PM. US withdraws combat troops from Iraq. US Congress passes health care reform legislation. Oil spill in Gulf of Mexico.	Films: *Toy Story 3. Alice in Wonderland*. Vancouver Winter Olympics.

Bibliography

Unpublished sources
CAB and FO papers in the National Archive, Kew
Curzon papers in the British Library
Tallents papers in family hands

Newspapers and periodicals
The Economist
The Guardian
The Times

Place of Publication for all books is London, unless otherwise noted

Published documents
Bourne, K and Watt, D C (eds). *British Documents on Foreign Affairs: Reports and Papers from the Foreign Office Confidential Print: The Paris Peace Conference of 1919* 7 vols (University Publications of America, Maryland, 1989).

Butler, R, Bury, J and Woodward, E L (eds). *Documents on British Foreign Policy 1919–1939* (First Series, HMSO, 1947 onwards).

Cmd 2169 *Papers Respecting Negotiations for an Anglo-French Pact* (HMSO, 1924).

The Treaty of Versailles and After: Annotations of the Text of the Treaty (Greenwood reprint, New York, 1968, of original U.S. Government Printing Office, 1944).

Papers relating to the Foreign Relations of the United States: Paris Peace Conference 1919 13 vols (Washington Government Printing Office 1942–47).

Diaries, letters, memoirs, speeches

Baker, R S. *Woodrow Wilson and World Settlement* 3 vols (Doubleday Page, New York: 1923).

Bonsal, S. *Unfinished Business* (Michael Joseph, 1944).

Chamberlain, N. *The Struggle for Peace* (Hutchinson, 1940).

Clemenceau, G. *Grandeur and Misery of Victory* (Harrap, 1930).

Headlam-Morley, A, Bryant, R and Cienciala, A (eds). *Sir James Headlam-Morley: A Memoir of the Paris Peace Conference 1919* (Methuen, 1972).

Kennan, G F. *At a Century's Ending: Reflections 1982–1995* (W W Norton and Co, New York: 1996).

Lansing, R. *The Peace Negotiations: A Personal Narrative* (Houghton Mifflin, Boston: 1921).

Lloyd George, D. *War Memoirs* 2 vols (Odhams, 1938).

_____. *The Truth about the Peace Treaties* 2 vols (Gollancz, 1938).

Monnet, J. *Memoirs* translated by R Mayne (Collins, 1978).

Nicolson, H. *Peacemaking 1919* (Constable, 1933).

Nicolson, N (ed). *Vita and Harold: The Letters of Vita Sackville-West and Harold Nicolson* (Putnam's Sons, New York: 1992).

Orpen, Sir W. *An Onlooker in France 1917–1919* (Dodo Press reprint of the original Williams and Norgate publication, 1921).

Saint-Aulaire, Comte de. *Confession d'un Vieux Diplomate* (Flammarion, Paris: 1953).

The Makers of the Modern World

Alston, C. *Piip, Meierovics & Voldemaras: Estonia, Latvia and Lithuania* (Haus, 2010).

Bulloch, J. *Karl Renner: Austria* (Haus, 2010).

Cartledge, B. *Mihály Károlyi and István Bethlen: Hungary* (Haus, 2009).

Clements, J. *Wellington Koo: China* (Haus, 2008).

_____. *Prince Saionji: Japan* (Haus, 2008).

Crampton, R J. *Aleksandŭr Stamboliĭski: Bulgaria* (Haus, 2009).

Dalby, A. *Eleftherios Venizelos: Greece* (Haus, 2010).

_____. *Prince Charoon et al: South-East Asia* (Haus, 2010).

Djokic, D. *Pašić and Trumbić: The Kingdom of the Serbs, Croats and Slovenes* (Haus, 2010).

Fraser, T G. *Chaim Weizmann: The Zionist Dream* (Haus, 2009).

Harmer, H. *Friedrich Ebert: Germany* (Haus, 2008).

Henig, R. *The League of Nations* (Haus, 2010).

Lentin, A. *General Smuts: South Africa* (Haus, 2010).

Mango, A. *From the Sultan to Atatürk: Turkey* (Haus, 2009).

Marks, S. *Paul Hymans: Belgium* (Haus, 2010).

McNamara, R. *The Hashemites: The Dream of Arabia* (Haus, 2009).

Morton, B. *Woodrow Wilson: United States* (Haus, 2008).

Neville, P. *Beneš, Masaryk: Czechoslovakia* (Haus, 2010).

Prazmowska. A. *Ignacy Paderewski: Poland* (Haus, 2009).

Purcell, H. *Maharajah of Bikaner: India* (Haus, 2010).

Scala, S Di. *Vittorio Orlando: Italy* (Haus, 2010).

Sharp, A. *David Lloyd George: Great Britain* (Haus, 2008).

Streeter, M. *South America* (Haus, 2010).

Watson, D. *Georges Clemenceau: France* (Haus, 2008).

Secondary material

Adamthwaite, A. *The Making of the Second World War* (Allen and Unwin, 1977).

Alcock, A. *A History of the Protection of Regional Cultural Minorities in Europe: From the Edict of Nantes to the Present Day* (Macmillan, Basingstoke: 2000).

Ambrose, S. *The Rise to Globalism: American Foreign Policy, 1938–1970* (Penguin, 1971).

Andrew, C. *Secret Service: The Making of the British Intelligence Community* (Heinemann, 1985).

Andrew, C and Kany-Forstner, A. *France Overseas: The Great War and the Climax of French Imperial Expansion* (Thames and Hudson, 1981).

Andelman, D. *A Shattered Peace: Versailles 1919 and the Price We Pay Today* (John Wiley and Sons, New Jersey: 2008).

Armstrong, D. *The Rise of the International Organisation: A Short History* (Macmillan, Basingstoke: 1982).

Azcárate, P de. *The League of Nations and National Minorities: An Experiment* (Carnegie Endowment, Washington: 1945).

Barnett, R J. *Allies: America, Europe, Japan since the War* (Jonathan Cape, 1984).

Bass, G. *Stay the Hand of Vengeance: The Politics of War Crimes Tribunals* (Princeton University Press, NJ: 2002 ed.).

Bell, P. *The World Since 1945: An International History* (Arnold 2001).

Beloff, M. *The United States and the Unity of Europe* (Faber, 1963).

Best, A, Hanhimaki, J, Maiolo, J and Schulze, K. *International History of the Twentieth Century* (Routledge, 2004).

Betts, R. *France and Decolonisation, 1900–1960* (Macmillan, Basingstoke: 1991).

Boyce, R. *The Great Interwar Crisis and the Collapse of Globalization* (Palgrave Macmillan, Basingstoke: 2009).

Cohrs, P. *The Unfinished Peace after World War I: America, Britain and the Stabilisation of Europe 1919–1932* (Cambridge University Press, 2006).

Churchill, W S *The Second World War*: Volume I *The Gathering Storm* 6 vols (Cassell and Co, 1949 ed.).

Darwin, J. *Britain and Decolonisation* (Macmillan, Basingstoke: 1988).

Debo, R. *Survival and Consolidation: The Foreign Policy of Soviet Russia 1918–1921* (McGill-Queen's University Press, Montreal: 1992).

Dinan, D. *Ever Closer Union: An Introduction to European Integration* (Palgrave Macmillan, Basingstoke: , 2005 Third ed.).

Duschene, F. *Jean Monnet: the First Statesman of Interdependence* (Norton and Co, New York: 1994).

Dunbabin, J D P. The *Cold War: The Great Powers and Their Allies* (Longman, 1994).

Duroselle, J. *Clemenceau* (Fayard, Paris: 1988).

Eubank, K. *The Summit Conferences 1919–1960* (Oklahoma University Press, OK: 1966).

Feis, H. *Churchill, Roosevelt, Stalin: The War They Waged and The Peace They Sought* (Princeton University Press, NJ: 1957).

Ferguson, N (ed). *Virtual History: Alternatives and Counterfactuals* (Picador, Basingstoke: 1997).

Fischer, F. *Griff Nach Der Weltmacht* (Droste, Dusseldorff: 1961) – English translation *Germany's Aims in the First World War* (Chatto and Windus, 1967).

_____. *Krieg der Illusionen* (Droste, Dusseldorff: 1969) – English translation *The War of Illusions* (Chatto and Windus, 1975).

Fraser, T G. *The Arab-Israeli Conflict* (Palgrave Macmillan, Basingstoke: 2008 Third ed.).

Fromkin, D. *In The Time of the Americans: The Generation That Changed America's Role in the World* (Papermac, 1995).

_____. *A Peace to End all Peace: The Fall of the Ottoman Empire and the Creation of the Modern Middle East* (Phoenix Press, 2000 paperback ed.).

Gaddis, J L. *The Cold War* (Allen Lane, 2005).

Grayson, R. *Austen Chamberlain and the Commitment to Europe: British Foreign Policy 1924–29* (Frank Cass, 1997).

Grosser, A. *The Western Alliance: European-American Relations since 1945* (Continuum, New York: 1980).

Heater, D. *National Self-Determination: Woodrow Wilson and His Legacy* (Macmillan, Basingstoke: 1994).

Hitchcock, W. *The Struggle for Europe: The History of the Continent since 1945* (Profile Books, 2004).

Hobsbawm, E. *Age of Extremes: The Short Twentieth Century 1914–1991* (Michael Joseph, 1994).

Horak, S et al. *Eastern European National Minorities, 1919–1980: A Handbook* (Littleton, Colorado: 1980).

Howard, M. *The Continental Commitment: The Dilemma of British Defence Policy in the Era of Two World Wars* (Pelican, 1974).

Hurd, D. *The Search for Peace: A Century of Peace Diplomacy* (Warner Books, 1997).

Ickenberry, G J. *After Victory: Institutions, Strategic Restraint, and the Rebuilding of Order After Major Wars* (Princeton University Press, NJ: 2001).

Jeannesson, S. *Poincaré, La France et La Ruhr (1922–1924): Histoire d'une Occupation* (Presses Universitaires de Strasbourg, 1998).

Kaiser, D. *Politics and War: European Conflict from Philip II to Hitler* (Tauris, 1990).

Kennedy, M. *Ireland and the League of Nations 1919–1946: International Relations, Diplomacy and Politics* (Irish Academic Press, Dublin: 1996).

Kennedy, P. *The Rise and Fall of the Great Powers: Economic Change and Military Conflict from 1500–2000* (Fontana, 1988).

_____. *The Parliament of Man: The United Nations and the Quest for World Government* (Allen Lane, 2006).

Keynes, J M. *The Economic Consequences of the Peace* (Macmillan, 1919).

Kershaw, I. *Fateful Choices: Ten Decisions that Changed the World 1940–1941* (Penguin, 2008).

Kissinger, H. *Diplomacy* (Simon and Schuster, 1995 ed.).

Kitching, C. *Britain and the Problem of International Disarmament 1919–1934* (Routledge, 1999).

Kramer, A. *Dynamic of Destruction: Culture and Mass Killing in the First World War* (Oxford University Press, 2007).

Kyle, K. *Suez* (Weidenfeld and Nicolson, 1991).

Lane, A. *Yugoslavia: When Ideals Collide* (Palgrave Macmillan, Basingstoke: 2004).

Lentin, A. *Lloyd George and the Lost Peace: From Versailles to Hitler* (Palgrave Macmillan, Basingstoke: 2001).

Loth, W. *The Division of the World 1945–1951* (Routledge, 1988).

Macartney, C A. *National States and National Minorities* (Oxford University Press, 1934).

MacMillan, M. *Peacemakers: The Peace Conference of 1919 and Its Attempt to End War* (John Murray, 2001).

_____. *Nixon and Mao: The Week That Changed the World* (Random House, New York: 2007).

Manela, E. *The Wilsonian Moment: Self-Determination and the International Origins of Anticolonial Nationalism* (Oxford University Press, 2007).

Marks, S. *The Illusion of Peace: International Relations in Europe, 1918–1933* (Palgrave Macmillan, Basingstoke: 2003 Second ed.).

_____. *The Ebbing of European Ascendancy: An International History of the World 1914–1945* (Arnold, 2002).

Mayer, A J. *Politics and Diplomacy of Peacemaking: Containment and Counter-Revolution at Versailles 1918–1919* (Weidenfeld and Nicolson, 1968).

Mayne, R. *The Recovery of Europe: From Devastation to Unity* (Weidenfeld and Nicolson, 1970).

Mee, C. *The Marshall Plan* (Simon and Schuster, New York: 1984).

Mellanson, R. *Reconstructing Consensus: American Foreign Policy since the Vietnam War* (St Martin's Press, New York: 1991).

Morgan, J H. *Assize of Arms* (Methuen, 1945).

Moynihan, D P. *Pandaemonium: Ethnicity in International Politics* (Oxford University Press, 1994).

Murray, L. *Clinton, Peacekeeping and Humanitarian Interventionism: Rise and Fall of a Policy* (Routledge, 2008).

Overy, R. *Why the Allies Won* (Norton, New York: 1996).

Perman, D. *The Shaping of the Czechoslovak State* (Brill, Leiden: 1962).

Recouly, R. *Où en est l'Allemagne: Comment La Faire Payer* (Hachette, Paris: 1922).

Ryan, S. *The United Nations and International Politics* (Macmillan, Basingstoke: 2000).

Schabas, W. *The UN International Criminal Tribunals: The Former Yugoslavia, Rwanda and Sierra Leone* (Cambridge University Press, 2006).

Schuker, S. *American 'Reparations' to Germany, 1919–1933: Implications for the Third World Debt Crisis* (Princeton University Press, NJ: 1988).

Sellar, W C and Yeatman , R J. *1066 And All That* (Penguin reprint, 1960, originally published by Methuen, 1930).

Servan-Schreiber, J. *American Challenge* (Penguin, 1969), originally published as *Le Défi Americain* (Editions De Nöel, Paris: 1967).

Sharp, A. *The Versailles Settlement: Peacemaking after the First World War, 1919–1923* (Palgrave Macmillan, Basingstoke: 2008 Second ed.).

Shaw, B. *Peace Conference Hints* (Constable, 1919).

Shaw, M N. *International Law* (Cambridge University Press, 1994 Third ed.).

Steiner, Z. *The Lights that Failed: European International History 1919–1933* (Oxford University Press, 2005).

Temperley, H W V (ed). *A History of the Paris Peace Conference* 6 vols (Oxford University Press, 1920, 1969 reprint).

Thompson, S H. *Czechoslovakia in European History* (Frank Cass, 1965).

Towle, P. *Enforced Disarmament: From the Napoleonic Campaigns to the Gulf War* (Oxford University Press, 1997).

Wandycz, P. *The Price of Freedom: A History of East Central Europe from the Middle Ages to the Present* (Routledge, 1992).

Watt, D. *Succeeding John Bull: America in Britain's Place* (Cambridge University Press, 1984).

Willett, R. *The Americanization of Germany, 1945–1949* (Routledge, 1989).

Willis, J. *Prologue to Nuremberg: The Politics and Diplomacy of Punishing War Criminals of the First World War* (Greenwood, New York: 1982).

Winter, J and Baggett, B. *1914–1918: The Great War and the Shaping of the Twentieth Century* (BBC Books, 1996).

Wright, J. *Gustav Stresemann: Weimar's Greatest Statesman* (Oxford University Press, 2002).

Articles and book chapters

Barros, A. 'Disarmament as a Weapon: Anglo-French Relations and the Problems of Enforcing German

Disarmament', *Journal of Strategic Studies,* Vol 29, No 6, April 2006, pp 301–21.

Dunbabin, J P. 'The League of Nations' Place in the International System', *History*, Vol 78, No 254, October 1993, pp 421–42.

Feldman, G. 'The Reparations Debate' in Fischer, Conan and Sharp (eds) *After the Versailles Treaty: Enforcement, Compliance, Contested Identities* (Routledge 2008) pp 69–80.

Fink, C. 'The Minorities Question at the Paris Peace Conference', in Boemeke, M, Feldman, G and Glaser, E (eds) *The Treaty of Versailles: A Reassessment after 75 Years* (Cambridge University Press, 1998) pp 249–74.

_____. 'Revisionism' in Martel, G. (ed) *A Companion to Europe, 1900–1945 (*Blackwell, Oxford, 2006) pp 326–40.

Fraser, T G. 'Germany and Indian Revolution, 1914–1918', *Journal of Contemporary History,* Vol 12, 1977, pp 255–72.

Fukuyama, F. 'The End of History?', *The National Interest* (1989) reprinted in Ó Tuathail, G, Dalby, S, and Routledge, P (eds) *The Geopolitics Reader* (Routledge, 2006 Second ed.) pp 107–14.

Henig, R. 'Britain, France and the League of Nations in the 1920s' in Sharp, A and Stone, G *Anglo-French Relations in the Twentieth Century: Rivalry and Cooperation* (Routledge, 2000) pp 138–57.

Howard, M. 'The Legacy of the First World War' in Boyce, R and Roberston, E M (eds) *Paths to War: New Essays on the Origins of the Second World War* (St Martin's Press, 1989) pp 33–54.

Huntington, S. 'The Clash of Civilizations', *Foreign Affairs*, 72, July/August 1993, pp 22–49.

Jackson, P. 'France and the Problem of Security and International Disarmament after the First World War', *Journal of Strategic Studies*, Vol 29, No 6, April 2006, pp 247–80.

Johnson, E. 'Britain and an International Force: The Experience of the League of Nations and the United Nations Military Staff Committee' in Hamilton, K and Johnson, E (eds) *Arms and Disarmament in Diplomacy* (Vallentine Mitchell, 2008) pp 173–93.

Kuisel, R. 'Coca-Cola and the Cold War: the French Face Americanization, 1948–1953', *French Historical Studies*, Spring 1991, pp 96–116.

Martel, G. 'From Round Table to New Europe: Some Intellectual Origins of the Institute of International Affairs' in Bosco, A and Navari, C (eds) *Chatham House and British Foreign Policy 1919–1945* (Lothian Foundation Press, 1994) pp 13–39.

Pearson, R. 'Hungary: a State Truncated, a Nation Dismembered' in Dunn, S and Fraser, T G (eds) *Europe and Ethnicity: World War I and Contemporary Ethnic Conflict* (Routledge, 1996) pp 88–109.

Preece, J J. 'Minority Rights in Europe: from Westphalia to Helsinki', *Review of International Studies* (1997) No. 23, pp 75–92.

Sharp, A. 'Britain and the Protection of Minorities at the Paris Peace Conference, 1919' in Hepburn, A C (ed) *Minorities in History* (Edward Arnold, 1978), pp 170–88.

_____. 'Quelqu'un Nous Ecoute: French Interception of German Telegraphic and Telephonic Communications during the Paris Peace Conference, 1919' in *Intelligence and National Security*, Vol 3, No 4, October 1988, pp 124–7.

_____. 'Mission Accomplished? Britain and the Disarmament of Germany, 1918–1923' in Hamilton, K and Johnson, E (eds) *Arms and Disarmament in Diplomacy* (Vallentine Mitchell, 2008) pp 73–90.

_____, and Ward, K. 'The United States and Europe, 1945 to 1991' in Waites, B (ed) *Europe and the Wider World* (Open University, 1993) pp 119–64.

Smith, M. ' "The devil you know": The United States and a Changing European Community', *International Affairs*, Vol 68, January 1993, pp 103–20.

Stevenson, D. 'Britain, France and the Origins of German Disarmament, 1916–1919', *Journal of Strategic Studies*, Vol 29, No 6, April 2006, pp 195–224.

Trachtenberg, M. 'Versailles after Sixty Years', *Journal of Contemporary History*, Vol 17, No 3, July 1982, pp 487–506.

White, R. ' "Through a Glass Darkly": The Foreign Office Investigation of French Federalism, January–May 1930' in Dutton, D (ed) *Statecraft and Diplomacy in the Twentieth Century* (Liverpool University Press, 1995) pp 75–97.

Internet sources

Benedikter, T. 'Legal Instruments of Minority Protection in Europe – An Overview' (Bolzano/Bozen, 2006) http://www.gfbv.it/3dossier/eu-min/autonomy-eu.html.

Bush, President G H, State of the Union Address, 28 January 1992 http://www.fas.org/spp/starwars/offdocs/union92.htm.

US General Accounting Office, *Military Presence: United States Personnel in NATO* (October 1989) http://siadapp.dmdc.osd.mil/personnel/MILITARY/history/hst0709.pdf.

Picture Sources

The author and publishers wish to express their thanks to the following sources of illustrative material and/or permission to reproduce it. They will make proper acknowledgements in future editions in the event that any omissions have occurred.

Page x: Topfoto; Page 7: Getty Images; Page 62: Roger Viollet/Getty Images; Page 68: Popperfoto/Getty Images; Page 89: John Lindsay/AP/Press Association Images; Page 198: Corbis; Page 170: Top: Time & Life Pictures/Getty Images   Bottom: AP/Press Association Images; Page 210: Courtesy of the Imperial War Museum.

Endpapers
The Signing of Peace in the Hall of Mirrors, Versailles, 28th June 1919 by Sir William Orpen (Imperial War Museum: akg-images)
Front row: Dr Johannes Bell (Germany) signing with Herr Hermann Müller leaning over him
Middle row (seated, left to right): General Tasker H Bliss, Col E M House, Mr Henry White, Mr Robert Lansing,

President Woodrow Wilson (United States); M Georges
Clemenceau (France); Mr David Lloyd George, Mr Andrew
Bonar Law, Mr Arthur J Balfour, Viscount Milner, Mr G N
Barnes (Great Britain); Prince Saionji (Japan)
Back row (left to right): M Eleftherios Venizelos (Greece);
Dr Afonso Costa (Portugal); Lord Riddell (British Press);
Sir George E Foster (Canada); M Nikola Pašić (Serbia);
M Stephen Pichon (France); Col Sir Maurice Hankey,
Mr Edwin S Montagu (Great Britain); the Maharajah of
Bikaner (India); Signor Vittorio Emanuele Orlando (Italy);
M Paul Hymans (Belgium); General Louis Botha (South
Africa); Mr W M Hughes (Australia)

Jacket images

(Front): Imperial War Museum: akg Images.
(Back): *Peace Conference at the Quai d'Orsay* by Sir William
Orpen (Imperial War Museum: akg Images).
Left to right (seated): Signor Orlando (Italy); Mr Robert
Lansing, President Woodrow Wilson (United States); M
Georges Clemenceau (France); Mr David Lloyd George, Mr
Andrew Bonar Law, Mr Arthur J Balfour (Great Britain);
Left to right (standing): M Paul Hymans (Belgium); Mr
Eleftherios Venizelos (Greece); The Emir Feisal (The
Hashemite Kingdom); Mr W F Massey (New Zealand);
General Jan Smuts (South Africa); Col E M House (United
States); General Louis Botha (South Africa); Prince Saionji
(Japan); Mr W M Hughes (Australia); Sir Robert Borden
(Canada); Mr G N Barnes (Great Britain); M Ignacy
Paderewski (Poland)

Index

Makers of the Modern World

UK PUBLICATION: November 2008 to December 2010
CLASSIFICATION: Biography/History/
    International Relations
FORMAT: 198 × 128mm
EXTENT: 208pp
ILLUSTRATIONS: 6 photographs plus 4 maps
TERRITORY: world

Chronology of life in context, full index, bibliography innovative layout
with sidebars